SYDNEY CEMETERIES

LISA MURRAY is a public historian and works as the City Historian at the City of Sydney Council. With over 15 years' experience in the field of public history, Lisa is passionate about making history accessible to the public. Lisa is an award-winning author of planning histories and a regular contributor to debates around public history, including being a speaker at TEDxSydney 2013. She wrote her doctoral thesis on the history of cemeteries in 19th-century New South Wales and is a current member of the National Trust (NSW)'s Cemeteries Conservation Committee.

T0363722

SYDNEY CEMETERIES

A FIELD GUIDE

Lisa Murray

NEWSOUTH

A NewSouth book

Published by
NewSouth Publishing
University of New South Wales Press Ltd
University of New South Wales
Sydney NSW 2052
AUSTRALIA
newsouthpublishing.com

National Library of Australia Cataloguing-in-Publication entry
Creator: Murray, Lisa, author.
Title: Sydney Cemeteries: A field guide / Lisa Murray.
ISBN: 9781742234489 (paperback)
        9781742248011 (ePDF)
Subjects: Cemeteries – New South Wales – Sydney.
        Sepulchral monuments – New South Wales – Sydney.
        Epitaphs – New South Wales – Sydney.
        Sydney (NSW) – History.
Dewey Number: 929.5099441

Design Emma Bennetts
Images All photographs by Mark Dunn. For historical images, see image credits section.
Cover images Front, top: Waverley Cemetery. Front, below: Methodist Cemetery, McGraths Hill.
Back, top: Sir John Jamison's Catholic Cemetery, Regentville. Back, below left: South Head
General Cemetery, Vaucluse. Back, below right: Rookwood Necropolis.
Maps Josephine Pajor-Markus
Printer Everbest, China

All reasonable efforts were taken to obtain permission to use copyright material reproduced in this book,
but in some cases copyright could not be traced. The author welcomes information in this regard.

This book is printed on paper using fibre supplied from plantation or sustainably managed forests.

UNSW
AUSTRALIA

CONTENTS

INTRODUCTION

I love cemeteries. They are a heady mix of art, architecture, garden design, history and belief. Sydney's cemeteries form beautiful open spaces – part garden, part outdoor sculpture park, part museum – that are a pleasure to wander around. There is much to admire in the skilled carving demonstrated on the headstones in our cemeteries. The inscriptions record the names and dates, occupations and virtues of Sydneysiders. Together these monuments provide an invaluable social, literary and economic record of the district. And did you know that a headstone may be the only place where the life and death of a colonist was recorded? It was only in 1856, with the establishment of civil registration, that it became compulsory for all births, deaths and marriages to be registered.

I find it staggering how undervalued Sydney cemeteries are. This field guide aims to change that. I want to share with you the unique qualities of Sydney's cemeteries. I have been visiting cemeteries for over 20 years. My doctorate was on the history of cemeteries, and I have volunteered on the National Trust Cemeteries Conservation Committee, undertaking cemetery surveys across the state. I reckon I know a thing or two about cemeteries, and I want to let you in on a few secrets.

Cemetery design and the burial of the dead are bound by regulations, religious and cultural values. The government established the majority of cemeteries in New South Wales through a grant of crown land. A surveyor mapped and laid out the cemetery after the government approved a request for a burial ground, or when a new town was being planned. After the land was set aside, trustees were appointed, the cemetery was fenced, cleared and made ready for burials, and regulations, fees and charges were gazetted. The cemetery was subsequently consecrated; although there were no hard and fast rules about when this might take place. Many parishes waited years for a visit from the church hierarchy. The dead, however, did not wait and burials occurred as soon as the cemetery was ready. The same basic process was followed for denominational burial grounds donated by individual parishioners, but with less official intervention.

There are two main types of burial grounds in Sydney: church cemeteries and general cemeteries. A church cemetery is a burial ground for one religious denomination. It is usually located beside or near a church, though very few traditional churchyards in Sydney actually surround the church. A general cemetery caters for many religious groups and is subdivided and laid out into denominational areas. I describe the evolution of cemetery design and the reason for the shift from churchyards to church cemeteries to general cemeteries in the essay 'Gothic romance: the cemetery ideal in Sydney'.

If you are not driven by family history to visit a cemetery, it can sometimes be difficult to know where to start looking. The field guide explains how to 'read' cemetery memorials to increase your enjoyment of sepulchral art. 'What headstone is that?' provides a simple guide to the different shapes and types of memorials you will encounter in cemeteries and how to describe them. A short essay on 'Monumental masons' depicts major trends in the design, material and production of memorials. 'Symbolic gestures', reveals the hidden meanings of headstones expressed through their ornamentation and symbolism. The art of reading headstones will greatly enhance your enjoyment visiting cemeteries.

You won't be the first to take advantage of this knowledge. Visiting cemeteries was once considered fashionable. In the essay 'A stroll in a cemetery' I outline Sydney's love affair with cemeteries. But cemetery visitation had waned by the mid-20th-century, and as the cemetery landscape matured, grave plantings began to smother the graves. Cemetery managers became aware that the ongoing maintenance costs of ornate 19th-century cemetery landscapes would be a constant drain on their funds.

In response to these maintenance challenges, cemetery managers sought alternative designs for cemetery landscapes, which led to the rise of the lawn cemetery. At the same time, there were growing calls for old cemeteries to be converted into pioneer parks. The neglected landscape of the closed abandoned cemetery is a graphic illustration of the shifting attachments of memory in the cemetery landscape. Between the 1940s and the 1960s trustees handed control of many early Sydney cemeteries over to local councils, who cleared their

headstones and converted them for community use or open park space.
A few of these sites are included in my book; many more have disappeared.
This management approach was formalised in legislation when the New South
Wales government passed the *Conversion of Cemeteries Act* in 1974. Incredibly,
the legislation was only repealed in November 2014.

Every Sydney cemetery is unique and has its own charm. For each cemetery
in this field guide, I give a short description, potted history and point out some
unique, rare or interesting features. Each entry has at least one contemporary
photograph included. Mark Dunn took all the photographs, unless otherwise
acknowledged. A date range for known burials is provided, although the
technicalities of whether a cemetery is formally closed and exactly when this
occurred has sometimes escaped me. And I list a handful of notable burials too.
I'm sure you will recognise other names prominent in the local area's history
and development; my list is by no means definitive. I have also included tips for
preparing for a visit and some suggestions about what else you can take in nearby.

The field guide is roughly divided into regions, so you can explore an area and
find cemeteries close by: East, South, Inner West and West, Parramatta, North,
North West, Outer West, Hawkesbury and South West. This division is somewhat
arbitrary; Inner West and West for instance extends south and west of the
traditional Sydney 'inner west' to take in Canterbury, Kinsgrove, Punchbowl,

St John's Anglican Cemetery, Parramatta

Bankstown and Rookwood. Parramatta gets its own region due to the cluster of noteworthy historic cemeteries situated there. Maps for each region help illustrate the extent and included cemeteries. Within each region, cemeteries are clustered geographically so you can travel from one cemetery to the next. I have also shared with you some of my favourite cemetery features in a series of top fives, which provides an alternative thematic way to explore Sydney's cemeteries: top five cemeteries for picnics, top five cemeteries for views, and so on.

Of course, I am not the first to appreciate the historical value of cemeteries. Many active historical societies, genealogists and family history groups have over the years recorded the inscriptions in our cemeteries. This book would not have been possible without their hard work and commitment to documenting our history and heritage. I take my hat off to you all. The resources included at the end of each entry, that show where you can find out more about a particular cemetery, highlight the amazing contribution of these groups. These resources are also combined in a comprehensive bibliography which I have published as a Trove list: *Sydney cemeteries* <trove.nla.gov.au/list?id=64285>.

Composing a field guide has many methodological challenges. Over the last twelve months my partner and I have visited pretty much every cemetery, churchyard and lone grave in Sydney. But you will not find them all included in this guide. There are some ground rules. It has to be publicly accessible; not on private property. It has to be a general cemetery or a denominational cemetery; not a single headstone or headstones moved from elsewhere. It has to be within the Sydney metropolitan area; I have used the Hawkesbury and Nepean rivers as my rough boundary of the Sydney basin. The bodies should still be there. Finally, and this is my 'get out of gaol free' card, there are always exceptions to the rules. To find out more about my methodological approach, other cemetery histories and commentary on cemetery features, visit my blog *Sydney Cemetery Adventures* <sydneycemeteryadventures.wordpress.com>.

Left All Saints Anglican Cemetery, North Parramatta   *Right* Catholic Cemetery, Windsor

GOTHIC ROMANCE:
THE CEMETERY IDEAL IN SYDNEY

S ydney was at the forefront of the new cemetery design movement that swept across Britain, Europe and America in the 19th century. Traditionally in Great Britain the dead were buried in graveyards surrounding churches. Church graveyards were part of the cultural baggage that came to Australia with the Brits too, but new thinking and new ideas were also trialled in colonial Sydney. Sydney had vast amounts of land upon which to impart the latest ideas in city planning, including the 'cemetery ideal'. The general cemetery is so ubiquitous in Sydney today that it might be hard to believe it was a new concept in the 19th century. John Timbs singled out the new trend in his *Curiosities of London* (1876): 'Cemeteries, or public burial-grounds, planted and laid out as gardens around the metropolis, are a novelty of our times.'

The 'cemetery ideal' was a creation of 19th-century architects and clergy, administrators and arbiters of taste, designed to regulate and control the bodies of both the living and the dead. The cemetery was seen as the answer to the sanitary problems of the overcrowded churchyards, scruples over the treatment and integrity of the corpse, and various religious and political contests.

The cemetery ideal was promoted in Britain by a number of reformers, along with contemporary journals such as the *Gardener's Magazine*, *The Gentleman's Magazine*, the *Builder* and the *Lancet* (although the latter's interest was more health than design related). This call for appropriately designed and tasteful extramural cemeteries (that is, outside the city centre) later became known as the 'garden cemetery movement' and was dominated by two Scotsmen, John Strang and John Claudius Loudon, who wrote influential treatises on the subject. Cemeteries could fulfil public and private commemorative functions, and provide both moral guidance and good examples of virtuous lives. An emphasis on moral improvement through meditation upon the grave or memorial encouraged 'contemplative recreation' in the cemetery. Consequently, 19th-century cemeteries were deemed to be appropriate places for walks and promenades by the city's citizens.

Utilitarian planning was helped along by cultural trends. In the late 18th century the cult of melancholy and emulation was popularised by the school of poetry known as the Graveyard Poets, men like Edward Young, James Hervey and Thomas Gray. The allure of the grave, with its glimpses of mortality and the sublime, was associated with Romanticism. Percy Bysshe Shelley summed it up in his Preface to *Adonais* (1821): 'The cemetery is an open space among the ruins, covered in winter with violets and daisies. It might make one in love with death, to think that one should be buried in so sweet a place.'

To many 19th-century cemetery reformers, the Père-Lachaise cemetery in Paris, created in 1804, was just such a place. So much so that it soon came to be seen as the 'model cemetery'. Indeed, the *Encyclopaedia Britannica* in 1876 identified Père-Lachaise as 'the prototype of the garden cemeteries of Western Europe'. The atmosphere and features of Père-Lachaise were written about so prolifically and were so widely admired in the 19th century that it became central to the populace's understanding of what a cemetery actually was.

Père-Lachaise was frequently referred to as a model for cemeteries in Sydney. The Presbyterian minister, Reverend Dr McGarvie, for example, was particularly impressed with Père-Lachaise, declaring at a parliamentary inquiry into the General Cemetery Bill in 1845 that it was well worth emulating:

I think it would be very desirable, for many reasons, to have a similar General Cemetery [to Père-Lachaise] here, laid out under a good arrangement, and public management; leaving other considerations out of question, the erection of handsome tombs and monuments, would give a stimulus to art, and would be more extensively adopted, when parties were assured by perpetual property in the ground, that such monuments would be duly respected, and preserved in a Public Necropolis ... the chief reasons with many persons, for incurring expense in erecting memorials to deceased friends, and family burial places.

Government officials in Sydney were equally aware of developments in Britain – both the rejection of intramural burials and the development of large metropolitan

Devonshire Street Cemeteries, c.1900

cemeteries run by joint-stock companies. Colonial Architect Mortimer W Lewis, for example, informed the general cemetery select committee inquiry of 1845 about the latest cemetery developments in London. He discussed Kensal Green, Norwood, Highgate, and Abney Park cemeteries, all located in and around London, as well as cemeteries at Liverpool, Gravesend and the Necropolis in Glasgow. Lewis pointed out that 'all the Cemeteries are ornamented more or less, with plantations of trees and flowers, after the manner of the *Pere la Chaise*, at Paris'.

Sydney embraced the cemetery ideal by developing larger spaces for burial grounds in locations outside the city or town centre, marked by the orderly arrangement of graves in rows or grids, major avenues and sweeping pathways and the conspicuous placement of vaults and monuments to the prominent and wealthy. The churchyard did not disappear immediately; however, the trend was to separate the cemetery from the church, even if it was just in the next paddock. Gradually denominational burial grounds came to be clustered side by side in the same space (rather than with their churches) and the Australian concept of a general cemetery evolved.

The Devonshire Street Cemeteries, established between 1820 and 1836 on the site of what is now Central Station, were at the cutting edge of cemetery design. For the first time the surveyor-general grouped a set of denominational burial grounds together outside the town. This was also the first attempt to seriously regulate burials and order the cemetery landscape.

The *Australian* newspaper on 12 December 1842 knew that Sydney was on trend with its 'new cemetery':

The practice of having large cemeteries on the outskirts of populous towns and cities, is one that is rapidly growing into practice ... Sydney in this respect is well provided. The new cemetery is a large and commodious one, situated on an open and airy ascent, and commanding a picturesque view of the city and harbour. The tombs and monuments which are erected over the dead, are many of them handsome pieces of sculpture. We are adverse [sic] to there being any exclusion from this spot, as we are aware that a walk through it must be interesting to all.

This newspaper article is one of the earliest articulations of the cemetery ideal in colonial Sydney.

Several proposed schemes also demonstrate the Gothic Romance colonists envisaged for the cemetery landscape. Colonial arbiters of taste in 1845 considered Garden Island, located in Sydney Harbour, as eminently suitable for a cemetery. Its 'seclusion' and 'picturesque features' would be favoured by persons wishing 'to erect Funeral Monuments, of a more durable and expensive character, to the memory of their deceased relatives, or friends' as Charles Cowper, chairman of the select committee inquiry, put it. Memorials on Garden Island to two prominent and respectable Sydney residents, Ellis Bent (d.1815) and Major John Ovens (d.1825) heightened its appeal. While this idyllic spot was never formally established as a cemetery, it remained a picturesque beauty much admired in the 19th century.

The vision of the original proposal to maintain the Old Sydney Burial Ground in George Street, attributed to architect Francis Greenway, also conformed to garden cemetery ideas. If the tombs were kept, the ground put in order, ornamented with trees and opened to public visitation, the monumental public square would become according to the Reverends William Cowper and John McEncroe a 'place which would afford solemn and agreeable recreation'. This never happened. Commercial pragmatism overcame Gothic Romanticism when the memorials were cleared in 1869 to make way for the building of the Sydney Town Hall.

More radical schemes were a step too far. The government established a non-denominational general cemetery on the Sydney Common (Moore Park) in

Promenading visitors at the Necropolis, Haslem's Creek, in 1875

1845, when the Devonshire Street grounds were crowded, but it was never used. The churches rejected such an ecumenical approach to death. It was not the dead they were worried about, but the living; visions of clashing funerals and religious beliefs showed Sydney's true colours. We may have had a separation of church and state, but we were not a secular society. So the colonial architects and government surveyors backed off and instead created a range of designs for general cemeteries with denominational divisions – a distinctive Australian response to death. The shift to general cemeteries was swift. This became the preferred burial ground design for new townships from the 1850s. However, single denominational burial grounds continued to be granted until 1867, the year Rookwood Necropolis opened.

Rookwood Necropolis was the elaborate pinnacle of Gothic Romance in Sydney. It provided for Sydneysiders an acceptable burial in individual graves for virtually all classes, and a landscaped public space that fused recreation with moral contemplation. The landform and layout of the 80 hectares were picturesque and romantic, being beautified with specimen trees and winding walks. The cemetery site was appropriate and commanding, with views to Seven Hills, Prospect and Parramatta. At its centre was an impressive Gothic mortuary railway station. The cemetery was linked to the city by train, providing an economic and decorous way for funerals to proceed to the Necropolis.

Other cemeteries in Sydney were sprinkled with the cemetery ideal. Gore Hill, Waverley, Field of Mars and Woronora all have elements of the cemetery ideal in their landscape design. Both Field of Mars and Woronora cemeteries were laid out in a gardenesque manner, with circular focal points and curving pathways. Gore Hill was more angular, but avenue plantings of cabbage palm trees drew the eye and created vistas to prominent family vaults.

Built structures, such as gatehouses, chapels, robing rooms and rest houses were equally important features in the garden cemetery. Waverley Cemetery had a picturesque Gothic sandstone lodge near the entrance gates and several small Gothic sandstone rest houses dotted across its landscape. Their picturesque design complemented the cemetery office. Rest houses provided protection to mourners during inclement weather and encouraged visitors to utilise the cemetery for passive recreation. Rookwood Necropolis, not surprisingly given its ornate landscaping, featured many rest houses and shelter sheds that invited the visitor to linger and contemplate the sublime environment. Providing less shelter, but equally welcome to the tired or emotional visitor, were garden seats. These were found in many cemeteries throughout the 19th century. Memorial seats in cemeteries and other landscapes such as public parks and private gardens still perform this function today.

With the cemetery ideal in place, the stage was set for Sydneysiders to indulge in some Gothic Romance, wandering among the tombs in 'solemn and agreeable recreation'. As I discuss in 'A Stroll in a Cemetery' later in this guide, Sydney's cemeteries became a popular destination on weekends.

Lychgate, Gore Hill Memorial Cemetery

TOP 5
VIEWS

Waverley Cemetery, Bronte

Third Quarantine Station Cemetery, North Head

Coast Hospital Cemetery, Little Bay

Eastern Suburbs Memorial Park, Matraville

St Bartholomew's Anglican Cemetery, Prospect

Coast Hospital Cemetery, Little Bay

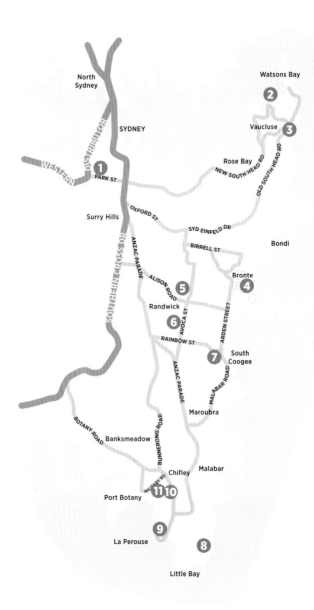

Opposite South Head General Cemetery

EAST

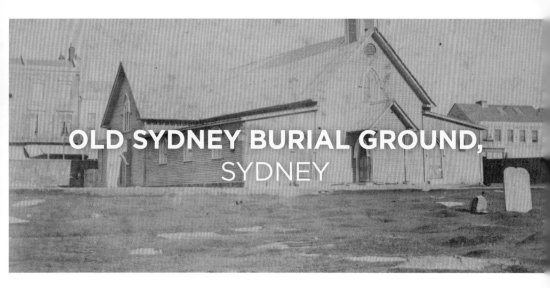

OLD SYDNEY BURIAL GROUND,
SYDNEY

483 GEORGE STREET, SYDNEY

Burials: 1792–1820 (removed)

The Old Sydney Burial Ground, as we now call it, was the first official cemetery for the town of Sydney. It once stood on the site of the Sydney Town Hall and has reached folkloric status due to regular archaeological discoveries. This cemetery, established in 1792, is not the oldest in Sydney – St John's Cemetery at Parramatta claims that status – and there is not much to see these days, but it was the first cemetery operating in the city.

Little is known about the burials during the first five years of the colony. What we know, thanks to extensive research by Keith Johnson and Malcolm Sainty, comes from early correspondence and diary entries. It is hard to reconcile the different descriptions, but the first informal burial grounds seem to have been close to the infant township. Johnson has found references to one at Dawes Point for mariners and seamen, another in the Rocks, possibly within the block today bounded by Essex, Gloucester, Grosvenor and Harrington streets, and a third behind the military barracks in Clarence Street.

When it was established, the Old Sydney Burial Ground was outside the little town. Sydney's first formal cemetery covered roughly 8000 square metres and was in use from 1792 until 1820. The burial ground served the entire population, burying convicts and free citizens, and all religions. Unlike today, there were no strict denominational divisions, although some social distinctions were made, with military burials in certain parts of the cemetery. No formal cemetery register or plan of the burials was kept. It was later estimated that about 2000 interments were conducted there. By 1820 the cemetery was full, commercial Sydney was enveloping the cemetery, and its clay soil and poor burial practices rendered it 'offensive to the inhabitants of the neighbourhood' (*Sydney Gazette*, 22 January 1820).

Consequently, the Devonshire Street Cemetery opened in 1820 at the southern end of the city and became the city's official cemetery (see Pioneer Memorial Park, Botany for more details). A few relatives transferred monuments to this new cemetery when the Old Sydney Burial Ground closed. This was a good move, as the old burial ground, although enclosed by a high brick wall, was neglected and suffered from vandalism. It became 'a resort for bad characters at night' and stray animals during the day. Kids from nearby St Andrew's schoolhouse played chasings in the cemetery.

Abandoned and unloved by its citizens, the city council dreamed of a better use for the site: a town hall. But it took them 20 years of lobbying to achieve their aim. The cemetery was supposedly cleared in 1869 to make way for the new town hall and exhumed remains taken to Rookwood Necropolis. Relatives could claim tombstones and we know that the headstone of Captain Gavin Hamilton (d.1798), commander of the *Sydney Cove*, was transferred to Rookwood, where it

Below George Street c.1842 with the walled burial ground on the left   *Previous page* The only known photograph of the Old Sydney Burial Ground, c.1867

still survives. As a mark of respect, the city council commissioned stonemason Francis Murphy to create a large classical monument to identify the remains it reburied out at Rookwood. The inscription records the name of the mayor, but due to gaps in the historical record does not list any names of those buried in the old cemetery.

The exhumation process overseen by undertaker Robert Stewart was basic, probably only clearing visible headstones and the original planned footings of the hall, so archaeological discoveries have been occurring ever since: 1871–72, 1888, 1890s, 1904, 1924, 1929, 1974, 1991, 2003 and 2007. For more information on these discoveries, check out my blog Sydney Cemetery Adventures.

Graves survive in a number of places beside and beneath the Town Hall, carefully preserved but invisible beneath the pavement. The City of Sydney Council installed a subtle memorial tablet in the paving outside the Druitt Street entrance to the Lower Town Hall commemorating the cemetery. They have also compiled an inventory of burials from historical documents providing a consolidated list of names for people probably buried in the Old Sydney Burial Ground.

> ## TIP
>
> Artefacts associated with the Old Sydney Burial Ground, including headstone fragments and a coffin plate, can only be viewed as part of guided tours by the Friends of Sydney Town Hall or during special Town Hall open days. The graves themselves are not visible.

MORE INFORMATION

- City of Sydney, 'Old Sydney Burial Ground', City of Sydney website, 2013, <www.cityofsydney.nsw.gov.au/learn/sydneys-history/people-and-places/old-sydney-burial-ground>.
- Keith Johnson & Malcolm Sainty, *Sydney Burial Ground 1819–1901 (Elizabeth and Devonshire Streets) and History of Sydney's Early Cemeteries from 1788*, Library of Australia History, Sydney, 2001.
- Judy Birmingham & Carol Liston, *Old Sydney Burial Ground 1974*, Studies in Historical Archaeology, No. 5, Sydney, 1976.

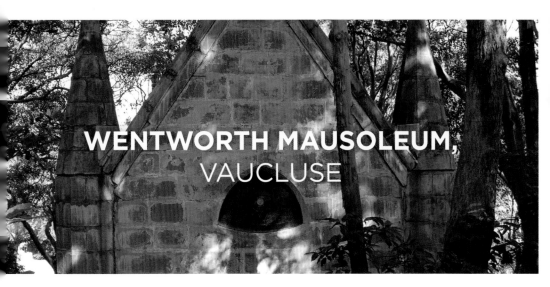

WENTWORTH MAUSOLEUM, VAUCLUSE

CHAPEL ROAD, VAUCLUSE

Private vault: 1873

When patriot William Charles Wentworth (1790–1872), explorer, author, barrister, landowner and statesman, was placed in the family vault on the Vaucluse Estate in 1873, Sir James Martin predicted that the mausoleum would be a revered site of pilgrimage for generations of Australians. This has not eventuated; yet the mausoleum, listed on the State Heritage Register, is a worthy stop for goths and history buffs alike.

Wentworth was admired in the 19th century for championing representative government and he was tenacious in pursuing judicial rights for convicts. He also helped found the colony's first university, the University of Sydney. His death in England on 20 March 1872 was a shock to the colony. The government voted a public funeral, Sydney's first official 'state funeral', which was held at St Andrews Cathedral. The governor declared the day of the funeral, Tuesday 6 May 1873,

The Wentworth Mausoleum in 1880

a public holiday. Between 50,000 and 70,000 Sydneysiders flocked to various vantage points to view the procession. The funeral cortege was extremely long, containing 133 carriages and 2200 mourners, and took several hours to pass. According to the *Empire* newspaper, when the first portion had reached the tollbar at Rushcutters Bay, the last of the carriages had not left George Street.

The design and location of the Wentworth Mausoleum embodies the Picturesque and Gothic Revival styles favoured by the Wentworths on the Vaucluse Estate. The family vault is built into the natural sandstone outcrop of Parsley Hill, a favourite harbour vantage point for Wentworth on his estate. Originally the mausoleum was visible from the verandah of Vaucluse House, the Wentworth family home. Such sight lines between family homesteads and private burial vaults were once common, acting as a visual assertion of dynastic estates. Residential subdivision has since destroyed this vista and today a eucalypt grove overshadows the mausoleum.

Mansfield Brothers, architects, designed the mausoleum in 1872–74, under directions from Sarah Wentworth, William Charles' widow. Sarah herself travelled from the UK to Brussels to select the marble sarcophagus and she also personally selected the iron palisading that encloses the mausoleum.

The interior of the mausoleum chapel can be viewed through a door to the east. A set of stained glass windows featuring the Wentworth coat of arms frames the sarcophagus. On the threshold of the door is a black and white tile mosaic of Triton, the son of Neptune. This is a copy of a 2nd-century AD Roman mosaic acquired by the Wentworth family on their Grand Tour in 1858–59.

TIP

There are two other significant private vaults surviving in Sydney: the vault of William Carss and the Rodd Family vault. Neither are technically cemeteries, but both are well worth a visit. See my blog Sydney Cemetery Adventures for more details.

MORE INFORMATION

- NSW Heritage Office, 'Wentworth Mausoleum and site', State Heritage Register Listing, database ID 5045532, NSW Office of Environment and Heritage website, 2015, <www.environment.nsw.gov.au/heritageapp/ViewHeritageItemDetails.aspx?ID=5045532>.
- Lisa Murray, 'First State funeral', Dictionary of Sydney website, 2013, <dictionaryofsydney.org/entry/first_state_funeral>.

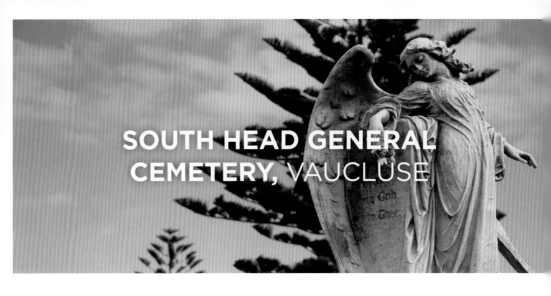

SOUTH HEAD GENERAL CEMETERY, VAUCLUSE

South Head General Cemetery is one of my favourite cemeteries. You pass by it if you run in the City to Surf. Often overshadowed by its more spectacular, younger neighbour at Waverley, South Head is an impressive cemetery that hosts an array of substantial memorials and the graves of many prominent Sydneysiders.

South Head Cemetery is up on the ridge overlooking Diamond Bay. There are ocean views, but the cemetery does not extend down to the cliff. Elegant cast-iron gates bearing the monograph SHC hang between hefty sandstone piers and usher the visitor through to the main avenue. Norfolk pines define its perimeter and a low fence encloses the cemetery. Other quaint entrance ways survive: there is a lychgate entrance on Burge Street and an arched entrance from Old South Head Road.

From the main gates, a sweeping avenue leads down to the ornately carved Celtic cross, erected by the people of Sydney, to commemorate the grave of Sir Walter Edward Davidson (d.1923), governor of New South Wales (1918–23). Large and expensive family monuments line this avenue, one of the best places to be buried in this cemetery. South Head Cemetery is still in use, managed by Waverley Council, and this means that some of the landscape design has been compromised. Lawn burials cluster in every spare avenue and pathway.

The size of the cemetery – just 1.6 hectares – means that it is easy to wander around and spot memorials to the rich and famous. The cemetery is notable for some fine examples of art deco memorials dating from the 1920s and 1930s – including the Wheeler memorial by sculptor Rayner Hoff – and for a preponderance of large granite memorials marking family plots. One of the most famous monuments is the marble bust to motor car racer Phil Garlick, complete with steering wheel and racing cap with

Two headstones representing occupations: motor car racer Phil Garlick (d.1927) and sea captains James Green (d.1857) and Malcolm Green (d.1904)

flaps. Towards the southern part of the cemetery there are some early sandstone altar tombs dating from the 1850s that were transferred from the Devonshire Street Cemeteries. The cemetery also features a number of naval burials, often marked with anchors – commanders and captains who now enjoy ocean views.

A few mausoleums and family vaults are dotted through the site. A fabulous pair of Grecian and Gothic mausoleums memorialise the Foy and Smith families on the southern part of the site. The family plot includes a simple Celtic cross memorial to the activist Juanita Nielsen who disappeared in 1975.

South Head also boasts local wildlife. Watch out for the kestrel that sometimes perches on headstones and uses the ocean breezes to hover and hunt lizards.

NOTABLE BURIALS

- Sir John Robertson (1816–1891), land reformer and politician, NSW premier
- Sir Edmund (Toby) Barton (1849–1920), federationist, first prime minister and judge
- Sir Walter Edward Davidson (1859–1923), NSW governor
- Reginald Gordon (Phil) Garlick (1887–1927), racing car driver
- George Washington Thomas Lambert (1873–1930), artist
- Francis Foy (c.1856–1918) and Mark Foy (1865–1950), businessmen, founders of Sydney's Mark Foy's, and sportsmen
- Gladys Lillian Moncrieff (1892–1976), soprano
- Packer Family Vault, including Robert Clyde Packer (1879–1934) and Sir Douglas Frank Hewson Packer (1906–1974), newspapermen and media proprietors

MORE INFORMATION
- *Waverley and South Head general cemeteries transcriptions*, CD ROM, Society of Australian Genealogists, Sydney, 2005.
- BT Dowd (ed.), *The Centenary of the Municipality of Waverley, 1859–1959*, Waverley Council, Sydney, 1959, pp. 175–77.

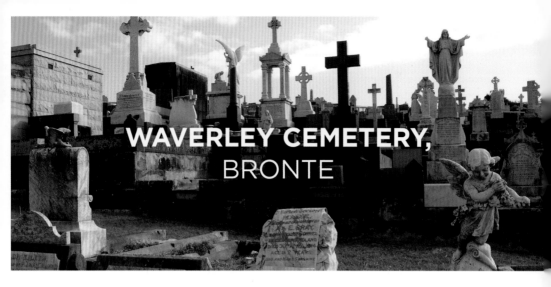

WAVERLEY CEMETERY,
BRONTE

**ST THOMAS STREET,
CORNER TRAFALGAR STREET, BRONTE**

Burials: 1877–present

Waverley Cemetery is Sydney's most famous cemetery. Spectacularly located on the cliff top above Bronte, it's a feature of the Bondi to Coogee coastal walk. With its ocean views and marble monuments glistening in the sun, few can resist exploring this cemetery. It has always been thus. Almost as soon as it was established in 1877, Waverley Cemetery was one of the most admired cemeteries in Sydney. Its position among the healthier and wealthier eastern suburbs, combined with its sublime aspect, quickly made Waverley Cemetery a popular choice for burials of the rich and famous.

Agitation for a cemetery in the eastern suburbs began in 1863 when alderman Joseph Dickson raised the issue at a Waverley Council meeting. In 1868 the New South Wales government finally allocated £1200 for a cemetery. In an unusual move, the colonial government asked Waverley Council to take control of the cemetery. They agreed, providing they did not incur the initial expense. The council acquired bits of land during the 1870s using the government's money. By-laws for Waverley Cemetery were gazetted in 1877, and the first burial took place on 4 August.

Waverley Cemetery was not the first general cemetery in the eastern suburbs. That distinction goes to South Head Cemetery. But, despite grand plans to extend South Head Cemetery down to the ocean, it remained small, about 1.6 hectares. In comparison, Waverley Cemetery covers about 16 hectares and has approximately 250,000 burials in 48,000 graves.

From the beginning, descriptions of Waverley Cemetery have focused upon its close proximity to the ocean and the pleasing effect this had on visitors. Cemeteries by the sea were, and still are, considered as 'beautiful', 'picturesque' and 'peaceful' – all essential qualities of a sublime landscape to encourage meditations and moral improvement. The sandstone cemetery lodge built in the Gothic Revival style and picturesque little Gothic rest houses dotted around the cemetery enhanced these Romantic associations.

The layout of the cemetery is a simple grid pattern, based on a north–south axis, so the graves face east and west. Waverley is remarkable for the strong sense of verticality and the overall quality of the formalised monumental art. Stylistically the monuments have an air of restrained classicism. Despite many large monuments, there is a lack of ostentation both in monument design and layout, particularly when compared to Rookwood Necropolis or even Gore Hill Cemetery. Waverley is a stark landscape relying upon its position by the sea to create a picturesque atmosphere. Sandstone headstones are scattered throughout the site, but the marble monuments, which stand out against the blue ocean and sky, define the cemetery's character.

One unusual feature of Waverley's design is the denominational layout. There are only three areas: Church of England, Roman Catholic and a general section. This reflects the different management and set up of the cemetery. Had the colonial government laid out the cemetery, there would have been more denominational areas. But Waverley Council catered only for the two main religions – everyone else was relegated to the general area.

The largest memorial in the

cemetery is the Irish Monument. It commemorates the rebels of 1798 who were exiled to Sydney. The remains of Michael Dwyer, the Wicklow Chief, and his wife Mary were exhumed from Devonshire Street Catholic Cemetery and reinterred in Waverley on the 100th anniversary of the uprising. It was one of the largest events Sydney had ever seen. Dr Charles William MacCarthy laid the foundation stone for the memorial. Two years later, the marble, bronze and mosaic monument designed by architects Sheerin and Hennessy was opened. The names of 79 people connected with the 1798 uprising were inscribed on the southern wall; all except Robert Emmet, who proclaimed at his execution in 1803 'when my country takes her place among the nations of the earth, then, and not till then, let my epitaph be written'. In 1947 the names of the 17 participants executed after the

1916 Easter uprising were added. The monument, one of the grandest to the 1798 Irish Rebellion in the world, is an important historical and spiritual link for Australia's Irish.

There are many famous people buried in Waverley Cemetery: businessmen, actors, poets, sportsmen and hit men. One of my favourite headstones of all time can be found in this cemetery. It is a marble headstone erected to Charles Peart (d.1896), a high diver in the Fitzgerald Brothers circus. He tragically died performing his circus act in Sydney and fellow performers erected the memorial. The gravestone features a diver carved at the top of the headstone poised in readiness, looking down to the tank carved at the bottom of the headstone.

Burials are still taking place at Waverley Cemetery and it remains a popular cemetery with walkers, film directors, goths and historians. The cemetery is extremely crowded so there is not that much room for a picnic, although there are some sandstone rest houses with benches scattered through the site. Freesias have naturalised across the site, so I recommend visiting in early spring.

TIP

Download the self-guided thematic walking tours of the cemetery from Waverley Council Library, 'Waverley Cemetery Who's Who'.

NOTABLE BURIALS

- John Sands (1818–1873), engraver, printer and stationer
- Thomas Henry Kendall (1839–1882), poet
- Sir James Martin (1820–1886), politician and chief justice, namesake of Martin Place
- Sir Robert William Duff (1835–1895), NSW governor
- William Henry Paling (1825–1895), musician, merchant, founder of Palings Music Store and philanthropist
- Ethel Charlotte Pedley (1859–1898), musician and writer, best remembered for her children's book *Dot and the Kangaroo*
- William Dymock (1861–1900), bookseller, founder of Dymock's Book Arcade
- George Sargent (1859–1921) and Charlotte Sargent (1856–1924), pastry-cooks and caterers, of Sargent Pies
- Henry Lawson (1867–1922), short story writer and balladist

- Sarah (Fanny) Durack (1889–1956), champion swimmer
- Isobel Marion Dorothea Mackellar (1885–1968), writer, best known for the poem 'My Country' (I love a sunburnt country)
- George Freeman (1934–1990), infamous Sydney racing identity, alleged links to Sydney's underworld

MORE INFORMATION

- Waverley Council, Waverley Cemetery website, 2015, <www.waverleycemetery.com>.
- Waverley Council Library, 'Waverley Cemetery Who's Who', Waverley Council website, 2016, <www.waverley.nsw.gov.au/services/library/local_studies/waverley_cemetery_whos_who>.
- *Waverley and South Head general cemeteries transcriptions*, CD ROM, Society of Australian Genealogists, Sydney, 2005.
- Michael O'Sullivan, '1798 Memorial, Waverley Cemetery', Dictionary of Sydney website, 2012, <dictionaryofsydney.org/entry/1798_memorial_waverley_cemetery>.

Crowds watch as a funeral cortege makes its way through Waverley Cemetery, c.1900

ST JUDE'S ANGLICAN CEMETERY, RANDWICK

106 AVOCA STREET, RANDWICK (ACCESS VIA CHURCH CAR PARK IN FRANCES STREET)

Burials: 1858–present

A more sublime church cemetery would be hard to find. Well kept, respected and full of fascinating characters, this cemetery exudes local history. The burial ground is located behind the quaint sandstone St Jude's church and was in use before the current church was completed. The first burial was Edwin David Daintrey, infant son of Edwin and Susan, who died 2 September 1858, just 11 weeks and 3 days old.

The well-heeled residents of the Eastern Suburbs have erected some impressive monuments here at St Jude's. Many of the iron grave surrounds are intact and form a neat catalogue of designs. It is a veritable rollcall of the rich and famous in the late 19th century. Even those with little historical knowledge will recognise some of the names carved in stone. At least eight religious ministers are

Archibald Mosman's white painted sarcophagus marks a large family vault

memorialised, including Archdeacon William Cowper (d.1858) whose remains were reinterred from the Devonshire Street Anglican Cemetery.

The cemetery is still in use and a columbarium and memorial garden at the rear of the cemetery are peaceful additions that continue the commemorative tradition at St Jude's.

There is room for a quiet picnic and in spring the cemetery is coated with freesias, which have naturalised across the cemetery from original grave plantings. The cemetery closes quite early – at 4 pm daily – so don't be caught out! The parishioners of St Jude's take an active interest and hold a monthly working bee to care for the historic cemetery.

NOTABLE BURIALS

- Archibald Mosman (1799–1863), merchant and pastoralist, namesake of the Sydney suburb
- Ann Hordern (c.1792–1871), matriarch of the retail empire Anthony Hordern & Sons

- Simeon Henry Pearce (1821–1886), civil servant, land agent, 'father of Randwick'
- William Busby (1813–1887), pastoralist, politician, son of John Busby of Busby's Bore fame
- Sir Alfred Stephen (1802–1894), chief justice and legislator

MORE INFORMATION

- St Jude's Anglican Church, 'Cemetery', St Jude's Anglican Church Randwick website, 2016, <www.stjudesrandwick.org.au/cemetery>.
- *St Jude's Cemetery, Randwick*, Randwick and District Historical Society, Randwick, 1991.
- Joseph Waugh, *The Living Among the Dead: Tales from St Jude's Cemetery, Randwick*, Randwick and District Historical Society, Randwick, 2005.

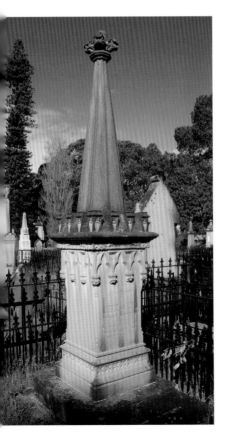

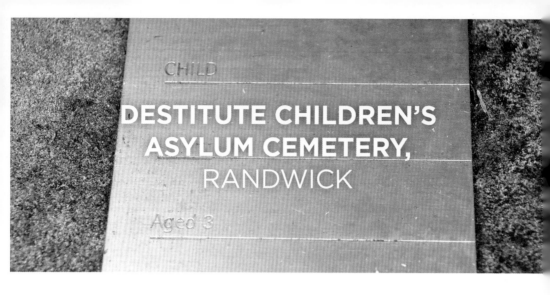

DESTITUTE CHILDREN'S ASYLUM CEMETERY, RANDWICK

MEMORIAL GARDEN, EASY STREET (OFF BARKER STREET), PRINCE OF WALES HOSPITAL, RANDWICK

Burials: 1858–1915

Sydney philanthropists established the Destitute Children's Asylum in Paddington in 1852. By the late 1850s the asylum had outgrown its first home at Ormond House and in 1858 the institution moved into a three-storey building in Randwick, designed by Edmund Blacket. The asylum operated from 1858 to 1915, providing a safety net for abandoned children in an age where social services and pensions did not exist. Children were housed, given a basic education and undertook farming and domestic tasks.

In a barracks-style institution crowded with children, infectious diseases such as measles and whooping cough could spread like wildfire. A burial ground was established to accommodate these tragic deaths. It is unknown exactly how many children died at the institution, but painstaking reconstruction of historical records has identified the names of 174 children who were buried in the cemetery.

The institution was requisitioned as a military hospital during the First World War and subsequently became a repatriation hospital. The cemetery with its unmarked graves lay neglected and forgotten.

In the mid-1990s redevelopment at the Prince of Wales Hospital shone a light on the cemetery once again. An archaeological excavation took place in 1995–96 to exhume the remains of the asylum children and rebury them in a dedicated memorial garden, which covers the southern end of the former cemetery, on the hospital grounds. An astounding 65 individual burials were identified and a further 215 individual pieces of bone were excavated. Detailed forensic analysis and historical research has revealed details of gender, age, ethnicity and in some cases even the names of these forgotten children.

Two long memorial plaques record the names of all the known burials in the cemetery, while plaques detail the 65 individuals reburied in the gardens. The memorial garden was officially opened in 2000. This is a place of quiet contemplation and a site that should never again be forgotten.

MORE INFORMATION

- 'Archives in Brief 66 – Randwick Asylum for Destitute Children', State Records NSW website, <www.records.nsw.gov.au/state-archives/guides-and-finding-aids/archives-in-brief/archives-in-brief-66>.
- Beverley Smith, *Randwick Destitute Children's Asylum: Deaths and Burials 1853–1916*, Cape Banks Family History Society, Maroubra, 1995.

Left Randwick's Destitute Children's Asylum in 1866   *Right* The memorial garden today

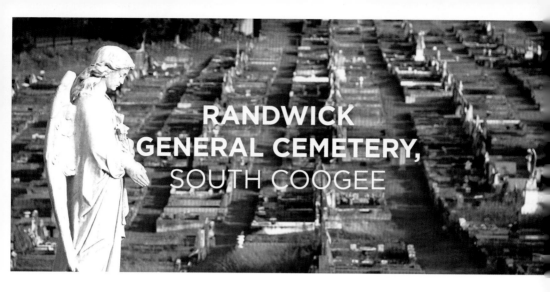

RANDWICK GENERAL CEMETERY, SOUTH COOGEE

MALABAR ROAD, NEAR ARDEN STREET, SOUTH COOGEE

Burials: 1874–present

Most Sydneysiders are unaware of this cemetery, but the locals love it: walking their dogs, including it on their jogging routes, visiting graves. The cemetery is on a sloping sandhill beside Emily McCarthy Park and forms a convenient shortcut. There are not many trees in the cemetery itself, except for some banksias around the edges, and the low sandstone wall contributes to the open feeling of the cemetery.

Yellow-tailed black cockatoos were enjoying the banksia flowers when we visited, their mournful cries providing an appropriate soundtrack to our graveyard rambles.

Randwick General Cemetery was dedicated in 1873 and the first burial took place on 10 September 1874. Impressive green iron gates mark the entrance and main avenue into Randwick General Cemetery. The layout illustrates a hierarchy of burial plot position based on class and wealth. The vaults and large select graves were surveyed and placed near the main avenue or main pathway for each denomination, ensuring cemetery visitors could easily view the high-class memorials.

One of the most historic monuments is the large granite obelisk that marks the family grave of former New South Wales premier, Sir John See. A circular fence encloses the grave plot and two cypress trees flank the memorial, making it easy to spot in the southern part of the cemetery. Twentieth-century lower memorials dominate the cemetery but there is a goodly amount of granite too. You can usually spot the earlier

graves by their use of sandstone or marble, and the cast-iron surrounds. Although not as spectacular as Waverley or South Head, Randwick General Cemetery has some historic burials and the cemetery lover should not underestimate it.

In the past, the cemetery was sometimes referred to as Long Bay Cemetery because Malabar Road was originally called Long Bay Road.

TIP

You can download a cemetery map from Randwick City Council's website.

NOTABLE BURIALS

- James Pemell (1816–1906), flour miller and baker, politician
- Sir John See (1845–1907), merchant, politician, mayor of Randwick and NSW premier
- Archibald Forsyth (1826–1908), rope maker and politician
- Thomas (Tom) Payten (1855–1920), horse trainer of Newmarket stables in Randwick
- William Henry Lambert (1881–1928), politician and union leader
- Bertram (Bert) Howell (1893–1961), musician, bandleader and collector

MORE INFORMATION

- Randwick City Council, 'About Randwick Cemetery', Randwick City Council website, 2016, <www.randwick.nsw.gov.au/facilities-and-recreation/randwick-cemetery/about-randwick-cemetery>.
- June Adams & Warwick Adams, *Randwick General Cemetery: transcripts of monumental inscriptions*, Cape Banks Family History Society, Maroubra, 1993.
- Ian Thomas Cripps, *A Guide to the Historical Significance of Randwick General Cemetery*, Historical Monograph No. 4, Randwick and District Historical Society, Randwick, 1987.

Left The grave of Sir John See (d.1907)

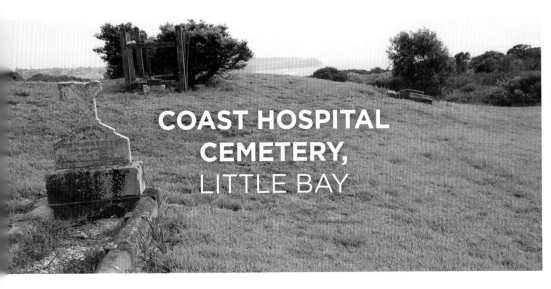

COAST HOSPITAL CEMETERY, LITTLE BAY

**BOTANY BAY NATIONAL PARK,
CAPE BANKS ROAD, LITTLE BAY**

Burials: 1897–1952;
Dharawal Resting Place 2002–present

The wind buffets as you emerge from the scrub to enter this melancholy spot. Nestled on the cliffs of Little Bay, the Coast Hospital Cemetery is a poignant reminder of the devastating effects of epidemics in Sydney. The Coast Hospital was established in 1881 during the smallpox epidemic. This cemetery was the second burial place for the hospital from 1897 to 1952. It was not within the hospital grounds itself, but away to the south in an isolated position to minimise the spread of disease. There is still a visual link between the cemetery and the hospital across the cliffs. It is a spectacular view.

You can feel the press of history in this cemetery. The scattered monuments among the mown grass testify to grief of losing a loved one to disease, quickly and unprepared.

Children, wives, husbands, nurses and doctors are all buried here. Some graves are just marked by kerbing; one by a little timber picket fence. The majority of graves are unmarked; it is estimated there are over 2000 burials here. Only 78 graves are still visible.

A row of grave markers to nurses and staff can be seen to the right as you walk into the cemetery. It must have been devastating for staff to lose a colleague, succumbing to their dedication and duty. There are two simple Gothic arch headstones to Chinamen, Tong Dong (d.1902) and Ah Wong (d.1902), both of whom died of the plague. The most unusual monuments are the two matching grave makers to the Rouse family, Enid Pearl (d.1907) and her mother Alice (d.1917). A semicircular barrel-top sarcophagus covered in tiles defines each grave plot; a little sandstone headstone records the inscription. Each is enclosed in matching cast-iron fence. Executed by monumental mason James Cunningham, Sydney, this style of funerary monument is rarely seen in New South Wales.

The cemetery has ongoing significance for the Aboriginal community as the Dharawal Resting Place, where ancestral remains of

Left The grave of Tong Dong (d.1902), one of several Chinese plague victims buried at the Coast Hospital

the La Perouse Aboriginal people, returned from both Australian and international museums, can be returned to country and buried. The first reburial took place in June 2002.

The cemetery is now within Botany Bay National Park and pressed by golf courses. Enter the National Park from Bunnerong Road and keep driving along the road until you see the 'Botany Bay National Park Cemetery Trail' sign. Pull off here; the cemetery is just a short walk down the trail.

MORE INFORMATION
- Joseph Waugh, *Deaths at the Coast Hospital and Burials at Little Bay: 1881–1952*, Randwick and District Historical Society, Randwick, 1999.
- Peter Olsen, 'Coast Hospital Cemetery', Australian Cemeteries Index website, 2014, <austcemindex.com/cemetery?cemid=1276>.

A rare surviving timber grave surround; the marker, if there was one, is no longer

PIONEER MEMORIAL PARK,
BOTANY

**LOCATED WITHIN EASTERN SUBURBS MEMORIAL PARK,
BUNNERONG ROAD, MATRAVILLE**

Headstones only: 1819–1880s

This is a remnant of the Devonshire Street Cemeteries which once stood on the site of Central Railway Station and tracks. The fact that these 746 memorials have survived at all is a miracle in itself. The Pioneer Memorial Park is the third resting place for these headstones.

The Devonshire Street Cemeteries were a cluster of seven denominational burial grounds established between 1820 and 1836, located on the southern outskirts of Sydney, beside the Benevolent Asylum and Carter's Barracks which both fronted Pitt Street. Originally 1.6 hectares of land was dedicated for a Church of England burial ground to replace the Old Sydney Burial Ground in George Street. The cemetery was consecrated in January 1820, but the first burial took place the previous year. Subsequently, the colonial government allotted adjacent land to other denominations. The layout of the Devonshire Street Cemeteries was an ad hoc arrangement, responding to the needs of the different religious communities for burial space. The Roman Catholics and Presbyterians were given land in 1825. Over the next 14 years, land was also granted to the Jewish, Wesleyan, Quaker and Congregationalist communities. By 1836, there were seven burial grounds covering about 4.8 hectares.

At the time they were established, the location, design and layout of the Devonshire Street Cemeteries demonstrated the latest thinking in the burial of the dead. They were located on the outskirts of town and graves were regulated to encourage orderly and economical use of the ground. A separate area was set aside for vaults. The *Australian* newspaper on 12 December 1842 praised the cemetery's commanding views of the city and harbour and encouraged readers to take a stroll there to admire the monuments. Evidently there were some fine pieces of sculpture.

The Devonshire Street Cemeteries were the principal burial grounds for Sydney between 1820 and 1866. It is often called the Sandhills Cemetery, a colloquial name ascribed on some death certificates that reflects the nature of the land at the edge of Surry Hills. Many prominent historical figures were buried in the

cemetery. There were First Fleeters, such as the brewer James Squire (d.1822). There were colonial firsts, such as Isaac Nichols (d.1819) the first postmaster and George Howe (d.1821) the first government printer. Allan Cunningham (d.1839), botanist and explorer, was buried there and merchants and businessmen such as Samuel Terry (d.1838) and Simeon Lord (d.1840). Cora Gooseberry (d.1852), wife of Broken Bay elder Bungaree and daughter of Moorooboora, leader of the Murro-ore-dial clan south of Port Jackson, was also buried here. Mrs Stewart and Mr Edward Berton, publican of the Sydney Arms Hotel who gave her shelter for several years, erected a tombstone in her memory recognising her as 'Queen of the Sydney tribe of Aborigines'.

By the 1840s these burial grounds were crowded and the orderly regulation of burials was falling by the wayside. In 1848 the Reverend Walsh reported 'it is now scarcely possible to dig a grave without disturbing or dis-interring the remains of dead bodies'. Problems were not confined to the Church of England portion. Henry Graham, the City Council Health Officer, described to a parliamentary inquiry the poor depth of burials in all the grounds. He claimed to have seen bodies in the

Sydney cemeteries 'so near the surface that you could just touch them with a walking-stick or umbrella'.

In the end the Church of England gave up and set up their own burial ground by purchasing land at Camperdown while William Patten, James Martyn Combes and Alexander Henry Brown took advantage of the situation, by establishing the commercially driven Balmain Cemetery. The Devonshire Street Cemeteries were finally closed to new burials in 1867, following the opening of Sydney's new Necropolis at Haslem's Creek. Subsequent burials in family vaults and graves at Devonshire Street required permission from the Colonial Secretary.

By 1878 the cemeteries were thoroughly neglected and the grounds were no longer on the outskirts of the city but surrounded by commercial and residential development as well as a bustling transport hub. Newspapers argued for government money to put the grounds in good order; the *Sydney Illustrated News* editorialised for its complete closure and removal on 13 July 1878; other papers pointed out the need to clean up the neglected grounds. Parliament seriously considered a proposal to resume the cemeteries for railway purposes in 1882, and finally did so in 1901 to make way for Central Railway Station. Relatives and descendants were invited to

1842 plan showing the denominational Devonshire Street Cemeteries

claim remains and monuments and have them removed at government expense to other cemeteries.

The unruly manner in which burials were conducted in these cemeteries became all too apparent when the cemetery was cleared. Bodies were discovered buried beneath paths, and in all the spare ground regardless of line or order. The total number of burials may never be known with certainty. Approximately 8500 remains were claimed by descendants and removed with their associated monumentation to other cemeteries. Those remains left unclaimed – somewhere around 30,000 – were exhumed and removed to Bunnerong Cemetery, an extension of Botany General Cemetery (now Eastern Suburbs Memorial Park), along with about 2800 memorials. A special tramway was laid down to transport the remains to their new home. Many have not survived to this day.

In 1972 when Botany Cemetery needed land for new burials, the government passed legislation to allow re-use of the Bunnerong Cemetery. The memorials were consolidated in 1976 to create the Pioneer Memorial Park. Weathered and broken headstones were discarded and the 746 memorials that survived now stand neatly in a geometrical pattern. Large memorials, ledgers and altar tombs form the perimeter on the south. In the centre of the park is the imposing Blake family monument, a large pedestal with diamond-shaped inscription panels surmounted by a pinnacle, executed by stonemason and sculptor Joseph Popplewell. Many of the sandstone headstones are covered in red lichen, making them very photogenic.

There are some ornate examples of early stonemasonry, especially Catholic iconography with seraphs, angels, sacred hearts and crosses, as well as incised Corinthian columns, draped urns and Georgian fan motifs. Look out in particular for cricketer Richard Murray's (d.1861) headstone which sports a pair of stumps, two cricket bats and a ball.

TIPS

For an engaging discussion of some of those buried in the Devonshire Street Cemeteries see Foster (1919).

To track down where headstones were relocated by relatives in 1901 consult Johnson & Sainty (2001).

For the transcription of all the headstones in Bunnerong Cemetery undertaken in 1969 prior to their consolidation see Johnson & Sainty (2001).

NOTABLE BURIALS

- John William Lewin (1770–1819), artist and naturalist
- George Howe (1769–1821), publisher of *Sydney Gazette*, first government printer
- Hannah Cooper (c.1774–1836), wife of Daniel Cooper (1785–1853), merchant and investor
- Mary Reibey (1777–1855), convict, businesswoman and trader
- Richard Murray (c.1831–1861), cricketer

MORE INFORMATION

- AG Foster, 'The Sandhills: an historic cemetery', *Journal of the Royal Australian Historical Society*, vol. 5, no. 4, 1919, pp. 153–195.
- Keith Johnson & Malcolm Sainty, *Sydney Burial Ground 1819–1901 (Elizabeth and Devonshire Streets) and History of Sydney's Early Cemeteries from 1788*, Library of Australian History, Sydney, 2001.
- *Pioneer Memorial Park at Botany Cemetery*, Cape Banks Family History Society, Maroubra, 1988.
- Sue Zelinka, *Tender Sympathies: A Social History of Botany Cemetery*, Hale and Iremonger, Sydney, 1991.

The Devonshire Street Cemeteries, c.1900

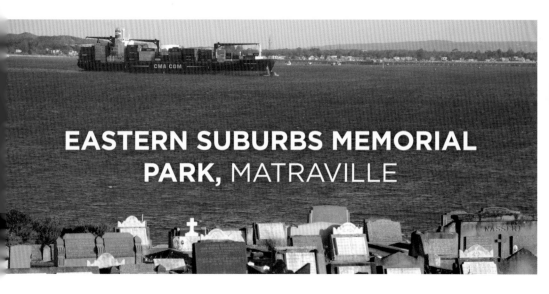

EASTERN SUBURBS MEMORIAL PARK, MATRAVILLE

12 MILITARY ROAD, MATRAVILLE

Burials: 1893–present

Eastern Suburbs Memorial Park began life as Botany Cemetery in the late 19th century. The Botany Progress Association formed in 1885 and lobbied the government for a local burial ground from its inception. The government selected the association's preferred site behind Bumborah Point but it took until 10 January 1888 to gazette the 11.7 hectare cemetery.

The cemetery trustees then had to fence and clear the site and adopt regulations and fees. It took another five years before the cemetery was open for business. The first burial, within the Church of England portion, was a simple one for Emily Cox, a 24-year-old from La Perouse, on 21 August 1893. The Presbyterians recorded their first burial on 11 February 1894, with a lavish funeral for Mary Wiggins, wife of Honorary Secretary to the Botany Cemetery Trust, Joshua Wiggins. The other sections soon followed: the first Roman Catholic interment on 9 March 1894; Congregationalist on 20 November 1897; and finally Wesleyan on 8 June 1898.

The original entrance to the cemetery was on Bunnerong Road and the earliest sections can be found in this area. The burial area has been expanded several times. Unclaimed remains from the Devonshire Street Cemeteries were reburied within an extension known as Bunnerong Cemetery that was later reclaimed. (See the separate entry for Botany Pioneer Memorial Park for its history.) The sleek modern Eastern Suburbs Crematorium was added in 1938, surrounded by memorial gardens. The site is sandy with water courses running through it, so there is a diversity of landscaping throughout. The main entrance is now on Military Road and the cemetery has expanded across to the northern side of the road. The cemetery is still in operation and there have been over 65,000 burials here.

Eastern Suburbs Memorial Park demonstrates the evolution of memorialisation through the 20th-century. There are many fine art deco slab and desk monuments, lawn burials with monumental niches, crypts and vaults. Lots of interesting Sydneysiders are buried here, including many from the Aboriginal community at La Perouse. It is a rollcall of modern Sydney.

There are great views from the cemetery of Yarra Bay and Port Botany, and also of the remaining Chinese market gardens that border the site. A rest house on the hill of Botany Circle affords some of the best views.

TIP

You can search the online database of burials and download maps from the cemetery's website.

NOTABLE BURIALS

- Emma Timbery (c.1842–1916) Aboriginal shell worker, elder of La Perouse community
- Harry Sidney Foy (1901–1942), nightclub entertainer and Sydney's best known female impersonator
- Herbert Henry (Dally) Messenger (1883–1959), footballer, commemorated by SCG grandstand and Dally M. medal
- Kathleen Mary Josephine (Kate) Leigh (1881–1964), sly-grogger

- Benny Wearing (1901–1968), footballer, record breaking winger for Souths
- Mary Elizabeth Kathleen Dulcie Deamer (1890–1972), writer and Bohemian
- Percival John (Perce) Galea (1910–1977) milkman, punter and bookmaker, illegal casino operator

MORE INFORMATION

- Eastern Suburbs Memorial Park website, 2009, <www.easternsuburbsmemorialpark.com.au>.
- *Botany Cemetery transcripts*, multiple volumes, Cape Banks Family History Society, Maroubra, 1988–95.
- Sue Zelinka, *Tender Sympathies: A Social History of Botany Cemetery*, Hale and Iremonger, Sydney, 1991.
- Maureen Reynolds, *Buried at Botany: A cemetery comes alive*, Cape Banks Family History Society, Maroubra, 2012.

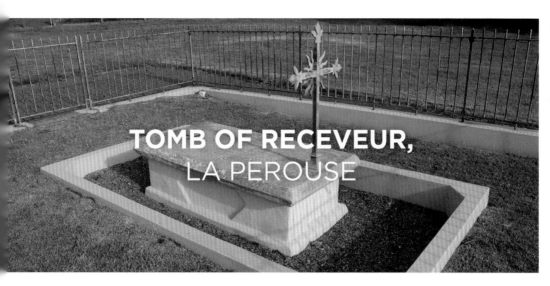

TOMB OF RECEVEUR, LA PEROUSE

ANZAC PARADE, LA PEROUSE

Lone grave: 1788

This is technically a lone grave, not a cemetery. However, it has the distinction of being the earliest marked European burial that survives on Sydney soil, so I thought it deserved a mention. Claude-Francois-Joseph Receveur (1757–1788) was a member of the French scientific expedition commanded by Jean-François La Perouse. Receveur, also known as Père Laurent Receveur, was a Catholic priest and one of two chaplains on the voyage.

A competent scientist, Receveur also performed astronomical observations and naturalist recordings on the expedition.

The ships the *Astrolabe* and *Boussole* anchored in Botany Bay for five weeks in January–February 1788, just as the British were settling into Sydney Cove. Receveur had been wounded in mid-December 1787 during an encounter with locals in Samoa. It seems his wounds, which he described to his brother in a letter as 'very trifling', did not heal as anticipated. He died on 17 February 1788 and was buried on the northern shore of Botany Bay.

Initially a sign marked Receveur's grave, then a plaque nailed to a nearby tree and then an inscription carved into the tree trunk. (The latter is now in a Parisian maritime museum.) The present sandstone altar tomb, surmounted by a crucifix, was erected at the direction and expense of visiting Frenchman Hyacinthe de Bougainville in 1825, with the blessing of Governor Brisbane. It was completed in 1829. The nearby monument to La Perouse was also erected at this time. The tomb was enclosed by a fence to protect it in the 1870s and the memorial has been restored several times over the years.

TIP

Time your visit for the first Sunday of the month so you can wander around the Blak markets on Bare Island, featuring Aboriginal arts, crafts and culture.

MORE INFORMATION

- Edward Duyker, 'Receveur, Laurent', Dictionary of Sydney website, 2011, <dictionaryofsydney.org/entry/receveur_laurent>.
- 'Receveur Monument', *Lapérouse Museum and Monuments*, 2016, <laperousemuseum.org/receveur-monument>.

Left Oswald Brierly's sketch of Receveur's tomb and the nearby tree, 1842

TOP 5

TOOLS OF TRADE GRAVESTONES

PHIL GARLICK Racing Car Driver	**South Head General Cemetery, Vaucluse**
OWEN PEART High Diver	**Waverley Cemetery, Bronte**
JAMES ROSS LOGAN Tram Driver	**Presbyterian No. 1 cemetery, Rookwood Necropolis**
RICHARD MURRAY Cricketer	**Pioneer Memorial Park, Botany**
JOHN LEYS Engineer, Mort's Dock	**Camperdown Cemetery, Newtown**

Cricketer Richard Murray's (d.1861) headstone, Pioneer Memorial Park, Botany

① Woronora General Cemetery, Sutherland *p. 66*
② Former Methodist Cemetery, Rockdale *p. 64*

Opposite Detail of inscription for Charles Clarke (d.1889), Former Methodist Cemetery, Rockdale

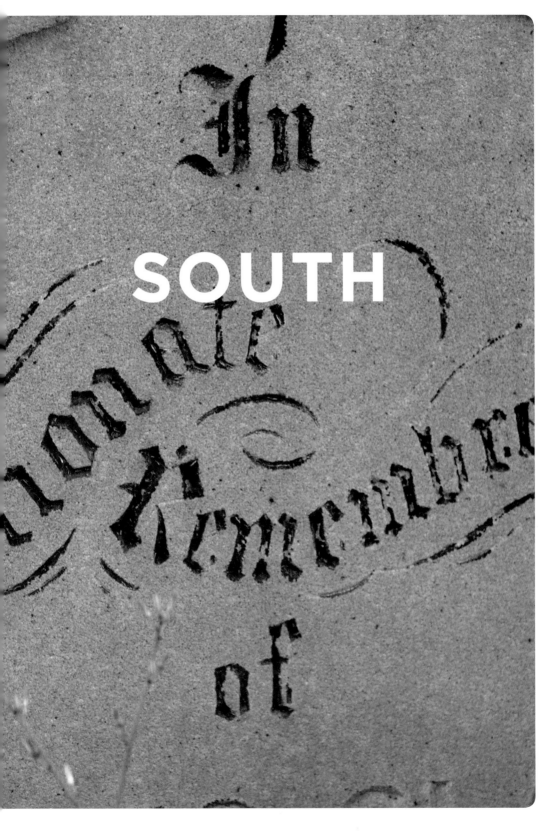

SOUTH

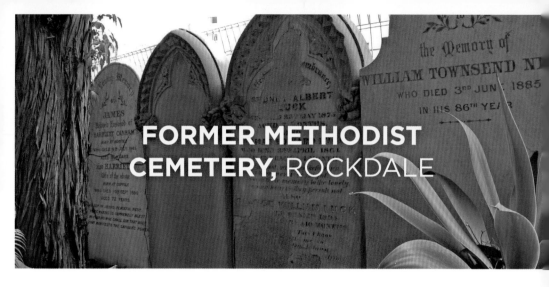

FORMER METHODIST CEMETERY, ROCKDALE

BAY STREET, ROCKDALE

Burials: 1865–1890s (converted 1936)

I was surprised to discover that a few remnant headstones survive from the former Wesleyan Methodist Cemetery at Rockdale. This was a very early cemetery in the area. James Beehag donated 4000 square metres of land for a Wesleyan Chapel and burial ground in 1858. It was known as the Rocky Point Wesleyan Chapel and was the first church built in the municipality.

By 1895 this was considered an 'old' cemetery located within the bustling and growing area of Rockdale. Burials had virtually ceased in the cemetery apart from family vaults and some of the headstones had been enclosed within the yard of the minister's house. The government gave church authorities permission in 1936 to clear the cemetery and create a Remembrance Wall from the suitable headstones and slabs elsewhere on their land. The bodies were not disturbed or removed; the former cemetery area was to be maintained as 'gardens, lawns or grass plots'.

Given the cemetery was converted so long ago, I honestly thought the chance that any headstones remained was relatively slim. But there they are, lined up along the cyclone fence with their backs to Chapel Lane, a silent reminder of the area's early history. There are now just 28 headstones recording the deaths of 36 locals between 1865 and 1890. The earliest that survive are two dating from 1865, commemorating Walter Cook and James Canham. The majority of headstones are sandstone, with just four marble ones, reflecting the period when the cemetery was active. Many headstones have been truncated, some severed in half. They are a sad remnant of a modest church cemetery.

MORE INFORMATION

- Rockdale Uniting Church, 'Our Church's History – the Story so far...', Rockdale Uniting Church website, 2016, <www.rockdaleuc.org.au>.
- *Methodist Church, Rockdale, Cemetery Act, 1936* <www.austlii.edu.au/au/legis/nsw/num_act/mcrca1936n29354.pdf>
- Ray Cork, 'Rockdale Uniting Church Cemetery', Australian Cemeteries Index website, 2011, <austcemindex.com/cemetery?cemid=799>.

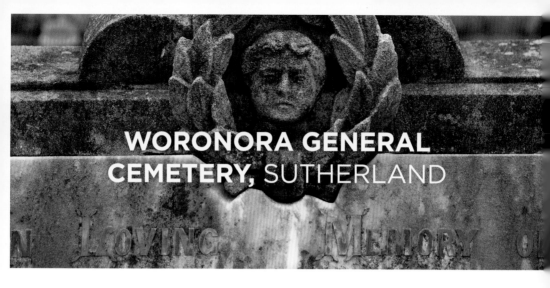

WORONORA GENERAL CEMETERY, SUTHERLAND

121 LINDEN STREET, SUTHERLAND

Burials: 1895–present

Woronora Cemetery, the major cemetery for southern Sydney, aspired to be a mini-Rookwood, but didn't quite make the mark. This late 19th-century cemetery was originally designed around a central circle, much like Rookwood, with denominational areas swirling off like flower petals. A short railway branch line brought mourners into the cemetery from the Sutherland line. The landscape design has been compromised over the years, although remnants of the

original intention endure in the main road structure and key avenue plantings of camphor laurels.

The cemetery was established in 1895. The first burial was Helen Willow, who died 30 March 1895. Her burial took place hurriedly on the day before the cemetery's official opening, rushed through because of her suspected tuberculosis. Helen Willow's grave in the Methodist section (behind the Holy Trinity Macedonian temple) is marked by a little marble Calvary cross.

The funeral train operated from 1900 to 1944. The terminus in the central circle had a platform lined with cabbage tree palms and a small waiting room. Sadly, the platform, waiting room and palms have all disappeared, replaced by the main office building.

Today the cemetery is comprised of three main elements: monumental burials, lawn burials and a crematorium with memorial gardens. Start your visit in the centre of the cemetery at the main office. From here you can easily wander around the earliest graves which are the closest. They are also easy to spot as they are generally taller in stature. The grave markers shrink throughout the 20th-century, till they become plaques in the ground on the outskirts of the cemetery. The cemetery feels densely occupied, which it is, an atmosphere reinforced by the visual impact of row upon row of lower desk and monuments unbroken by any vegetation or visual diversity. A close reading of memorials, however, is rewarding. Look out for the little differences: a footstone set into the kerbing noting a nickname, the regard of workmates, or a touching farewell epitaph.

Wandering around the Anglican 1 Section is sobering, as you encounter a conspicuous number of private family memorials to soldiers killed during the First World War. Look out in particular for the marble medallion portrait of John Percy James Derwent, killed in France 27 February 1917. A number of grave markers were transferred from the Devonshire Street Cemeteries when it was cleared in 1901. These are conspicuous by their early designs and death dates predating 1895. I spotted a few in the Presbyterian 1 Section. The grave furniture in Woronora is remarkably intact and you will see porcelain immortelles under glass domes, colourful earthenware floral wreaths, and a large number of swan vases. Little cast-iron signs for Annual Care and Perpetual Care also poke up from various graves.

The trustees first considered a crematorium in 1929. Architect Louis Robertson designed a moderne, art deco-style crematorium constructed between 1933 and 1934 by local contractor Norman Smith of Bexley. It was the third crematorium in Sydney, after Rookwood in 1925, and Northern Suburbs Crematorium in 1933. At its opening on 21 April 1934, officials and journalists described the structure at Woronora as one of 'stateliness and beauty',

Left John Percy James Derwent, killed in France 27 February 1917

'huge and elaborate' and 'modern and imposing'. Robertson subsequently designed the Eastern Suburbs Crematorium in 1938 along similar lines. The Woronora Crematorium is surrounded by immaculate memorial gardens. When we visited in February the roses were in full bloom, providing colourful relief to the dense uniformity and greyness of desk monuments found elsewhere.

Woronora Cemetery has been at the forefront of memorial innovation and was the first Sydney metropolitan cemetery to establish a lawn cemetery section. It began considering the idea in 1950 and an area was gazetted in late 1953. More recently the cemetery has introduced a number of contemporary memorial structures which reflect the changing role of the cemetery landscape supporting

mourning and grief. Woronora has a garden for miscarriages and stillborn babies, a children's area as well as memorials recognising road trauma and emergency services, missing people, the police and the military. A Stations of the Cross is another circular focal point for the cemetery. There are some areas for individual crypts and two larger mausoleums for above-ground crypt burial. The cemetery is still in use and expanding, managed by the Southern Metropolitan Cemeteries Trust.

TIP

Pick up a self-guided tour brochure from the cemetery office to see the major memorial structures in the cemetery.

NOTABLE BURIALS

- Helena Sumner Locke (1881–1917), author
- Karl Reginald Cramp (1878–1956), public school inspector and historian
- Herbert Stanley (Bert) Groves (1907–1970), Aboriginal activist

MORE INFORMATION

- Woronora Cemetery website, <www.woronoracemetery.org.au>.
- Peter Olsen & Ray Cork, 'Woronora Cemetery', Australian Cemeteries Index website, 2014, <austcemindex.com/cemetery?cemid=907>.
- Michael Boyd, *Woronora Cemetery and Crematorium, 1895–1995: 'Where Beauty Softens Grief'*, Woronora General Cemetery and Crematorium Trust, Sutherland, 1995.

WHAT HEADSTONE IS THAT?

As you wander around Sydney's cemeteries, you will start to notice trends in grave marker styles and materials. The popularity of styles shifts and changes over the decades. Sepulchral memorial styles tend to replicate trends in architectural styles. This is not a recent phenomenon; English sepulchral monuments have followed architectural fashions since the medieval period.

The majority of grave markers in Sydney's cemeteries are executed in stone. Sandstone was the most common material used for memorials in the first half of the 19th century, as it was widely available and easy to carve. Mass-produced iron grave markers were a cheaper alternative to stone and a few still survive in Sydney's cemeteries. Marble became the material of choice in the second half of the 19th century. Granite, in turn, became popular for expensive monuments in the late 19th century and was widely used in the 20th-century. Concrete and metal plaques became more common in the second half of the 20th-century.

Funerary monuments in Sydney can be divided into five main categories: stelae (or headstones), horizontal slabs, pillars and sculpture, crosses, and crypts and mausoleums. These categories were originally developed by the Cemeteries Conservation Committee at the National Trust (NSW) in the 1980s to help establish some common terminology concerning sepulchral memorials. I have used these terms throughout the book to highlight different grave markers worth seeing in each cemetery, so familiarise yourself with them. It will enhance your enjoyment of this book, as well as your cemetery visits.

A sandstone altar tomb and a small neoclassical family mausoleum, South Head General Cemetery

HEADSTONES

Stelae, or headstones as I tend to call them, were the most common type of grave marker and can be found around Sydney from the 1790s through to the 1930s. Prior to the 1860s a grave would often be marked with a matching headstone and footstone. The footstone usually records the initials of the deceased and often also noted the year of death. From the 1860s onwards, it became more usual to mark the grave plot with stone kerbing, sometimes with iron railings. This was partly due to cemetery regulations many of which required owners to enclose their plots shortly after purchase.

There are lots of headstone variations, particularly in how the overall stone was shaped and whether the shoulders of the headstone were cut away or carved. The basic shapes are rectangular, cambered, semicircular, gabled or Gothic. More unusual were the ogee and anthropomorphic headstones, which tend to be found prior to 1860. Within each of these styles the shoulders of the headstone might be shaped, cutaway, stepped or formed with acroteria. Headstone shapes might also have a pediment or surmount.

Left Lower slab and desk monuments, Frenchs Forest Bushland Cemetery   *Right* Black granite Celtic cross, Richmond Lawn Cemet

HORIZONTAL SLABS

Horizontal slabs in the 19th century consisted of ledger stones, altar tombs and table tombs, along with the occasional sarcophagus. These monuments were inspired from English church memorials and were prestigious grave markers that often stood over a brick vault. Some of Sydney's earliest burial grounds have altar tombs, including St John's Anglican Cemetery at Parramatta and St John's Catholic Cemetery at Campbelltown. The tombs did not contain the bodies themselves, but functioned as commemorative monuments. The misconception that these tombs might contain the bodies has led to much vandalism in the 20th and 21st centuries..

Lower horizontal styles of monumentation returned in the 20th-century with slab and desk markers, or more simply desk markers with kerbing. The sloping desk usually featured an inscription panel. Historians have frequently identified the First World War as a turning point in the history of mourning and cemetery landscapes. However, analysis of patterns of consumption in monumental masons' records suggests that the immediate impact of the war was a lot less dramatic. The trend towards simpler monumentation was evident as early as 1902. The shift to the lower-style desk memorial had become quite pronounced by the 1920s. Sandstone and marble were preferred in the 1920s but by the 1940s granite was more popular.

Left Marble draped urn on a pedestal, Gore Hill Memorial Cemetery *Right* Marble figurative sculptures, crosses, pillars and pedestals define the character of Waverley Cemetery

CROSSES

There are all sorts of crosses: Latin, Calvary (a Latin cross with a three-step base), Celtic, and rusticated crosses. Celtic crosses are particularly associated with the Irish and often feature symbols of Irish nationalism such as the shamrock as well as Celtic patterns. Vernacular timber crosses also fall into this category. Larger crosses were often placed on a pedestal with chamfered base or stepped base. Crosses were often incorporated into headstones, as either a major stylistic motif or a surmount, in addition to being sculptural elements.

PILLARS AND SCULPTURE

Pillars and sculpture had replaced altar tombs as the prestigious memorial of choice by the 1870s. The term pillars encompasses various forms of columns, obelisks and pedestals. A pedestal with a chamfered base often supported an urn or sculpture. Such monuments had been used since 1800, but did not become widespread until the 1870s. By this point large monumental masonry firms had been established in Sydney and they could offer an impressive range of local and imported cemetery monuments at more affordable prices. Pillars were mainly executed in imported marble from the 1870s to the 1890s, granite to a lesser extent.

Three-dimensional sculpture was another form of cemetery monument used to mark large family plots and brick vaults. Again, you tend to find these in Sydney's cemeteries in the late 19th and early 20th-century. Sculpture, typically an angel or allegorical figure, embellished mausoleums. Sculpture was often placed upon a pedestal to reinforce the landmark qualities of the grave marker.

MAUSOLEUMS, VAULTS AND CRYPTS

Mausoleums and vaults were the domain of the wealthy in the late 19th and early 20th centuries. They were an architectural statement inspired by mortuary chapels. Bodies were buried not in the ground, but on shelves within the building. Double-lined coffins, or coffins within caskets, were required and only the very rich could afford such things. This form of memorialisation promoted dynasties. European migration from the 1950s influenced a revival in mausoleums and vaults, and the introduction of crypts. A crypt is an above-ground burial chamber in a wall or structure, that you can buy as an alternative to a burial plot. Sometimes, a structure with crypt burials is referred to as a mausoleum but generally vaults and mausoleums are for individual families. The widespread introduction of the practice of embalming in the second half of the 20th-century has also facilitated the use of crypts. In the 21st century most active cemeteries have a vault and crypt section.

Family mausoleums line Frost Avenue, Eastern Suburbs Memorial Park

Left Art deco slab and desk memorial with majolica flowers, Eastern Suburbs Memorial Park   *Right* Crematorium rose gardens, Woronora General Cemetery

GRAVE FURNITURE

If you are a connoisseur of interior design, you might notice that grave furniture such as grave surrounds, grave coverings and flower vases particularly reflect domestic decoration and taste. Cast-iron surrounds in graveyards mimicked Victorian terrace verandah balustrades. Black and white marble tiles were popular between the 1890s and 1910s. Small octagonal tiles in two contrasting colours, common in bathrooms, were utilised to cover grave plots in the 1920s and 1930s. Australian pottery vases can be found on graves dating from the 1920s. Decorative pieces of grave furniture, such as wreaths and crosses, were made from majolica (earthenware), just like the flying ducks on living room walls. Glazed tiles were popular in the 1950s in bold modern colours such as pink, red, blue, oatmeal and beige.

LAWNS AND GARDENS

Cemetery regulations have always dictated the type of memorial style acceptable in any given area. Timber and concrete were banned in many cemeteries until the mid-20th-century. But as the ornate 19th-century cemetery landscapes became increasingly difficult to maintain, cemetery managers introduced lawn cemeteries. Simple plaques set into the ground or low monumentation placed on a concrete strip made lawn maintenance much easier.

The establishment of crematoria gardens – with their smaller commemorative plaques and neatly kept memorial gardens – may have helped to smooth the way for the introduction of lawn cemeteries in New South Wales after the Second World War. The secularisation of society may have also made lawn cemeteries more acceptable because the grave was no longer a source of consolation for many, or of faith; rather it was a reminder of loss. This made the grave less central to the memory and identity of the deceased.

Lawn cemeteries introduced specific regulations for memorial types and heights, and usually banned any form of enclosure or kerbing. Grave furniture was also kept to a minimum. For cemetery managers, lawn cemeteries were more economical in their land use and easier to maintain. A lawn cemetery did not need, nor did it encourage, regular grave visitation.

Over time, people, reacting to the minimalist simplicity of lawn cemeteries, began to decorate them with windmills, artificial flowers, photographs, flags and other personal memorabilia. In response some cemeteries introduced tighter regulations on different memorial sections; while others let such personal expressions flourish, allowing an intimate and less formal memorialisation to evolve in the 21st century.

You have now completed a crash-course in how to identify cemetery memorials. Go and test your knowledge at a cemetery near you and see how many styles you can identify.

Richmond Lawn Cemetery

TOP 5

CEMETERIES FOR PICNICS

St Jude's Anglican Cemetery, Randwick

St John's Anglican Cemetery, Ashfield

Presbyterian Cemetery, Ebenezer

St Thomas' Rest Park, Crows Nest

Rookwood Necropolis

St Jude's Anglican Cemetery, Randwick

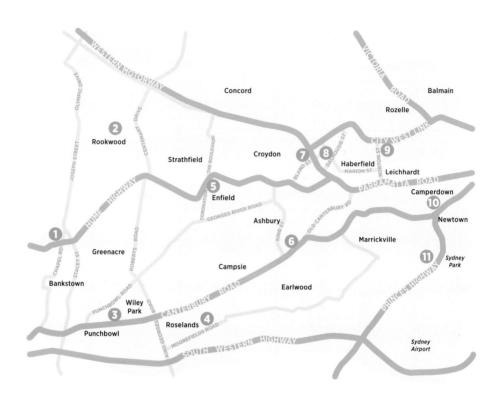

Opposite Detail of a weeping widow, Camperdown Cemetery

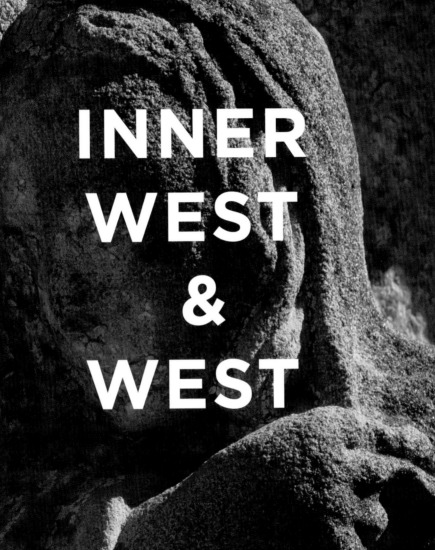

INNER
WEST
&
WEST

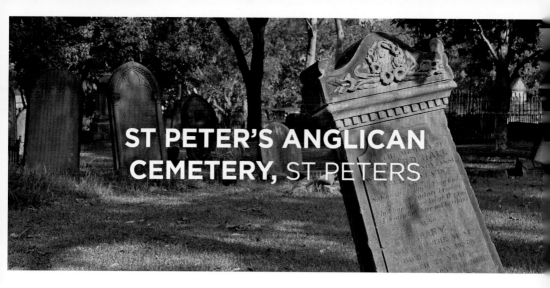

ST PETER'S ANGLICAN CEMETERY, ST PETERS

187–209 PRINCES HIGHWAY, ST PETERS

Burials: 1839–1896

This oft-overlooked cemetery is one of the earliest cemeteries surviving in the inner west. Established in 1838, St Peter's Anglican Church and Cemetery served the Cooks River parish and predates its more famous neighbour Camperdown Cemetery by 11 years. The small cemetery is nestled to the northern side of the early Gothic Revival style church. Stroll beneath the eucalypts that are dotted amongst the graves and you might hear a kookaburra. It's a grassy, tranquil setting; tranquil, that is, if you can ignore the traffic whizzing past along the highway and the aeroplanes screaming overhead about to land at the nearby airport.

St Peter's is a compact example of a 19th-century church cemetery, although many headstones and grave surrounds have disappeared and other monuments have collapsed. Don't be put off. This is a well cared for cemetery, much loved by the church parishioners. A series of large, finely carved neoclassical monuments, that stand atop large family vaults near the driveway and church entrance, signify the wealthier burials of prominent citizens and provide the cemetery's wow factor. Virtually all the markers are sandstone, giving the graveyard a pleasing aesthetic. Look out for some early cross-shaped sarcophagi, Egyptian symbolism and hourglasses.

There are 2515 burials entered in the burial register. Tragically, two-thirds of the burials were children under the age of ten, a testament to the high rate of infant and child mortality in the 19th century. The first burial on 4 March 1839 was of John Benfield, a soldier. The last on 10 April 1896 was Sarah Ann Sargant, a widow.

The church was built by brickmaker Henry Knight (d.1887), who is also buried here. The square tower once sported a church spire; this is now missing.

This small cemetery deserves exploring. Look for the modest but informative signs, installed in 2014 to celebrate the cemetery's 175th anniversary, that point out some of the cemetery's prominent residents.

TIP

The church runs cemetery tours on the first Saturday of the month.

Left St Peter's Anglican Church and Cemetery, taken between 1876 and 1895

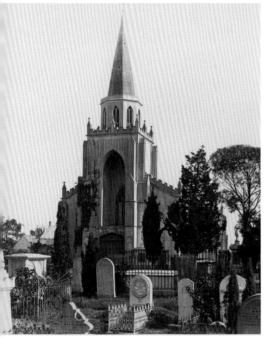

NOTABLE BURIALS

- Frederick Wright Unwin (1798–1852), solicitor and merchant, of Unwins Bridge Road
- Alexander Brodie Spark (1792–1856), merchant, of 'Tempe House'
- John Bibb (1810–1862), architect of Pitt Street Uniting Church, Sydney

MORE INFORMATION

- St Peter's Anglican Church, 'Our History', St Peter's Anglican Church website, 2015, <stpetersatstpeters.org.au>.
- St Peters Church, Cooks River, History Group website, 2015 <stpeterscooksriverhistory.wordpress.com>.
- Laurel Horton, *Grave Reflections: The Story of St Peters Graveyard, Cooks River*, St Peters Publications, St Peters, 1996.

CAMPERDOWN CEMETERY,
NEWTOWN

Burials: 1849–1926 (converted 1948)

Camperdown Cemetery is one of Sydney's favourite cemeteries. Located in the heart of Newtown, its flowing kangaroo grass and air of benign gothic neglect appeals especially to students and hipsters. You will regularly encounter dog walkers, photographers, strumming troubadours and picnickers lounging in the cemetery.

There is much more to this cemetery than meets the eye. Many people think it is a churchyard, but St Stephen's Anglican Church was built inside the grounds in the 1870s after the cemetery was partially closed to burials. And it's bigger than you think. The walls lined with headstones hint at an earlier history. Many people are stunned to learn the burial ground once covered the entire rest park area; and the bodies are still there.

Camperdown Cemetery can claim a special place in Sydney's cemetery history. Anglican parishioners were frustrated at the lack of government action in providing appropriate burial grounds for Sydneysiders. Their cemetery at Devonshire Street was overflowing and the Church of England had rejected as unworkable the proposal for a truly general cemetery on the Sydney Common (Moore Park), burying all denominations next to each other. So parishioners took matters into their own hands and founded the Church of England Cemetery Company, a joint-stock company formed to finance Camperdown Cemetery; 200 shares were issued at £10 each. The Camperdown Cemetery was one of only two company cemeteries established in 19th-century Sydney. The other was Balmain Cemetery, a totally different proposition.

Roughly 5 hectares of land were purchased by the company on the Camperdown Road (Church Street) for the exclusive burial of Church of England parishioners. The cemetery was consecrated on 16 January 1849. The company designed the cemetery with plantations and walks, like English model garden cemeteries. The cemetery company also adopted the English method of planning and locating grave plots. Rather than using a simple grid pattern, the cemetery was divided into imaginary squares of 100 feet (900 square metres each), ignoring any paths or landscape. Detailed plans of each square were kept and graves were numbered as formed and noted in the plans. Although following the latest English trends in cemetery design, the burial plot layout of Camperdown Cemetery was the exception rather than the rule. I have not found any other cemeteries planned on this principle in New South Wales.

The cemetery was divided into vaults, select graves and common graves. The common and pauper graves were located at the lowest point of the cemetery, far from the cemetery entrance; no monumentation was allowed in this section.

Camperdown Cemetery was the main burial ground for the Church of England from 1849 until 1867. During its first 18 years, there were over 15,700 burials here. The first symbolic

Camperdown Cemetery in 1951 just before its conversion; most of this area is now Camperdown Rest Park

interment was Sir Maurice Charles O'Connell (d.1848), who had sold the land to the company. He had died the previous year and was originally buried in the Devonshire Street Cemetery, but his remains were reinterred in the new cemetery. Other prominent figures include the surveyor-general Sir Thomas Livingstone Mitchell (d.1855), James Kidd (d.1867), superintendent of the Botanic Gardens, Commissioner of Police William Augustus Miles (d.1851), and politician Stephen Styles Goold (d.1876). There are two vaults for Robert Tooth's family, reflecting the wealth accrued from the brewing industry, and more

poetically Charles Bochsa (d.1856) a former harpist to Napoleon is buried in the cemetery. A finely carved, medieval-inspired canopied Gothic tomb is erected over the family grave of John Roote Andrews (d.1884). Andrews established his stoneyard next to the cemetery and he executed many of the monuments to be found here. His sons went on to become undertakers and monumental masons.

Camperdown Cemetery hosts a large number of memorials to mariners, naval officers and shipwrecks, silent testimony to Sydney's 19th-century character as a bustling maritime port. The most famous memorial is to the wreck of the *Dunbar*, which was dashed on the cliffs of The Gap on the night of 20 August 1857, leaving just one survivor. This was one of Sydney's worst maritime disasters; 121 passengers and crew drowned. Thousands of Sydneysiders attended the funeral of the victims, the government erected a memorial, and an old anchor from the *Dunbar* is by the mass grave and tomb. Memorial services commemorating the wreck of the *Dunbar* were an annual feature until at least the 1940s. In recent years interest in the graves of James Donnithorne (d.1852), East India Company judge and master of the mint in the Bengal civil service, and his daughter Eliza (d.1886) has surpassed the interest in the *Dunbar* memorial. Some claim that Eliza Donnithorne was the inspiration for the jilted, eccentric Miss Havisham in Charles Dickens' novel *Great Expectations*.

By the 1860s the cemetery was filling up. In addition, New South Wales parliamentary inquiries in 1855 and 1866 had exposed problems arising from the cemetery's apparently haphazard and unregulated burial practices. Parliamentarians, reported the *Sydney Morning Herald* on 5 September 1855, decried the Camperdown Cemetery as 'a shame and a disgrace to any community'. The cemetery exuded offensive smells and businesses beside it complained to the 1866 select committee inquiry

into the Camperdown and Randwick Cemeteries Bill of 'nasty greenish-blue' blowflies invading their workshops from the drainage sump and pauper graves. Camperdown Cemetery was closed to new burials in 1867 and after this date, vault owners had to apply to the Chief Secretary for special permission to bury. The following year the Sydney Church of England Cemetery Company was dissolved. The cemetery land was handed over to the Bishop of Sydney and Edmund Blacket designed St Stephen's church at this time. Between 1867 and 1900 there were a further 2183 burials, but very few more before it closed in 1926.

Today the cemetery is a shadow of its former self. The state government resumed the majority of the cemetery (3.6 hectares) and converted it into a memorial rest park in 1948. A high sandstone wall enclosed the remaining 1.6 hectares. Some of the headstones from the outlying areas were repositioned around the walls.

When Balmain Cemetery was converted in 1941, a few of its headstones were transferred here and managed to survive Camperdown's subsequent conversion. Look out for the large ship's propeller that marks the grave of John Leys (d.1883). Leys was a foreman engineer at Mort's Dock, Balmain, and this memorial was erected by his fellow workers. The headstone of architect Edmund Thomas Blacket (d.1883), which he actually designed for his wife Sarah (d.1869), also made the cut and can be found near the church main door. A number of headstones removed from the Anglican cemetery at Devonshire Street have also found their way to Camperdown Cemetery.

TIPS

The church runs guided tours on the first Sunday of the month.

The Society of Australian Genealogists has compiled an excellent guide to the records of Camperdown Cemetery.

An online database of cemetery headstones and a map is available on the church website.

NOTABLE BURIALS

- William Perry (d.1849) and Mogo (d.1850), Aboriginal men whose graves were marked with headstones in 1931; at least five other Aboriginal burials are known to have occurred in the 1860s and 1870s

- Sir Thomas Livingstone Mitchell (1792–1855), surveyor-general
- Robert Nicholas Charles Bochsa (1789–1856), musician, harpist to Napoleon
- Victims of the wreck of the *Dunbar* (1857)
- Frederick Casemero Terry (1825–1869), artist and engraver
- Stephen Styles Goold (1817–1876), politician, painter, contractor and political organiser
- John Roote Andrews (1801–1884), monumental mason
- Robert Tooth (1821–1893), merchant, pastoralist, brewer

MORE INFORMATION

- Newtown Erskineville Anglican Church, 'Cemetery Headstones', Newtown Erskineville Anglican Church website, 2014, <www.neac.com.au/bookings/cemetery-headstones>.
- Megan Martin, 'Society of Australian Genealogists' Primary Records Collection Guide: Camperdown Cemetery', Society of Australian Genealogists website, 2008, <www.sag.org.au/downloads/CamperdownCemetery.pdf>.
- Chrys Meader, *Beyond the Boundary Stone: a history of Camperdown Cemetery*, Marrickville Council Library Services, Petersham, 1997.
- PW Gledhill, *A stroll through the historic Camperdown Cemetery, NSW*, Robert Dey, Sydney, 1946.

Moreton Bay fig tree and Sexton's Cottage, built 1848; the surviving fig and oak trees are said to date from the cemetery's establishment

PIONEERS MEMORIAL PARK, LEICHHARDT

NORTON STREET, LEICHHARDT

Burials: 1868–1912 (converted 1941)

If you have ever wondered why there is such a large park in the crowded inner-city suburb of Leichhardt, the answer is simple: it was once Balmain Cemetery and the bodies are still there. The creation of the rest park and garden area, on the corner of Norton and William streets, was authorised by the *Old Balmain (Leichhardt) Cemetery Act (No. 12, 1941)*. Leichhardt Council was required to document the old cemetery, but it seems all they did was

lodge the old burial register. Removal of the headstones proceeded in 1942, during the Second World War. Very few relatives took the opportunity to move headstones elsewhere; though, thanks to the efforts of PW Gledhill a cluster went to Camperdown Cemetery. Leichhardt Council has a short list of where headstones went. The rest were cleared and some stone segments were re-used to create the sandstone retaining wall and memorial arch entrance. Researcher Tricia

Mack uncovered some extraordinary film footage showing the clearance and conversion of the cemetery in the National Film and Sound Archive. The park was dedicated on 18 November 1944 and officially named the Pioneers Memorial Park.

Apart from the memorial archway and retaining wall, no remnants of the headstones remain on site. The war memorial was moved there in 1949 and Leichhardt Council dedicated a rose garden to those buried in the cemetery. Despite the lack of headstones, the former Balmain Cemetery has a unique place in the history of Sydney's cemeteries.

In 1866 William Patten, James Martyn Combes and Alexander Henry Brown founded the private cemetery company that established the Balmain Cemetery. Cemetery companies,

both commercial enterprises and non-profit bodies, were common in 19th-century England and America; not so in Sydney. Only two cemetery companies were established here: one for the Camperdown Cemetery and one for the Balmain Cemetery.

The proprietors of the Balmain Cemetery Company were astute. They founded the company at a time when there was an acute shortage of burial space in metropolitan Sydney. The Devonshire Street Cemeteries were closed to new burials, a parliamentary inquiry into the burial grounds at Camperdown and Randwick threatened to close them down, and while the government had plans for a large cemetery at Haslem's Creek, it was yet to open. The proprietors already had an interest in the funeral industry and saw a market opportunity. William Patten was a stonemason who managed Patten Bros in Pitt Street in the city. Some of the land owners were also connected: Robert Stewart was an undertaker, and Josiah Treeve was the Secretary of the Camperdown Cemetery Company.

The Balmain Cemetery Company settled on a large block of land, just over 4.5 hectares in expanse, on the Balmain Road (now Norton Street) in Leichhardt. The cemetery had no denominational divisions and was simply divided into three sections: private selection (two guineas), middle selection (10 shillings) and ordinary area (10 shillings – if they could pay it), being the equivalent of first, second and pauper classes. Interment hours were fixed between 9 am and 4 pm.

The first burial took place on 26 January 1868. Harry Guttridge was a 46-year-old resident of Sussex Street, Sydney. The last burial occurred on 7 May 1912, farewelling George Holley of Balmain. Between 1868 and 1912, there were a total of 10,608 interments. Among those buried in the cemetery were architect Edmund Thomas Blacket (d.1883), shipbuilder Captain Thomas Stephenson Rowntree (d.1902), surveyor Ferdinand Hamilton Reuss (d.1896), mathematics professor Morris Birkbeck Pell (d.1879) and Stephen Campbell Brown, MLA (d.1882).

Leichhardt Council was formed in 1871 and councillors immediately began agitating for the cemetery's closure, citing poor sanitary conditions. *The Balmain Cemetery Act, 1881* was passed to clarify the cemetery company's commercial rights under local government by-laws. Complaints about the cemetery persisted through the 1880s and in 1887 the company transferred the land unconditionally to Leichhardt Council. The cemetery continued to operate into the first decade of the 20th-century, but was all but closed by 1908. Only 126 burials occurred in the final four years of operation to 1912. The cemetery remained closed and neglected, with various proposals to convert it through the 1920s and 1930s culminating in the official opening of the rest park in 1944.

TIP

Tricia Mack has transcribed the burial register, which is available online. She is now tracing the biographies of those buried in this forgotten cemetery.

MORE INFORMATION

• Leichhardt Council Library, 'Balmain Cemetery', Leichhardt Council website, 2013, <www.leichhardt.nsw.gov.au/Library/Local-History/Family-History/Balmain-Cemetery>.

• Tricia Mack, Balmain Cemetery website, 2010, <www.balmaincemetery.org>.

• Bonnie Davidson and Kathleen Hamey, *The Balmain Cemetery: Grave Concerns*, Balmain Association, Balmain, 1999.

ST DAVID'S PRESBYTERIAN CEMETERY, HABERFIELD

51-53 DALHOUSIE STREET, HABERFIELD

Burials: 1860–present

This 'cemetery' is actually a private family burial ground within the church grounds, but there is public access to the vault precinct behind the church. So don't be shy – St David's parish and the Ramsay family are proud of their ongoing connection to this site. The parish have erected a sign sharing the history of the site and the family continue to use the burial ground for inurnments (ashes).

The burial ground is for the Ramsay Family. Dr David Ramsay (1794–1860) married Sarah, the eldest daughter of wealthy emancipist Simeon Lord, in 1825 and took over 'Dobroyd Farm' from Lord in a complicated financial arrangement ensuring security for Sarah and any children.

David Ramsay died in 1860 and was buried on his property. His widow set aside land for a church, manse and school, with plans to establish a family burial ground. A large square family vault was constructed within the church allotment sometime between mid-1860 and mid-1862. Ramsay's remains were transferred from Dobroyd House grounds, along with two infants who had died in 1841 and 1858. There are 20 gravesites, including the vault, that host over 50 burials.

The immense size of the partially subterranean vault only becomes apparent as you wander around the solid sandstone structure to face the entrance which is located down the slope. The vault is enclosed by an iron palisade fence, denying the visitor close inspection. But you might be able to read the names on the inscription panels that flank the entrance.

There are a number of substantial monuments that surround the vault. The broken column encircled in ivy on a Grecian pedestal commemorates Ramsay's son-in-law, Alexander Learmonth (d.1877), of 'Yasmar'. Also worthy of note is the solid rusticated sandstone block to Archibald Ernest Ramsay (d.1924) and Muriel Woolnough Ramsay (d.1937).

Only two burials are interlopers: Annie Downie (d.1868), the wife of Reverend SF Mackenzie, first minister of St David's Church, has a chaste squat obelisk, and Percy Pope (d.1871), the infant son of the first mayor of Ashfield, a small headstone. Everyone else is related to the Ramsays by birth or marriage and this arrangement was confirmed by a formal agreement with the church in 1902.

This is the last surviving family burial ground in the inner city. Its only rivals are the Macarthur family cemetery and vault out at 'Camden Park' in Menangle and the Pearce family cemetery at Baulkham Hills, but neither is accessible to the public. The Ramsay burial ground is deservedly listed on the State Heritage Register, along with the church, manse and school hall.

MORE INFORMATION

- NSW Heritage Office, 'St David's Uniting Church', State Heritage Register listing ID 5053328, NSW Office of Environment and Heritage website, 2016, <www.environment.nsw.gov.au/heritageapp/ViewHeritageItemDetails.aspx?id=5053328>.
- Bob Irving & Chris Pratten, 'The Ramsay Family Vault', *Ashfield and District Historical Society Journal*, No. 11, 1994, pp. 35–43.

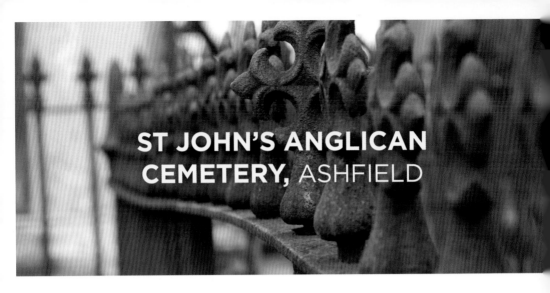

ST JOHN'S ANGLICAN CEMETERY, ASHFIELD

62-74 BLAND STREET, ASHFIELD

Burials: 1845–1970

St John's Cemetery is an unexpected gem in the bustling neighbourhood of Ashfield. Elizabeth Underwood, of Ashfield Park estate, donated the original portion of church land. It was part of the land she subdivided to create the village of Ashfield. The foundation stone for the church was laid in 1840 and infant Frederick Underwood was the first burial recorded in 1845. Surprisingly, Bishop Broughton did not consecrate the burial ground at the time of the church's dedication. The cemetery was only formally consecrated by Archbishop Mowll on 8 September 1934. The Archbishop gave a sense of historic solemnity to the consecration by using the book that Reverend Samuel Marsden had used when dedicating the first churchyard in Australia.

St John's provides a compact overview of headstone design from the mid-1840s through to the early 20th-century. It was the first Anglican cemetery to be established between Sydney and Parramatta. A central avenue runs through the cemetery and the graves embrace the pathway, facing inwards. This landscape layout reflects the growing attitude in the 19th century that cemeteries be appropriately romantic, yet also a chaste and instructive space for passive recreation; indeed the *Sydney Mail* on 2 August 1884 encouraged wandering among the tombs of this 'very picturesque' cemetery.

The *Sydney Mail* described St John's as 'rather fashionable', the inner west's rival of St Jude's Cemetery in Randwick. This reflects Ashfield's growing popularity among the merchant class who established suburban villas there. There are at least 1500 burials recorded in this early cemetery. Prominent suburban families abound, along with local luminaries, politicians and rectors.

One of the most celebrated burials is the long-lived convict John Limebourner, a First Fleeter who died on 4 September 1847, aged 104. Look out also for the headstone of 17-year-old Thomas Aitken (d.1874) who was 'accidentally killed at the Sydney Foundry'.

This is a must-see cemetery of the inner west, a delight to explore.

TIPS

This is a good cemetery for a picnic. It has areas of green space, a number of benches are scattered through the site, and there is even a children's playground in the church grounds.

The parish have a cemetery database and maps on their website, along with the original burial register.

NOTABLE BURIALS

- Elizabeth Underwood (1794–1858), 'Mother of Ashfield'
- Randolf John Want (1811–1869), solicitor and politician
- William Henry Hudson (1814–1882), woodworker, builder and contractor, founder of Hudson Bros
- Thomas Walker (1804–1886), merchant, banker and benefactor, of 'Yaralla' Concord
- Edward Thomas Jones Wrench (1828–1893), real estate agent, founding partner of Richardson & Wrench

MORE INFORMATION

- Christ Church Inner West Anglican Community, 'St John's Cemetery', Christ Church Inner West Anglican Community website, 2015, <cciw.org.au/#/resources/st-johns-cemetery>.

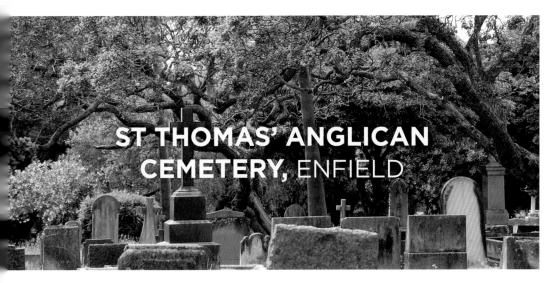

ST THOMAS' ANGLICAN CEMETERY, ENFIELD

CORONATION PARADE, ENFIELD

Burials: 1849–present (existing burial rights)

St Thomas' churchyard at Enfield is a surprisingly early cemetery for the inner west – just a little younger than St John's at Ashfield and the same age as Camperdown Cemetery. Unlike these cemeteries, St Thomas' has an urban feel – less grass, more brick – with a high proportion of marked graves and neat pathways throughout. Access to the churchyard is through a quaint stone lychgate; one of the few left in Sydney. It is densely populated, with approximately 4000 people buried here, and the cemetery envelops the church and school hall.

Thomas Hyndes and his wife Charlotte founded the church. Both convicts transported for life, they were granted land here after they received full pardons in 1812 and 1814 respectively. At first they travelled to St John's at Ashfield for church, but the onerous journey through the bush soon lost its charm. So Thomas Hyndes resolved to build his own church. He donated

2.2 hectares of land in 1847, and organised the cedar from his business, the stone from the quarry on his land, and the labour to build the church. Bishop Broughton laid the foundation stone on 1 February 1848.

Sadly, his wife Charlotte did not survive to see the church finished. She died on 6 January 1849, aged 69 years and was the first to be buried in the churchyard, just to the left of the church doorway. Stones and scaffolding had to be shifted to make room for the funeral cortege. Thomas erected a large classical vault with draped urn and downturned torches decorating the fat, square pedestal over her grave.

The church and vault exude success; Thomas and Charlotte Hyndes were convicts made good in every sense of the word. Thomas's

Left Charlotte Hyndes's (d.1849) imposing neoclassical vault Beale family graves

Right The ornate and unique cast iron cross marking the

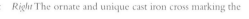

second wife Lucy Havens summed it up in a memorial tablet erected over the porch door when Thomas died in 1855: 'To the memory of Thomas Hyndes. This tablet was erected by his widow. If you would seek his memorial – look around.'

There are plenty of interesting people buried in the churchyard. A whopping 14 clergy are memorialised in the cemetery and remembrance wall, including four former rectors. Among the vaults and large monuments located in the prime position near the church on the left is a large Gothic altar tomb for Richard Wynne (d.1895), benefactor of the Wynne Prize at the Art Gallery of New South Wales. A unique, elaborate iron cross and art nouveau floral fence mark the graves of the Beale family. Octavius Beale (d.1930) established Australia's first piano factory in 1897 in Annandale; the cross was probably crafted at the factory.

The cemetery has high quality memorials from both the 19th and 20th centuries. Look out for the sandstone headstone with floral wreath, dove and laurel branches which stonemason William Partridge of Burwood erected over his son's grave (d.1883) and the headstone to local smithy Edmund Richard Collis (d.1888) which has an anvil, horseshoe and hammer carved in relief.

NOTABLE BURIALS

- Thomas Pinnick Hyndes (1778–1855), convict, timber merchant and church founder
- John Frederick Hilly (c.1833–1878), architect, designer of St Thomas' Church, Enfield
- Richard Wynne (c.1822–1895), Burwood's first mayor and benefactor of the Wynne Art Prize for landscape or sculpture
- Arthur Yates (1861–1926), seedsman, founder of the Yates seed company
- Octavius Charles Beale (1850–1930), piano manufacturer

MORE INFORMATION
- Sally Louisa Jackson, *A matter of importance: A glimpse into the lives of some of those buried in the cemetery at St Thomas' Anglican Church, Enfield, plus a complete listing of graves*, St Thomas' Church, Enfield, 1999.

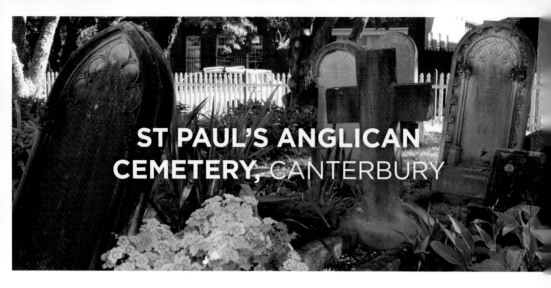

ST PAUL'S ANGLICAN CEMETERY, CANTERBURY

CHURCH STREET, CANTERBURY

Burials: 1860–1968

St Paul's Anglican church is a quaint little sandstone church designed by Edmund Blacket and constructed in 1858–59. The cemetery, directly beside the church and accessed through a neat timber picket fence, wins the prize for the most cared for cemetery by a church congregation. It is like a floral garden with irises, jonquils, geraniums, kangaroo paw and daisies, and that's just what was flowering in winter when I visited.

The church and cemetery are within Robert Campbell's Canterbury Estate. His daughter Sophia Ives Campbell donated the land. The first burial was a two-day-old baby Henry Monk, buried on 26 August 1860. This sad trend continued: of the 51 burials in its first ten years of operation, 30 were children.

Bishop Barker consecrated the cemetery on 27 June 1861 and the oldest surviving headstone is to Eliza Bell (d.1862), wife of the churchwarden William Bell. The last burial took placed in 1968.

The most dramatic death recorded here was Constable William Hird, brutally killed on 13 August 1885 while on duty. His body was found lying on the Canterbury Road near the bridge over the Cooks River; he had received serious blows to his head. Two men were convicted of manslaughter (the judge believed it was murder, but the jury decided manslaughter). About 400 relatives, friends, policemen and local residents attended the funeral which attracted widespread 'melancholy interest' according to the *Sydney Morning Herald* on 17 August 1885. Although an adherent of the Presbyterian faith, Hird was buried in the local cemetery after an ecumenical service. St Paul's Church bell tolled as the funeral cortege wended its way through the streets from his home to the cemetery. Locals expressed their deep sympathy by closing their shutters or pulling their blinds, and local shops closed as a mark of respect. Prominent locals raised £900 and set up a fund for his widow and five children. This paid the mortgage of the Hirds' cottage and the remainder was invested to supplement his widow's police pension.

NOTABLE BURIALS

- Francis Cornwall Bromhead Bell (c.1832– 1864), teacher at St Paul's parish school
- George Kenyon Holden (1808–1874), solicitor and politician
- William Hird (c.1853–1885), policeman killed on duty

MORE INFORMATION
- Audrey Barnes, *St. Paul's Church of England, Canterbury, burial records*, Canterbury and District Historical Society, Earlwood, 1986.

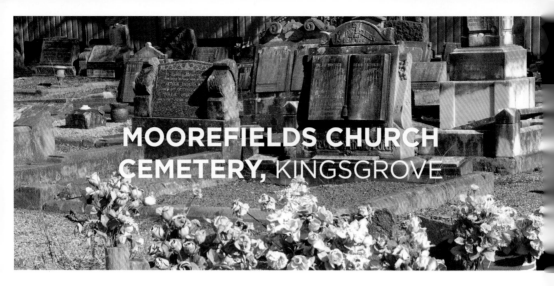

MOOREFIELDS CHURCH CEMETERY, KINGSGROVE

MARAMBA CLOSE, KINGSGROVE

Burials: 1855–1959 (existing burial rights)

A modest Wesleyan Chapel, established in 1851, once fronted Moorefields Road, with the cemetery situated behind it. John Chard, an early landholder, donated 4000 square metres of land for the church and cemetery. The original chapel was demolished in 1967 and the connection between the church and cemetery severed. Visitors to the cemetery now enter from Maramba Close via new cemetery gates.

When the church was founded in 1851, Canterbury village had a population of 473, of which a quarter were Wesleyans. The first burial took place in 1855 and this little cemetery serviced the Wesleyan community throughout the Canterbury district, with headstones recording family connections to Peakhurst, Hurstville, Kingsgrove, Campsie and Earlwood.

There are over 1100 known burials, and many more unmarked graves. Local heritage signs say that there are unmarked graves for both

Aboriginal people and convicts. The majority of headstones face east in neat rows. The trustees stopped selling plots in 1959 and Canterbury City Council took over the cemetery in the 1960s. The early burial registers were lost to a fire in 1905.

Look out for the headstone of James Chard (father of John who donated the land) which dates from 1856 and is the earliest extant headstone. There are at least four generations of the Chard family buried in the cemetery.

Of note are the pious marble draped pedestals with bibles atop. Also the finely carved sandstone desk headstones designed by Rofe of Lidcombe in the early 20th-century. Look for the ones that feature short epitaphs carved in bas-relief at the base of the desk.

TIP

Every headstone has been photographed by the council and is available online, along with an alphabetical list.

NOTABLE BURIALS

- James Chard (c.1777–1856), very early district settler
- John Robert Peake (c.1785–1886), namesake of Peakhurst suburb
- Francis Hill Beamish (c.1817–1907), teacher at the old Moorefields Public School

MORE INFORMATION

- Canterbury City Council Library Service, 'Moorefields Methodist Cemetery, Kingsgrove', Canterbury City Cemeteries Online, 2015, <www2.canterbury.nsw.gov.au/history/cemetery/moorefields/welcome.htm>.
- Joyce Ormsby, *Moorefields Cemetery Records*, Canterbury & District Historical Society, Earlwood, 1983.
- Chris Betteridge, *Moorefields Cemetery Kingsgrove: Conservation Management Plan*, prepared for Canterbury City Council, 2002, <www2.canterbury.nsw.gov.au/history/cemetery/moorecem_cmp.pdf>.

John Robert Peake's (d.1886) monument

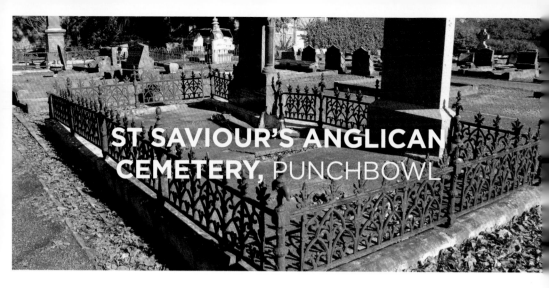

ST SAVIOUR'S ANGLICAN CEMETERY, PUNCHBOWL

1353 CANTERBURY ROAD, PUNCHBOWL (ACCESS VIA VIOLA STREET FOR PARKING)

Burials: 1878–1986

Most people would not even know that this cemetery exists. Tucked away behind St Saviour's Anglican Church on Canterbury Road, this modest church cemetery is a true local cemetery, known only to parishioners, nearby residents and possibly the students of the adjoining Punchbowl Public School. The cemetery was originally referred to as the Belmore Cemetery, but now resides within the suburb of Punchbowl.

The first recorded burial was a young woman, Catherine Elizabeth Pearson, who died on 19 February 1878. Although there is a smattering of 19th-century memorials, it is predominantly a 20th-century cemetery filled with low desk monuments. There are over 1000 burials in this little cemetery. You won't find the rich and famous residing here, just local residents who formed the burgeoning communities of Belmore and Punchbowl.

The Fenwicks are one such family; there are at least 15 of them buried here. John Fenwick built 'Belmore House' in the 1880s, which was demolished in the 1960s to make way for Roselands Shopping Centre. Also look for the sandstone headstones that mark the Bond family graves on the eastern boundary of the cemetery.

Most conspicuous in this little cemetery is the impact of the Great War back home: you can find the graves of at least 15 soldiers here, four of whom were killed in action. The most prominent soldier memorial is the grey granite obelisk that marks the grave of Sergeant Charles Gibson, 1st Australian Light Horse Brigade, who was killed in action, Dardanelles, 7 August 1915, aged 28 years. This small community would have been rocked by worry and grief.

St Saviour's Anglican cemetery is also the repository of remains from St Barnabas' Anglican Cemetery (Highclere Ave, Punchbowl) which was sold off by the church in the 1990s.

NOTABLE BURIALS

- Adam Bond (c.1811–1885), convict and namesake of Bond Road, Belmore.
- James Milner (c.1832–1889), first postmaster of Belmore Post Office
- John Fenwick (c.1837–1901), ship owner and patriarch of 'Belmore House' on 'Bellgrove Farm'
- William John Gibson (c.1862–1925), mayor of Bankstown

MORE INFORMATION
- Canterbury City Council Library Service, Saint Saviour's Cemetery, Punchbowl website, 2015, <www2.canterbury.nsw.gov.au/history/cemetery/st_saviours/welcome.htm>.
- Joyce Ormsby, *St. Saviour's Church of England, Canterbury road (opposite Belmore Road), Punchbowl, burial records*, Canterbury and District Historical Society, 1989.

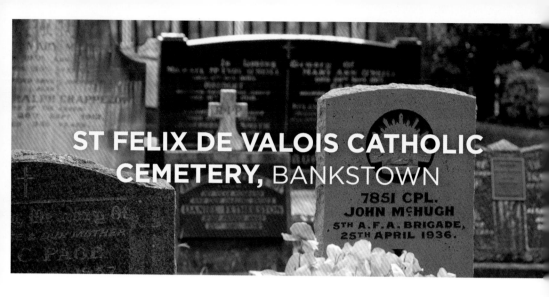

ST FELIX DE VALOIS CATHOLIC CEMETERY, BANKSTOWN

550 CHAPEL ROAD, BANKSTOWN

Burials: 1856–present

This tiny cemetery is boxed in between a church, school and playground, with a convent nearby. Enclosed by hedges and a fence, entry is by an iron arch gate on the corner nearest the church. John Abbott donated land for the original church in 1853. It was the first church in the district, which was then called Irish Town, due to the large number of Irish Catholics residing there. John Abbott also became the first inhabitant of the burial ground in 1856. This makes the cemetery 160 years old and it is still in use. The original little sandstone church (demolished in 1944) was sited in front of the current church, so the graveyard, as was traditional in Sydney, sat beside the church.

John Abbott's sandstone altar tomb survives, close to the cemetery gate. Also in sandstone, an early Gothic headstone with shoulders records the death of Margaret Hurley (d.1857). One of the most elaborately decorated gravestones is in affectionate remembrance of 18-year-old Annie Caird who died in 1884. It features a delicately carved angel leaning on a cross encircled with a garland of flowers, which surmounts a classical style headstone with dentils, a Celtic cross and flower festoon, and a fallen rose at its base.

There are around 230 known burials in the cemetery. Many headstones are densely crammed with multiple inscriptions, recording five or more deaths. The inscriptions often note Irish birth counties, reinforcing the veracity of the suburb's early name of Irish Town.

Recent conservation works in the 21st century installed interpretive signs on the back of new cremation memorial walls. The introduction of these memorial walls ensures that the cemetery will be an important commemorative space for the parish in years to come. The cemetery has been dedicated 'to all those pioneers whose faith and effort were instrumental in developing the Catholic faith in the district and in the establishment of Bankstown'.

NOTABLE BURIALS

- John McQuillan (c.1816–1884) and Mary McQuillan (c.1819–1887), proprietors of 'The Irish Harp', the first hotel in Bankstown
- Robert Ramsay Caird (c.1829–1892), postmaster and father of Annie Caird
- Sisters of St Joseph, associated with the school and convent (established 1886)

MORE INFORMATION
- Errol Lea-Scarlett, *The faith of Irishtown: a history of St. Felix Parish*, Bankstown, St Felix Presbytery, Bankstown, 1982.

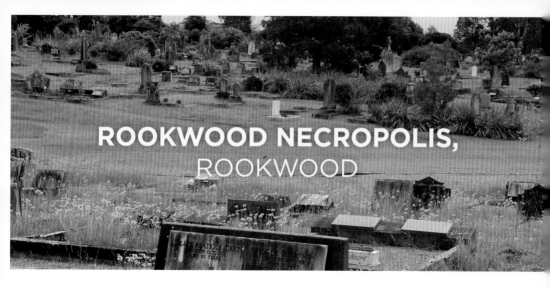

ROOKWOOD NECROPOLIS,
ROOKWOOD

WEEROONA ROAD, ROOKWOOD

Burials: 1867–present

Rookwood Necropolis was belatedly established in the 1860s to replace the Devonshire Street Cemeteries in Sydney. The colonial government had set aside land for a new cemetery in 1847 on the Sydney Common (Moore Park) facing South Dowling Street but it was never used. The churches opposed it because of its non-denominational emphasis, forcing the colonial government to redesign a new public cemetery for Sydney. In this, the government was the victim of its own earlier policy of divesting administrative powers to the church.

The challenge was to find appropriate land for a cemetery that was neither too close to the city, nor too far away. By 1860 the government had decided the railway was a practical solution to the distance issue and called for expressions of interest. In September 1862 the government purchased 81 hectares for Sydney's new general cemetery near Haslem's Creek Station on the Great Southern Railway.

The *Sydney Morning Herald* editorial on 1 April 1862 encouraged the government and the trustees to create a pleasant cemetery landscape for the recreational benefit of the city's population:

> It will be highly gratifying to the public 'if the house appointed for all living' shall be adorned with some care and in good taste. If the depth of graves be properly regulated, and everything noxious be obviated, there is no reason why the intended burial ground should not be a place of festive or pensive resort as in many other countries – whither the inhabitants of the city should often betake themselves.

While mourning and remembrance were of course important activities in the cemetery, the *Herald* also believed the cemetery could also be a place of recreation for the residents of Sydney, since 'an occasional stroll through the avenues of the well-kept cemetery will afford instruction with out depression'.

The Necropolis at Haslem's Creek (later known as Rookwood Necropolis) opened in 1867. Although it was a government-planned general cemetery, individual denominations and sections managed their own burial grounds, each appointing a committee of trustees. The original 81 hectares were laid out as separate denominational cemeteries, including a general cemetery with lay trustees, in the gardenesque style. The Necropolis featured sinuous paths, ornamental shrubberies, specimen trees, summerhouses, chapels, water features, and an elaborate network of deep, brick-lined serpentine drains. The ornamental layout has been attributed to Charles Moore, director of the Sydney Botanic Gardens, except for the large Church of England section which has been attributed to the cemetery trustee Simeon Henry Pearce (the 'father of Randwick', a resident of St Jude's Cemetery, Randwick). It appears that Pearce's landscaping ideas were based on his own tour of European and American cemeteries.

The first burial reported was a pauper, 18-year-old John Whalan. The burial apparently took place on 5 January 1867, although it was not officially recorded in the burial register. The first official burial is recorded two days later on 7 January, a 14-month-old baby christened Catherine McMullen who was buried in the Roman Catholic section. Either way, it was a modest yet symbolic start for Sydney's premier cemetery: an indication

Mortuary Station on Regent Street, 1871

that the cemetery would cater for the whole Sydney community.

One of the initial concerns for the government was the distance of the Necropolis from the populous suburbs. Funeral corteges were expensive and it was a long way to travel to bury the dead. Their solution was practical and innovative. A mortuary station was built at Redfern railway terminus to carry funeral corteges, mourners and visitors to the cemetery. A branch link of the main western railway line led into Rookwood where a grand mortuary station received the coffins and mourners. The mortuary stations attracted attention for their novelty and architectural taste, being praised by journalists and opinion-makers, such as the *Sydney Mail* on 16 March

1878, as 'appropriate in character, picturesque in form, and chaste in design'. They were even written up in the *London Illustrated News*.

The *Illustrated Sydney News* on 29 May 1875 gave its seal of approval to the new cemetery, declaring the Necropolis was 'picturesque' and 'tastefully laid out with shrubs and parterres, divided by neatly kept paths'. It drew attention to the 'modern Gothic' chapels and the 'light and elegant' Mortuary Station. The following year on 9 December, the *Town and Country Journal* praised the picturesque beauty of the landscape, concluding, 'Some of the monuments exhibit great taste on the part of their designers; and it is consoling and comforting to find that the metropolitan burial-ground is kept and ornamented in a highly creditable manner'.

Once the railway link opened, the Necropolis became a favourite weekend destination for Sydneysiders. Cemetery promenading was considered a genteel and respectable activity, which provided moral and artistic edification. (I explore this idea further in 'A Stroll in a Cemetery' later in this guide.) Like some cemeteries in London and America, the trees and shrubs in Rookwood were labelled for the interest and education of visitors. The trustees supplied garden seats, gazebos, fresh water and toilet facilities for the comfort of visitors, many of whom stayed for several hours and had a picnic lunch in the grounds. By the early 20th-century, tea rooms had been built in Rookwood Necropolis to cater to the weekend crowds.

Rookwood Necropolis is Sydney's most impressive interpretation of a garden cemetery; it is extraordinary in its size, scale and landscape design. Only the largest cemeteries in Sydney exhibited the major landscaping features of the garden cemetery movement. Gore Hill, Field of Mars and Woronora Cemetery exhibit some elements – such as avenue plantings, gardenesque layouts, major carriageways and rest houses – although the landscaping at Rookwood is far more ornate.

To get a sense of the cemetery's landscape and its evolution, start your visit in the original section around

Ornamental circular garden bed featuring Statue of Hope and urns, Anglican No. 1 cemetery, 1930s; note the water tap in the foreground

Left Publican Robert Hancock's (d.1876) statue *Centre* Decorative urn near the premium vault section in the Anglican No. 1 cemetery *Right* Exquisite mourning statue executed by Villeroy & Bosch commemorating Gustav Renz (d.1909) in the Lutheran section

Necropolis Circuit (enter via the East Street gates opposite Victoria Street). The Mortuary Station stood within the circuit until 1957. Then it was removed stone by stone and taken to Ainslie, Canberra where it has been adaptively re-used as All Saints Anglican Church. Footings now mark out the station site so you can imagine the scale. The stark black granite monument to the Holocaust designed by architect Harry Seidler and called the Martyrs Memorial, is located within Necropolis Circuit opposite the old Jewish ground. Each of the main denominational sections in the No. 1 cemetery area has standout elements. Be careful as you walk around, though, because some of the brick gutters and box drains are overgrown with grass.

The Catholic No. 1 cemetery is dominated by the Chapel of St Michael the Archangel, designed by Catholic architects Sheerin and Hennessy and completed in 1890. The belltower is surmounted by the Angel of the Resurrection, a smaller version of the original angel which has been destroyed by lightning twice, the second time in 1955. Large angels of Hope and Charity grace the chapel's main door. Rows of identical cross headstones mark the religious graves behind the chapel. The Catholic section feels a bit bare, as many of the iron grave surrounds have been removed. The marble Celtic cross towering over the Maher family vault is a standout. Angelo

Bertazzi of Carrara, Italy carved it to a design of Sheerin and Hennessy. Also keep an eye out for the vault of brewer John Toohey (d.1903).

The Anglican No. 1 section has the most intact landscape. Unlike other sections with gardenesque teardrop pathways, the Anglican section is more angular with long defined carriageways punctuated by feature trees and carriageway turning circles at pathway junctions. A deep serpentine drain intersects the site and connects a series of four ponds featuring water lilies, fountains and terracotta urns. This is the perfect spot for a picnic. A number of rest houses also survive in the No. 1 and No. 2 cemeteries. The polychrome brick federation building you might espy further across the cemetery was once a cemetery office and later converted to a rest house. The Anglican No. 1 cemetery has an impressive vault section, which includes the Gothic vault to politician James Watson (d.1907), designed by architects Wardell and Vernon, and the Italian renaissance mausoleum for the Sparke family. To the left of the vaults you will see the life-sized statue of Robert Hancock (d.1876). The statue, executed in 1844 by sculptor Charles Abrahams, used to embellish the gardens of Hancock's house in Ultimo.

Heading clockwise around the circuit the next section is the original Jewish No. 1 cemetery. An eye-catching classical domed monument with four Corinthian columns, covering a pedestal and urn, marks the grave of former convict Samuel Henry Harris (d.1867). Some of the best examples of Jewish symbolism can be found here and many of the inscriptions are only in Hebrew.

The original office for the Independent (Congregationalist) cemetery still survives. Don't miss the Dixson monument in the Independent ground, described as the most beautiful and graceful monument in Rookwood. Supported on a marble cloud, a life-sized figure of the Angel of the Resurrection, holding a trumpet and pointing to heaven, gracefully bears the beatific soul of the deceased to heaven with her wings outstretched. This outstanding piece of sculpture marks the family grave of Sir Hugh Dixson, tobacco manufacturer and philanthropist. Behind the office there is a unique cast-iron memorial. The broken Corinthian column was erected by the ironmonger JR Bubb over the grave of his son. Bubb & Son were also responsible for the elaborate denominational section signs you see around the original part of the cemetery.

Continuing clockwise, the old general cemetery seems unused, but this area was in fact the key burial ground for the Chinese community in the late 19th and early 20th centuries, many of whom exhumed remains and sent them back to China after a few years. In the centre of this cemetery is the Quong Sin Tong Shrine, erected in 1877. The Quong Sin Tong was a Chinese welfare association operating in early Sydney and the shrine formed a key part of Chinese burial rituals and funerary practices, for burning incense and offerings. Bea Miles (d.1973) is also buried in the general section.

Next around the circuit is the Presbyterian No. 1 cemetery, where you cannot help but notice the enormous Frazer Mausoleum down the slope with its multiple domes. London architect Maurice B Adams designed it in high Victorian Byzantine Gothic style. Gargoyles protrude from the roof and a teardrop-shaped iron railing with delicate wrought-iron flower finials surrounds the mausoleum. Built of sandstone, the Frazer Mausoleum dominates the Presbyterian skyline, but fits neatly into the overall form of the landscape design. This mausoleum no longer contains the family remains, but the alabaster sarcophagi are intact and the mausoleum is usually open for inspection as part of the Rookwood Open Day held in springtime. The architect James Barnet (d.1904) is, fittingly, buried in this section, since he designed the two mortuary stations at Regent Street

Left Waterlily pond with terracotta urns, Anglican No. 1 cemetery

Right Coreopsis lanceolata provides a cheery floral accent across the cemetery in late spring

and the Necropolis, as well as many significant public buildings including the General Post Office in Martin Place and the Balmain Courthouse and Post Office. Marble medallion portraits of James and his wife Amy, carved by Giovanni Fontana, adorn their red granite gravestone, which is easy to spot from Oliver Avenue. The Presbyterian No. 1 cemetery contains numerous, high quality examples of iron grave surrounds and substantial sandstone surrounds.

Finally, there is the smaller, more sedate Wesleyan No. 1 cemetery. Hedges, palms, rose gardens and paths hint at the sinuous landscaping that once embellished this section. Here you will find the family vault of the Allen family. George Allen (d.1877) was the first solicitor to receive his training in the colony and founder of the oldest legal firm in Australia which, after expansions, mergers and name changes, is today known as Allens. He was a man with a strong sense of civic and philanthropic duty. He was secretary of the Benevolent Society for many years, mayor of Sydney (1844–45), and Member of the Legislative Council (1856–1873). Here you will also find the grave of William Vial (d.1878), who saved Prince Alfred, the second son of Queen Victoria, from an assassination attempt down at Clontarf in 1868.

Necropolis Drive, lined with Canary Island date palms (*Phoenix canariensis*), connects the original cemetery with the various extensions. The Sydney War Cemetery is located within the Necropolis grounds on the

The Sparke family vault, one of the impressive 19th-century vaults in the premium section of the Anglican No. 1 cemetery

Left Portrait of architect James Barnet (d.1904) on his red granite headstone   *Right* A poignant rendition of 7-year-old Lucy Molloy (d.1877)

eastern side. It was established in 1942 and contains the graves of 732 service men and women, many of whom died in Concord Military Hospital. The entrance way to the cemetery forms a modernist arch framing the central cross and is also the site of the New South Wales Cremation Memorial. This commemorates by name 199 servicemen who died in New South Wales during the Second World War, and whose ashes were either scattered or buried across the state without proper commemoration.

Beside the war graves is the New South Wales Garden of Remembrance where plaques commemorate servicemen of the First World War who are buried elsewhere in New South Wales. The cemetery is immaculately maintained by the Commonwealth War Graves Commission and is best visited in spring or summer when the roses are in full bloom. There are also two naval cemeteries in the Anglican No. 1 cemetery and a Merchant Navy Memorial Cemetery in the Anglican No. 2 cemetery.

The Necropolis hosts the first crematorium building in the state, which opened in 1925. It was designed by Frank Bloomfield in the Spanish Mission style. Its interwar designed gardens are superb as well, with roses, water features and topiary hedges. Later gardens from the 1950s were by landscape designer Norman Weekes.

Monuments from a number of smaller Sydney cemeteries that were cleared have been relocated to

Left The Frazer Mausoleum dominates the Presbyterian No. 1 cemetery   *Right* An unusual iron structure commemorates George Lawton Bond (d.1909)

Rookwood. The remains exhumed from the Old Sydney Burial Ground in 1869 to make way for Sydney Town Hall are buried in a large plot in the Anglican No. 1 cemetery. A large classical urn and pedestal erected by the municipal council marks the graves. Rookwood also features the largest collection of monuments relocated from the Devonshire Street Cemeteries aside from the Pioneer Park at Botany. They are not in one place, however, but scattered around the Necropolis on family graves. In the Catholic No. 3 cemetery you will find a collection of headstones transferred from the St Thomas Catholic Cemetery at Lewisham (1865–1905). Remains were exhumed and headstones transferred in 1926–27 following the passing of the *Lewisham*

Cemetery Act (No. 24, 1925).

Now covering some 283 hectares, Rookwood Necropolis is Australia's largest cemetery, and is believed to be one of the largest Victorian-era burial grounds in the world. The cemetery is also one of the largest open public spaces in Sydney, bigger than either Centennial Park or the Botanic Gardens. The cemetery is still in use and today caters for 90 different religious and national groups. The cemetery's memorials form a visual social document of the origins of our community and the multicultural influence of immigration. The denominational trustees were amalgamated in 2012 to form three groups that manage the cemetery: Rookwood General Cemeteries Reserve Trust, the

INNER WEST & WEST

Catholic Metropolitan Cemeteries Trust, and the Rookwood Memorial Gardens and Crematorium.

During late spring and early summer, the cemetery is a bright blanket of yellow *Coreopsis lanceolata* which has become naturalised across the site, along with Watsonia. Rookwood Necropolis is also famous for its many heritage *Rosa* species. The cemetery is a haven for birdlife and native fauna; indeed, this is great location for twitchers in Sydney. You may also encounter some less welcome strays, such as hares and feral goats.

An intrepid group of volunteers from the Society of Australian Genealogists, with the support and encouragement of all the denominational trustees, transcribed the Necropolis between 1981 and 1988. It remains the largest single undertaking of the society's cemetery transcription program. Their dedicated work highlighted the historic values of the cemetery,

as well as its dilapidated condition. Out of this the Friends of Rookwood was formed, a community group which runs tours of the cemetery and raises funds to support the conservation of memorials. They are still running strong today. The best way to get an overview of the cemetery is to go on a tour with the Friends of Rookwood.

TIPS

The Friends of Rookwood conduct public tours on the first Sunday of the month, March to November.

The Catholic Cemetery Trust also has a self-guided walking tour brochure.

Hidden, an outdoor modern sculpture exhibition in among the graves, occurs annually in late September to early October.

The Cemetery Trusts have online searchable databases for locating graves.

NOTABLE BURIALS

CATHOLIC NO. 1 CEMETERY

- John Thomas Toohey (1839–1903) and James Matthew Toohey (1850–1895), brewers
- Charles O'Neill (1828–1900), founder of St Vincent de Paul Society in Australia
- Timothy Maher (1821–1905), upholsterer, auctioneer and pastoralist

Sydney War Cemetery

ANGLICAN NO. 1 CEMETERY

- Mei Quong Tart (1850–1903), tea merchant and philanthropist
- Charles Moore (1820–1905), botanist, Director of the Botanic Gardens, 1848–1896
- David Scott Mitchell (1836–1907), founder and benefactor of the Mitchell Library
- Louisa Lawson (1848–1920) newspaper proprietor and suffragette (her son Henry is buried in Waverley Cemetery)

JEWISH NO. 1 CEMETERY

- Harry Van Der Sluys (1892–1954), aka Roy Rene, comedian, burlesque and vaudeville artist, known for his character 'Mo', especially in the duo 'Stiffy and Mo'

INDEPENDENT NO. 1 CEMETERY

- David Jones (1793–1873), merchant, founder of David Jones store
- John Fairfax (1804–1877), newspaper proprietor, early partner of *Sydney Morning Herald*
- Sir Hugh Dixson (1841–1926), tobacco manufacturer and philanthropist

GENERAL NO. 1 CEMETERY

- Beatrice (Bea) Miles (1902–1973), Sydney eccentric and Bohemian rebel

PRESBYTERIAN NO. 1 CEMETERY

- John Frazer (1827–1884), merchant, company director and philanthropist
- James Barnet (1827–1904), colonial architect, designer of the mortuary stations
- Peter Dodds McCormick (c.1833–1916), composer, wrote 'Advance Australia Fair'

WESLEYAN NO. 1 CEMETERY

- George Allen (1800–1877), solicitor, founder of the oldest legal firm in Australia, now known as Allens

MORE INFORMATION

- Rookwood General Cemeteries Reserve Trust website, 2016, <www.rookwoodcemetery.com.au>.
- Rookwood Catholic Cemeteries and Crematoria Trust website, 2013, <www.catholiccemeteries.com.au/cemeteries/rookwood>.
- *Rookwood Cemetery Transcriptions*, v.1.10, (CD Rom), Society of Australian Genealogists, Sydney, 2002.
- Friends of Rookwood website, 2014, <www.friendsofrookwoodinc.org.au>.
- David A Weston (ed.), *The Sleeping City: The Story of Rookwood Necropolis*, Society of Australian Genealogists in conjunction with Hale & Iremonger, Sydney, 1989.

Crowds gather to witness the spectacle of a Chinese feast day at Rookwood, c.1930s

TOP 5

OLDEST (UNDISTURBED) CEMETERIES

1790   St John's Anglican Cemetery, Parramatta

1810   St Matthew's Anglican Cemetery, Windsor

1811   St Peter's Anglican Cemetery, Richmond

1811   Castlereagh Cemetery

1811   Wilberforce Cemetery

Castlereagh Cemetery

Opposite All Saints Anglican Cemetery, North Parramatta

PARRAMATTA

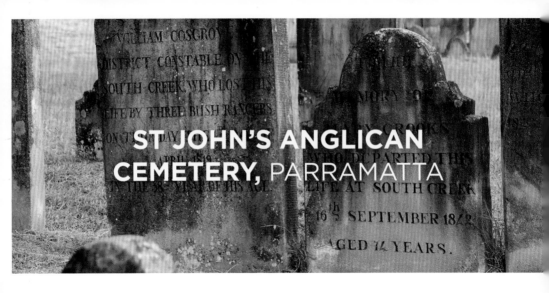

ST JOHN'S ANGLICAN CEMETERY, PARRAMATTA

O'CONNELL STREET, PARRAMATTA

Burials: 1790–1980

St John's Anglican Cemetery, established in 1790 for the growing township of Rose Hill (Parramatta), is the oldest surviving Christian burial ground in Australia. It was the first cemetery to be formally established in the penal colony, outstripping the Old Sydney Burial Ground by two years. Surprisingly, perhaps, it is also undisturbed, unlike the Old Sydney Burial Ground and the Devonshire Street Cemeteries which have both been removed. Here at St John's you will find inscribed some of the earliest headstones in Sydney and, it almost goes without saying, many First Fleeter graves. There are 17 marked graves of First Fleeters and many more go unmarked.

The location of St John's Cemetery, situated on a rise to the south of the original town square, demonstrates the governor's original preference to establish burial grounds outside the town areas and separate from the denominational churches. The cemetery is no longer on the edge of Rose Hill, however, but right in the heart of Parramatta. Glass office towers, a behemoth Westfield and redbrick residential apartments today cluster around the cemetery, modernity impinging on every viewpoint from this historic spot.

The first burial recorded in the register is James Magee, the child of a convict, who died 31 January 1790. The earliest marked grave in the cemetery is to Henry Edward Dodd, Superintendent of Convicts. He had come to the colony as Arthur Phillip's personal servant but was sent to Rose Hill when his farming knowledge became apparent, to oversee the convict cultivation of crops for the starving colony. In just over a year Dodd had supervised the clearing of 36 hectares and plantings of wheat, barley, oats and maize. The success of the Rose Hill gardens was celebrated. So proud was Dodd of his produce that in 1789 he sent a cabbage weighing 12 kilograms to Government House as a Christmas present. Henry Dodd died on 28 January 1791 after a lingering illness. Pride in his gardens may have been his downfall. David Collins, a reliable colonial observer, recorded in his account of New South Wales that his illness had been accelerated by ranging through the night in search of 'thieves' who had been 'plundering his garden'. His grave

Modernity encroaches on Sydney's oldest intact cemetery

St John's Anglican Cemetery, c.1870

is marked by a simple horizontal sandstone slab with the barest of information: 'H.E. Dodd 1791'.

The cemetery initially buried all denominations; it was, after all, the only one in Parramatta. The Catholics did not get their cemetery in the area until 1824, the Wesleyans and Presbyterians waited until 1839 and the Baptists finally got their own burial ground in 1848.

The wall enclosing the cemetery was constructed in 1821–23. Prior to that it had been protected by a fence with a bank and ditch. A similar brick wall enclosed the Old Sydney Burial Ground, Sydney's first major cemetery on the site of Sydney Town Hall, so we can start to imagine what that cemetery might have been like. The entrance lychgate came later in 1857 (reconstructed 1982); a rare entrance way in Sydney cemeteries at the time.

The cemetery is divided into four quarters by grass avenues. The majority of headstones face east so if you get here before noon it will be easier to read the weathered inscriptions. Footstones accompany many of the early headstones and wrought-iron palisade fencing encloses a few of the altar tombs, but overall there is an absence of grave enclosures or kerbing. An early photograph from 1870 indicates that many of the graves were once enclosed by low timber picket fences, but these have since disappeared.

There are many early memorial styles represented in St John's Cemetery. I particularly like the Georgian medallions on the base of some of the altar tombs. Many of the early headstones are plain semicircular styles, some with cutaway shoulders, and there are a small number of anthropomorphic-shaped headstones. The headstone to Brother William Toft (d.1849), on the left of the entrance by the wall, was 'erected by the brethren of his Lodge, as a mark of the esteem'. It features a heart on an open hand, a common symbol of Oddfellow friendly societies, that represents friendship, and particularly the idea that gestures of kindness (the hand) are meritless unless they come from the heart. Richard Turner erected a striking headstone to his first wife Sarah (d.1868), a woman with books is expertly carved into the pediment. Two large Gothic crosses mark the Dare family plots at the rear of the cemetery.

In some cases, the inscriptions, or their owners' virtues, are left to do the talking. Robert Lowe inscribed on his wife Barbara's (d.1818) table top monument, 'To Record her Virtues on a mouldering Stone 'twould be a vain attempt. Know o' Reader they are Registered elsewhere'. There are memorials to two policemen shot by bushrangers. William Cosgrove's (d.1819) epitaph notes he was a district constable on South Creek who 'lost his life by three bushrangers'. Benjamin Ratty's (d.1826) inscription is more effusive:

The deceased was a Constable in the Town of Parramatta, during seven Years; and this Stone was erected by its Inhabitents as a Mark of their Esteem for his Services on various occasion in apprehending Bushrangers; & particularly for his intrepid behaviours with the aid of P. Brennan in the night of the 23rd Septr when he received the Wound which caused his Death from Pistol shot; & which conduct led to immediate Apprehension of a Part of the Banditte.

The inscriptions in St John's Cemetery resonate with the names of prominent citizens who helped shape Sydney. Augustus Alt, Australia's first surveyor-general, is buried here; so is Charles Fraser (d.1831) first Superintendent of the Botanic Gardens in Sydney. There is Robert Campbell, of Campbell's Cove, John Harris of Ultimo fame and Harris Park, the Thorn family of Thornleigh, whose grave is marked by a tall pyramid on a pedestal, and the Blaxland family. The Reverend Samuel Marsden is buried in the cemetery he administered for so many years, as is Samuel Cook (d.1925), who was St John's sexton for 50 years.

There are the wives of two governors and many early churchmen and missionaries. Lady FitzRoy's demise was particularly tragic. She was travelling in a carriage driven by her husband in 1847, when the horses bolted and the carriage overturned on the driveway of Government House, Parramatta. Both Lady FitzRoy and Lieutenant Charles Masters, the governor's aide-de-camp, were thrown headlong into an oak tree and killed.

Governor FitzRoy was unhurt, but heartbroken; the funeral was one of the largest Parramatta had ever seen. Lady FitzRoy and Lieutenant Masters were laid to rest in the vault in St John's Cemetery. A marble obelisk in Parramatta Park perpetuates their memory. Erected in 1888 it marks the spot where the tragedy occurred.

Fittingly, William Freame (d.1933), a prolific local historian and newspaper contributor, and a strong advocate for Sydney's historic burial grounds, is also buried in St John's Cemetery.

St John's Cemetery at Parramatta is widely recognised as one of the most historic cemeteries in Australia and is listed on the State Heritage Register. Do yourself a favour and go visit it.

TIPS

To help you explore the cemetery, download the short guide that includes a basic map from St John's Cathedral website.

Historian Judith Dunn of Past Times Tours also does regular tours of St John's Cemetery.

Opposite A solid neoclassical pedestal marks the Tunks family vault; inscriptions cover every available space

IN LOVING REMEMBRANCE OF
CHARLES TUNKS,
DIED FEB. 5TH 1902.
AGED 21 YEARS.

ALSO CHARLES ROBINSON TUNKS
SON OF JAMES TUNKS.
WHO DEPARTED THIS LIFE JULY 27 1902.
AGED 30 YEARS.
Not lost but gone before

TO THE MEMORY OF
JOHN TUNKS.
WHO DEPARTED THIS LIFE
MAY 1ST 1848
AGED 53 YEARS.
IN THE MIDST OF LIFE WE ARE IN DEATH
ALSO OF
ALFRED FREDRICK THOMAS
TUNKS
GRANDSON OF THE ABOVE
DIED JANUARY 13TH 1865
AGED 1 YEAR AND 4 MONTHS
ALSO
EDWIN WALTER BARNETT
TUNKS
DIED SEPTEMBER 26 1867
AGED 7 MONTHS AND 18 DAYS
ALSO
HAROLD EDWIN TUNKS
GRANDSON OF THE ABOVE
WHO DEPARTED THIS LIFE
JANUARY 27 1878
AGED 5 YEARS
CURRAN   MASON
ALSO
HENRY TUNKS,

ALSO
MARY ANN
THE BELOVED WIFE OF
JAMES TUNKS
WHO DEPARTED THIS LIFE
JULY 28 1870
AGED 44 YEARS.
NOT LOST BUT GONE BEFORE
ALSO
PHOEBE McROBERTS
THE BELOVED WIFE OF
JOHN McROBERTS
AND RELICT OF THE LATE
JOHN TUNKS
WHO DEPARTED THIS LIFE
10TH JUNE 1888
AGED 70 YEARS
She knew a mothers love.
ALSO
JOHN McROBERTS
HUSBAND OF THE ABOVE
WHO DEPARTED THIS LIFE
10TH MAY 1889
AGED 76 YEARS.
ALSO
FREDERICK ARTHUR TUNKS
SON AND GRANDSON OF THE ABOVE
DEPARTED THIS LIFE 3RD SEPTEMBER 1889
AGED 36 YEARS.
not lost but gone before

NOTABLE BURIALS

- Augustus Theodore Henry Alt (1731–1815), soldier and surveyor, Australia's first surveyor-general
- Darcy Wentworth (1762–1827), medical practitioner and public servant
- Charles Fraser (1788–1831), gardener and colonial botanist, first Superintendent of the Botanic Gardens, Sydney
- Elizabeth Jane Bourke (c.1776–1832), wife of Sir Richard Bourke, NSW governor
- Reverend Samuel Marsden (1765–1838), chaplain, missionary and farmer
- John Harris (1754–1838), surgeon, public servant and landholder, of Ultimo and Harris Park
- John Thorn (1794–1838), policeman and estate owner, of Thornleigh
- John Blaxland (1769–1845), landowner and merchant, brother of Gregory Blaxland
- Robert Campbell (1769–1846), merchant, pastoralist, politician and philanthropist, of Campbell's Cove fame
- Mary FitzRoy (1790–1847), wife of Charles Augustus FitzRoy, NSW governor

MORE INFORMATION

- St John's Anglican Cathedral Parramatta, 'Our Heritage', St John's Anglican Cathedral Parramatta website, 2014, <stjohnscathedral.org.au/our-heritage>.
- Judith Dunn, *The Parramatta Cemeteries: St John's*, Parramatta and District Historical Society, Parramatta, 1991.
- Paul Fitzgerald & Michael Brookhouse, 'Parramatta St John's Cemetery', Australian Cemeteries Index website, 2011, <austcemindex.com/cemetery?cemid=789>.
- Michaela Ann Cameron, St John's Cemetery Parramatta website, 2015, <stjohnscemetery.jimdo.com>.

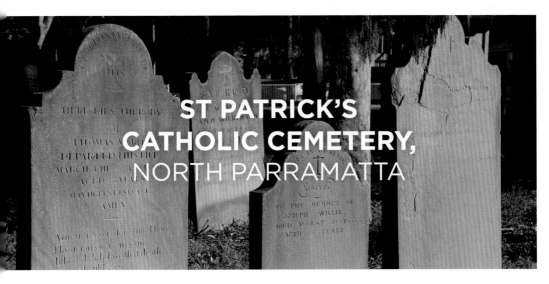

ST PATRICK'S CATHOLIC CEMETERY, NORTH PARRAMATTA

JUNCTION OF CHURCH STREET AND PENNANT HILLS ROAD, NORTH PARRAMATTA

Burials: 1824–1972

St Patrick's Catholic Cemetery is a very special cemetery. It is the oldest undisturbed Catholic cemetery in Australia and has at its centre the oldest mortuary chapel in Australia. Entry is via a modern timber lychgate entrance at the junction of Church Street and Pennant Hills Road or through the original (but shifted) cemetery gates on Church Street.

Around 1822, probably soon after Father John Joseph Therry started his public campaign for separate Catholic cemeteries, 2.2 hectares of land on the Pennant Hills Road was appropriated for a burial ground in Parramatta. Some officers within the surveyor-general's department, however, disputed the land which they felt was too valuable for a Catholic burial ground. They offered an alternative piece of land beside All Saints Cemetery. But the Catholics stuck to their guns and began utilising the promised land. The land grant was officially surveyed in 1834 and finally confirmed by the governor in 1835 (although the deeds weren't issued until 1846). The securing and dedication of Sydney's early cemeteries was often perilous.

Three marked graves date from 1824: the first belongs to Thomas Nugent, who died on 29 April 1824. There may have been earlier burials, but the burial registers only begin in 1840. When Father Thomas Francis McCarthy died in 1844, Bishop Polding decided to erect a mortuary chapel in the cemetery. The foundation stone was laid 20 August 1844 and the chapel built over Father McCarthy's grave. Four other priests are buried with McCarthy. The mortuary chapel is a small plain Gothic chapel executed in ashlar sandstone with a gable roof. It provides a central focus for the cemetery and imparts a solemnity to the landscape. Chinese funeral cypresses (*Cupressus funebris*) flank the entrance to the chapel and mark the avenue which leads down to the original cemetery entrance on Church Street.

The cemetery boundaries have been shaved and realigned to accommodate road widenings on both Church Street and Pennant Hills Road. The cemetery was closed to burials in 1972 and trusteeship of the cemetery passed to Parramatta Council in 1975

The mortuary chapel is the oldest in Australia

under the *Conversion of Cemeteries Act (1974)*. Thank goodness the Council did not do to St Patrick's what they did to the Methodist cemetery (see Walter Lawry Methodist Memorial Park)! Despite being used for seven decades in the 20th-century, overall St Patrick's Cemetery has a historic 19th-century aesthetic. It contains many early sandstone headstones of historic and sculptural interest.

As you enter from the modern corner entrance, look out for the interesting early headstones that have decoration picked out with simple incisions, a technique rarely seen in Sydney; it was more commonly deployed on harder and less pliable stones such as slate. Also around here is the grave of Ann Bellamy, a convict who died in 1843 at the grand old age of 100.

There are some fine examples of the sculptor's art, with scenes of Christ with doubting Thomas, cherubs mourning over a cross, mourning widows, even a rendition of Thorvaldsen's *Night with her children, sleep and death*. Also look out for seraphs, draped classical urns (some with downturned torches), the Lamb of God, the hand of God, Gothic angels, wreaths and floral swags.

TIP

This is a shady cemetery, with spotted gums and brush box scattered throughout the site. Better to go visit during the warmer months when you can enjoy the shade and not be cold.

NOTABLE BURIALS

• Hugh Taylor (1823–1897), local Parramatta politician and parliamentarian

MORE INFORMATION
• Judith Dunn, *The Parramatta Cemeteries: St Patrick's*, Parramatta and District Historical Society, Parramatta, 1988.
• Michael Brookhouse, 'Parramatta St Patrick's Catholic Cemetery', Australian Cemeteries Index website, 2011, <austcemindex.com/cemetery?cemid=785>.

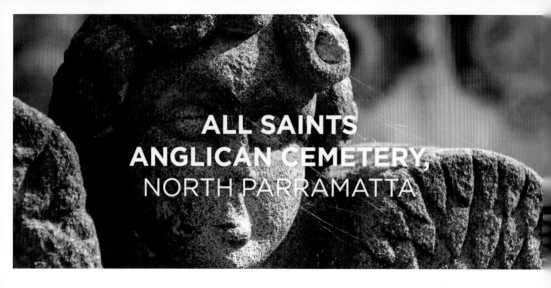

ALL SAINTS ANGLICAN CEMETERY, NORTH PARRAMATTA

FENNELL STREET, NORTH PARRAMATTA

Burials: 1844-1992 (existing burial rights)

This is the second Anglican cemetery in the Parramatta district. It seems the river was a bit of an impediment to the growing population of North Parramatta, so the cemetery was laid out in 1844. The first recorded burial in the register was a 13-year-old girl Mary Ann Ralph who died on 4 March 1844.

The first thing that strikes you is the open grassland of this plain, rectangular cemetery and the limited number of memorials. Only a small proportion of the graves appear to have been marked. Indeed, a closer inspection of the memorial wall in the south-west corner reveals that of the 2000 or so burials in the cemetery, at least 1500 are buried in unmarked graves. The memorial wall records the names, death date and ages of everyone recorded in the surviving burial registers. A central avenue leads from the original entrance and divides the grave areas. The largest monuments, to the Moxham and French families, are located beneath some trees on a little knoll in the north-east corner.

All Saints Cemetery has often been regarded as the poor cousin of St John's Cemetery, the receptacle of the poor, insane, destitute and abandoned. It is true that All Saints Cemetery buried the inmates of several public institutions, including the Parramatta Lunatic Asylum, Parramatta Gaol, the Female Orphan School and the hospital. But so did St John's, primarily from the public hospital and the George Street Asylum.

The memorials in the cemetery are all quality and style, finely executed with prominent, confident carving. A number of the graves are enclosed with wrought-iron palisade fences. There are some lovely sandstone headstones that feature symbolism carved in high relief. Look out for the thistle on James Douglas's (d.1878) headstone, the draped urn on Joseph Eyles (d.1856), the laurel wreath on Carson McBrien (d.1870), and the seraph on George Handley (d.1874). There are also some fine examples of wrought-iron surrounds.

The most famous resident in the cemetery is Gregory Blaxland of Blue Mountains fame. His modest, plain headstone is in stark contrast to the fine monuments of his colleagues to be found at Vaucluse and Prospect.

TIP

There is not much shade in this cemetery, so visit on a sunny autumn morning.

NOTABLE BURIALS

- Gregory Blaxland (1778–1853), grazier and winemaker, of Brush Farm and explorer fame
- Edward Waldegrave Wardley (c.1839–1872), superintendent of the Parramatta Lunatic Asylum
- Thomas Robert Moxham (1860–1916), pastoralist, politician and Parramatta mayor
- French family, of Cumberland Woollen Mills in Smith Street

MORE INFORMATION

- Judith Dunn and Rosemarie Morris, *The Parramatta Cemeteries: All Saints and Wesleyan*, Parramatta and District Historical Society, Parramatta, 2007.
- Michael Brookhouse, 'Parramatta All Saints Cemetery', Australian Cemeteries Index website, 2011, <austcemindex.com/cemetery?cemid=776>.

PARRAMATTA

Gregory Blaxland's (d.1853) headstone is modest compared to Wentworth's mausoleum at Vaucluse and Lawson's vault at Prospect

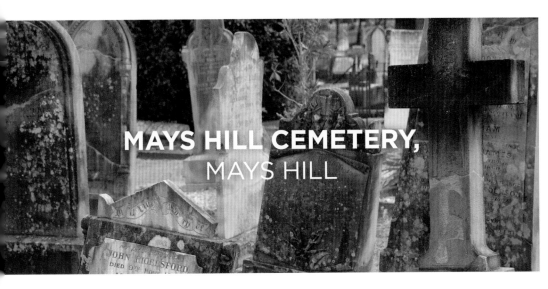

MAYS HILL CEMETERY, MAYS HILL

GREAT WESTERN HIGHWAY, BETWEEN STEEL AND FRANKLIN STREETS, MAYS HILL

Burials: 1843–present (existing burial rights)

At Mays Hill you get two for the price of one. The government dedicated a Presbyterian burial ground of 4000 square metres on the Western Road for the district of Parramatta in 1839 and then dedicated another 4000 square metres for a Baptist cemetery beside it in 1849. They originally functioned totally separately, with different trustees and different entrances. Today there is one fence, one entrance and one management – Holroyd Council.

These two cemeteries demonstrate the Land Department's evolving approach to cemetery design and management in the 1830s and 1840s. They located burial grounds on the outskirts of the township and while the secular administration aspired towards a truly general cemetery with no denominational divisions, religious feeling in Sydney forced them to reassess. St John's Cemetery

Parramatta (at least initially) and the Old Sydney Burial Ground had no divisions, but in the 1840s the proposed general cemetery at Sydney Common (Moore Park) was abandoned because of denominational resistance. When religious groups would not tolerate a truly general cemetery beyond pragmatism, individual religions began to be granted burial grounds. Clustering denominational cemeteries together made sense for town planning and ease of surveying, and so the Australian concept of the denominational general cemetery evolved. Mays Hill Cemetery is a forerunner in this regard with its two denominational cemeteries dedicated a decade apart. A third cemetery, for the Congregationalists, also 4000 square metres, was dedicated in 1876, but appears never to have been used.

The earliest burial in the Presbyterian cemetery is Elizabeth McKay, who died on 9 October 1843. Her death is recorded on the impressively substantial Greek Revival-style pedestal surmounted by a sarcophagus which was erected on the family plot in 1851. The earliest burial in the Baptist cemetery is for an infant Arthur Stapleton who died in 1853, and whose grave is marked by a simple sandstone headstone and footstone.

Despite the formal denominational divisions, the burying grounds accepted other religions. Congregationalists were buried in either the Baptist or Presbyterian cemeteries, and as St John's became crowded by the mid-1890s, the Anglicans were also accommodated in the two cemeteries on the Western Road.

As you face the cemetery today, with the Great Western Highway behind you, the Presbyterian cemetery is on the left and the Baptist cemetery is on the right. Entrance is through the Baptist brick lychgate. The cemetery features a range of 19th- and 20th-century headstones.

At first the cemetery and its monumentation appear unremarkable, but the observant visitor will be rewarded. The cemetery is well maintained and has an active friends group. The plantings throughout the cemetery make it a pleasant place to wander around, but I'd highly recommend a sunny winter's day when the snowdrops, jonquils and daffodils are in full bloom.

Look out to your left as you walk into the cemetery for the sandstone broken column on a pedestal with a broken stem rose, both symbols of a life cut short. This marks the Garlick family grave where the first burial was Mildred Essie Garlick who died in 1895 aged 6 years and 11 months. Another more unusual version of this symbolic motif is the lyre with the broken string that decorates the marble Gothic arch headstone to Frank Drysdale Henderson who died in 1908.

Further along the row you'll see another fine early classical pedestal with a gabled pediment that marks the enclosed Kell family plot. Smaller than the McKay monument, a female mourner who clutches an urn, while kneeling on a three-step base surmounts this pedestal. On the northern face, the deaths of two children in 1847 and 1854 are commemorated. Perhaps the mourner represents the children's mother.

NOTABLE BURIALS

- James Houison (1800–1876), builder and contractor, Parramatta alderman
- Thomas Hollier junior (1815–1895), farmer at Sherwood, connected with Baptist Chapel at Smithfield
- Edwin Case (1865–1936), drove first tram in Parramatta

MORE INFORMATION
- Judith Dunn, *The Parramatta Cemeteries: Mays Hill*, Parramatta and District Historical Society, Parramatta, 1996.
- Michael Brookhouse, 'Mays Hill Cemetery', Australian Cemeteries Index website, 2011, <austcemindex.com/cemetery?cemid=801>.
- *Tales from the Western Road Cemetery*, 3 vols, Friends of Mays Hill Cemetery, Merrylands, 2011–14.
- Friends of Mays Hill Cemetery website, 2016, <www.mayshillcemetery.org>.

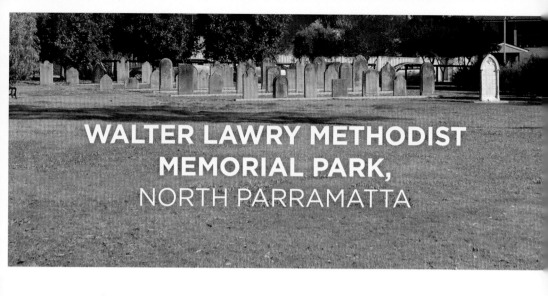

WALTER LAWRY METHODIST MEMORIAL PARK, NORTH PARRAMATTA

BULLER STREET, NORTH PARRAMATTA

Burials: 1841–1946 (converted 1961)

The Walter Lawry Methodist Memorial Park is just a shadow of what was once Parramatta's Wesleyan burial ground. Land set aside for a burial ground in 1839 was formally granted to the Wesleyans on 31 October 1843. The earliest surviving headstone commemorates William Weedon Robinson, who died at Newlands on 13 April 1842. There were 572 burials in the cemetery between 1841 and 1946.

The cemetery was closed by the *Parramatta Methodist Cemetery Act 1961* and control passed to Parramatta City Council so that the cemetery could be cleared and converted into a public park. Headstones and grave surrounds were cleared, but the bodies were not exhumed.

An interpretive sign at the park's entrance on Buller Street explains the cemetery's bleak history. A memorial wall enveloping a monument to Walter Lawry lists the name, death date and age of everyone known to be interred here.

This has to be one of the worst conversions of a cemetery to parkland that I have seen (although St James at Smithfield gives it a run for its money). Originally in 1965 many of the headstones were placed flat on the ground. Forty-eight memorials were salvaged in 2003 and re-erected upright in six rows in a corner of the park, but it remains a soulless, underutilised open space.

The memorial park is named in honour of Walter Lawry, considered the 'Father of Methodism' in Parramatta. Lawry organised the first Missionary Society, set up the Sunday School, and even built the first Wesleyan chapel in the district in 1821 at his own expense. If he could see the cemetery now, he would be turning in his grave.

NOTABLE BURIALS

- Walter Lawry (1793–1859), Methodist missionary
- John Allen Manton (1807–1864), Wesleyan minister, inaugural principal of Newington College
- Francis Rowland Oakes (1818–1866) and George Oakes (1813–1881), brothers, pastoralists and politicians
- Joseph Wearne (1832–1884), flour-miller and politician
- John William Pass (c.1818–1884), ironmonger, mayor of Prospect and Sherwood

MORE INFORMATION

- Judith Dunn & Rosemarie Morris, *The Parramatta Cemeteries: All Saints and Wesleyan*, Parramatta and District Historical Society, Parramatta, 2007.
- Michael Brookhouse, 'Parramatta Methodist Cemetery', Australian Cemeteries Index website, 2011 <austcemindex.com/cemetery?cemid=778>.

MONUMENTAL MASONS

In 1802 when the French explorer and historian François Péron was visiting Sydney, he recorded in his notebook that the public burial ground on George Street was already an 'object of curiosity' and interest for the 'several striking monuments' erected therein. He was surprised by the quality of cemetery memorials, commenting that its execution 'is much better than could reasonably have been expected from the state of the arts in so young a colony'. This is one of the earliest descriptions of monumental masonry in the colony. After only 14 years, Sydney was supporting a small but creative group of stonemasons, who were carving memorials to perpetuate the memory and identity of the deceased. In the newly settled colony, the cemetery became an important cultural institution to establish the religious, moral and social order and to define a person's identity.

MODES OF PRODUCTION

In the 19th century, cemetery memorials were generally ordered from a stonemason or monumental mason. Cemetery memorial designs in Sydney were essentially modified derivatives from Great Britain and to a lesser extent Europe, utilising the established 'language' of funerary memorials and symbolism. The earliest craftsmen brought their knowledge of design from their native country. The development of the monumental masonry industry in New South Wales followed a similar pattern to that of England, but later, and over a more compressed time period.

Andrew Bros monumental masonry yard, Elizabeth Street, Sydney, 1910 (established 1879)

Up until the 1850s in New South Wales, individual artisans produced funerary monuments. Some had their own business and a yard to display their wares. As the 19th century progressed, the monumental trade became increasingly organised and specialised into larger firms. The carving and lettering of monuments was usually completed at the mason's workshop, commonly a large shed. The space was organised so that the stone was worked sequentially along a quasi-production line. It remained at heart, though, an artisan trade, highly skilled and able to respond to individual needs. There was often a direct interaction between the stonemason and the customer.

The monumental masonry industry was a conservative, close-knit hereditary craft built on family businesses. Training was supplied on the job in the form of an apprenticeship. Between the 1840s and the 1860s, several skilled masons immigrated to the colony. The growing market created by urbanisation and the consequent development of many suburban general cemeteries, along with union organisation, led to an increasingly organised and specialised monumental trade. The Operative Stonemason Society (formed in 1853) was an integral part of the development of the industry both in terms of conditions and social status. The union was a strong proponent behind professionalisation in the late 19th century. It fought hard for the eight-hour day, opposed piecework, and promoted training and education. Stonemasons were the first trade in Australia to establish the eight-hour day.

Prior to 1870 firms were generally a family concern, but by the end of the 19th century many businesses employed several masons (anywhere between three and fifteen men) and at least one apprentice. In the early 1900s, stonemasons had reduced their hours to the 40-hour working week. Their work began to be classified into various tasks; an industrial award in 1916 formalised their work arrangements.

Changes in technology and machinery in the 20th-century had a dramatic impact on the production of memorials and favoured materials. What was previously done by hand could now be done by machine. F Arnold & Sons explained in their catalogue issued around 1930 that:

> The stone-saw cuts all stones without waste, the marble-cutter accomplishes three operations in one, and the planing machine runs mouldings accurately in the shortest possible time. In fact, all the machinery used enables us to manufacture a better product (for less cost) than hand methods would.

This increasing mechanisation meant that hard, durable stones like granite and trachyte, difficult and expensive to carve by hand, were now more easily worked. Sandblasting could incise inscriptions in granite and produce decorative motifs. Relief lettering in granite was now possible for inscriptions (previously only family names would be given such treatment – it was just too labour intensive to do a whole inscription by hand). Thus mechanisation made some materials cheaper and easier to work. Granite, once an expensive material and the domain of the rich, was more affordable by the 1940s and could be easily worked in smaller quantities.

Sandblasting and computer-guided cutting of headstones in the late 20th-century has allowed for greater intricacy and personalisation of incised decoration.

CHOOSING A MONUMENT

Two things are consistently emphasised in memorial advertisements in Sydney: economy and choice. J Hanson claimed in 1882 to have 'the largest and best stock in Australia to select from', boasting that 'the designs are the choicest, combined with prices to suit all classes of purchasers'. More succinctly R Clark offered 'first-class workmanship at lowest prices' at his yard at Rookwood in 1904. So what was

Opposite An example of stonemason Shea's work at St Peter's Anglican Cemetery, Campbelltown; his distinctive 'memento mori' headstones can be found around the district

the average cost of a memorial? Could 'all classes of purchasers' really afford to buy a headstone as the advertisements of these firms suggested?

The cheapest stone memorials available in the late 19th century – generally plain sandstone headstones – ranged between £4 and £5. This was the equivalent of one and a half to two weeks' wages for a tradesman. A sandstone headstone with some simple decorative carving cost £8 to £12, or approximately four weeks wages for a tradesman.

Marble was more expensive than sandstone, but along with granite, gained rapid favour over the last three decades of the 19th century. It was popular for a number of reasons. Associations with classical Greece and Rome helped to define marble as an enlightened and refined choice, and its use by the English aristocracy for church memorials gave it cachet. Prestigious and expensive, marble expressed social differentiation. Marble's pure white colour was admired for its contrast against the dark green foliage of a cemetery, and our vibrant blue sky. It was also more durable than sandstone, making it appropriate for memorial art. Inscriptions could be incised and filled with what was described as 'imperishable' lead lettering, improving the legibility and lifespan of the monument.

Marble was imported from Italy, Belgium, the United Kingdom and North America for monumental work in Sydney. Some monumental masons also used local marble. William Patten had a marble quarry on the Wollondilly River and his firm Patten Bros advertised that they used both Italian and Australian marble.

The choice of a marble memorial implied greater wealth, taste and social status. This is illustrated not only in the comparative cost of marble and

Left The distinctive shape produced by stonemasons George Peters and Joseph Craig in Parramatta   *Right* George Peters, monumental masonry yard, Parramatta, c.1870

sandstone, but also in the composition of catalogues themselves. Marble monuments were placed at the front of the catalogue and cost two to three times more than their sandstone counterparts. A plain semicircular marble headstone, the simplest marble memorial available, cost £10. The ubiquitous draped urn on a pedestal with three-step base – which is found all around Sydney's cemeteries – cost £50 10s, one-third of a tradesman's annual wage. The erection of a grave marker was a requisite part of a respectable burial, yet for many this expression of mourning and remembrance was unobtainable. It was too costly for many within the lower classes.

The wider availability of granite for cemetery monuments followed in marble's footsteps. A variety of granite colours and types were available by the early 20th-century. A large quantity of monumental granite was imported from Scotland, but other sources came from Sweden, Finland and North America. There were also some local sources, including dark grey granite from Marulan and trachyte from Bowral. Other granite quarries in New South Wales were at Anarel, Mudgee and Uralla.

Like marble, granite was more expensive than sandstone. A granite headstone or monument ranged in price from £16 to £67, or approximately four times more expensive than the average sandstone headstone at the time, and about a third more than marble.

By the 1940s granite was the most popular material for cemetery memorials, big or small. The memorial catalogue no. 5 issued by F Arnold & Sons around 1930 demonstrates the shift in style. Gone are the multitude of marble headstones, replaced by a chart showing the colour and grain of four granites along with illustrations of lower desk headstones and wider headstones designed for double

Left Granite desk monuments, Frenchs Forest Bushland Cemetery   *Right* A matching pair of marble draped urns on pedestals, Manly General Cemetery

plots. The height of headstones has lowered, but the height of kerbing has risen to create a more built-up, enclosed tomb-like space. In the early 1940s the average cost of a memorial at F Arnold & Sons was nearly £32, the equivalent of five and a half weeks' wages. By the early 1950s people spent £102 on a memorial, or about seven times the average weekly wage. Memorials were becoming more expensive, even while their overall size and impact on the landscape was shrinking.

Further innovations in memorial styles in the 1960s responded to the demand from postwar European immigrants. Memorial designs had vases executed in sandstone, marble or terrazzo built in, they included ceramic photos, or incorporated niches for statues and candles. The different needs of Sydney's diverse ethnic and religious communities have continued to shape the style and range of memorials in Sydney's cemeteries into the 21st century.

MARKETING AND AVAILABILITY

Cemetery memorials were heavily marketed in the 19th century. The position of a monumental masonry yard near, or even adjacent to, a cemetery was not only a convenient practicality but also an invaluable marketing tool. Completed monuments were displayed in the front yard of the workshop and office, advertising the designs available as well as the skill of the mason. Anywhere between 10 and 40 monuments were displayed in the average yard. Today's monumental masons still have their yards close to cemeteries, although the industry has diversified with both cemeteries and funeral directors now offering memorials.

Apart from the show yard, the simplest marketing technique was to sign a memorial. A cemetery visitor could then attribute a pleasing design to a particular sculptor or firm. Monumental masons F Arnold & Sons encouraged prospective customers to 'inspect our memorial works in the cemeteries of this country', thereby drawing attention to their market penetration, popularity, reliability and durability. They were essentially saying, 'our monuments have stood the test of time'. Monumental masons continue to sign their work to this day, proclaiming their skill and touting for business.

Some masons directly canvassed for work inside cemeteries, much to the consternation of visitors. Several correspondents to the *Sydney Morning Herald* in 1890 complained a visit to Rookwood Necropolis had been made 'intolerable' by the 'unfeeling and untimely practices' of masons touting for business. Masons 'thrust' their cards into the hands of visitors as they arrived and even approached people attending graves. They brandished photo albums of their work and price lists. Such practices were in contravention of cemetery regulations, but difficult to stamp out.

Promotional materials, such as price lists, design sheets, photo albums and catalogues, were the main way a mason could illustrate and disseminate memorial designs. Many monumental masons advertised that they could post a free sheet of designs to prospective customers. The development of such broadsheets from the late 19th century allowed large Sydney firms to expand further into country areas. This meant that the latest designs from Sydney and overseas were available throughout the state.

Monumental masons also promoted their wares through advertisements in post office and commercial directories, church newspapers and the popular daily press. The advertisements not only listed services; the entire layout was a testimonial to the mason's skill and taste. The ads could display different lettering styles and show balance and spacing in its presentation, like the layout of an inscription.

Patten Bros advertisement, 1889

Fine or famous examples of a firm's work could be illustrated, too. Ross & Bowman had the honour to erect the memorial to New South Wales governor Sir Robert Duff; T Andrews & Sons claimed an association with the tomb of the wreck of the *Dunbar*; while Patten Bros had a brush with sporting fame, carving the memorial for world champion sculler Henry Ernest Searle.

Symbolic motifs carved on the pediment of the headstone became the central focus of most grave markers in the late 19th century. The symbolism itself became subsumed in a self-conscious desire to keep up with the latest trends. Mix and match was the principal idea behind much of the ornamentation on headstones. Clients often chose elements from several different designs in a pattern book or catalogue and asked the mason to combine them on the one gravestone.

The localised repetition of headstone designs across rows of unrelated family graves hints at gravestone designs being chosen by families on the basis of examples nearby, reflecting an 'I'll have what she's having' mentality that assured class-conscious purchasers that their memorial was appropriate and met social standards.

Regrettably the desire for a 'chaste' memorial led to the decline in true individualism in cemetery memorial design in Sydney. Pattern books, while bringing the latest fashions to Sydney served to further standardise the appearance of the average headstone. Many masons produced a hybrid style.

Cemeteries are like outdoor sculpture parks and there is much to admire in the skilled carving demonstrated on so many grave markers erected in the 19th century. As you wander around cemeteries today, how many variations on a theme can you spot? Look out for the truly original headstones and see if you can find the signature of the mason who crafted it. Look at the base of the headstone, the plinth of the pedestal or on the kerbing around the grave plot.

Left A unique medieval-style canopy tomb marks the family grave of monumental mason John Roote Andrews, Camperdown Cemetery   *Right* A child's face, lizards and birds decorate the pedestal commemorating John Nimrod Monk (d.1864), St Peter's Anglican Cemetery, Campbelltown

TOP 5

FLORAL DISPLAYS

ROSES	**Rookwood Necropolis**
FREESIAS	**Waverley Cemetery, Bronte**
SNOWDROPS, JONQUILS AND DAFFODILS	**Mays Hill Cemetery**
IRISES, AS WELL AS JONQUILS, KANGAROO PAW, DAISIES AND GERANIUMS	**St Paul's Anglican Cemetery, Canterbury**
COREOPSIS	**Gore Hill Memorial Cemetery, St Leonards**

St Paul's Anglican Cemetery, Canterbury

Bar Point

Mooney
Mooney

Umina Beach

1

2

Brooklyn

Patonga

Pearl Beach

Palm Beach

Berowra

Cottage Point

Elvina Bay

Avalon Beach

3

MCCARRS CREEK RD

Bayview

Newport

4

Mona Vale

Terrey Hills

Ingleside

St Ives

Narrabeen

FOREST WAY

Davidson

5

Pymble

6

Gordon

WARRINGAH ROAD

Dee Why

Brookvale

Freshwater

Macquarie
Park

7

DELHI ROAD

11

KENNETH

SYDNEY RD

8

Chatswood

Manly

Lane Cove

9

10

12

St Leonards

Mosman

PACIFIC MOTORWAY

MONA VALE ROAD

PITTWATER ROAD

PACIFIC HIGHWAY

M2 MOTORWAY

PITTWATER RD

KINGS ROAD

Opposite Detail of altar tomb of Ellis Bent (d.1815), St Thomas' Rest Park, Crows Nest

NORTH

ST THOMAS' REST PARK, CROWS NEST

250 WEST STREET, CROWS NEST (PARKING ON ATCHISON STREET)

Burials: 1845–1950 (converted 1974)

Although converted from a cemetery into a rest park in 1974, St Thomas' is still worth a visit. Many North Shore luminaries found their resting place here after Alexander Berry donated the land to the Anglican Parish of St Leonards in 1845 following the death of his wife. It was the first cemetery on the North Shore and fascinating memorials survive here, clumped around the park.

There were over 4000 burials in the 1.6 hectare cemetery between 1845 and 1950. The parish registers record what is not so evident from the surviving memorials: about half the burials were children under the age of ten. The cemetery was located some distance from St Thomas' parish church, so the sexton who worked, and later lived, onsite supervised the burials. The Sexton's Cottage survives and is one of the oldest buildings remaining in North Sydney.

Two large monuments that have remained in situ particularly demand attention. The Berry monument in the eastern section of the park is a massive sandstone pyramid that sits atop the family vault. Merchant Alexander Berry and his business partner Edward Wollstonecraft at various times worked and lived at Crow's Nest House. The death of Elizabeth Berry (nee Wollstonecraft) prompted Berry to donate the land for the cemetery.

Much smaller, but exquisitely carved, is the Bent / Ovens memorial in the western area of the park. This is the earliest memorial in the park and if you look carefully you can see the sculptor's name 'Tyler'. Judge Advocate Ellis Bent (d.1815) was first buried in the Old Sydney Burial Ground, but a new memorial was created when his friend Major John Ovens died in 1825. For many years this monument was a picturesque landmark on Garden Island.

There are some impressive examples of headstone and monument designs between the 1840s and the 1860s. Of particular note is the weeping widow that adorns an altar tomb erected by William Williams for his 'beloved and deeply regretted wife' Annie Fitz Williams (d.1865), just 32 years of age.

A number of mariners are buried here, bearing witness to the importance of the harbour and sea trade in Sydney's economic development. The most prominent memorial is to James Graham Goodenough (d.1875), Commodore of the Australian Station of the Royal Navy, who died from arrow wounds sustained while trying to settle a dispute with Pacific Islanders in 1875. Commodore Goodenough's simple

Left Conrad Martens' (d.1878) memorial impresses visitors   *Right* The massive scale and unusual design of the Berry monument still

marble Celtic cross is enclosed with a chain bearing crossed anchors. Other mariners buried at St Thomas' include Captain Owen Stanley (d.1850), commander of HMS *Rattlesnake*, Merion Marshall Moriarty (d.1864), Port-Master of New South Wales 1842–57, and marine surveyor John Thomas Ewing Gowlland (drowned off Dobroyd Point 1874).

This is a busy, much-loved park, favoured by dog walkers. An enclosed children's playground in the north-west corner makes this the perfect family picnic spot.

NOTABLE BURIALS

- Alexander Berry (1781–1873), merchant and settler, namesake of Berry's Bay and the South Coast town
- Conrad Martens (1801–1878), artist and designer of the first St Thomas' Church
- John Jago (c.1835–1896), stonemason and builder of many buildings on the North Shore, including the Uniting Church at Chatswood South
- Hannah McLeod (1857–1912), first matron of Crown Street Women's Hospital

MORE INFORMATION

- Heritage Centre, *St Thomas' Cemetery Headstones Index*, North Sydney Council, 2016, <photosau.com.au/StantonHeadstones/scripts/home.asp>.
- North Sydney Council Library, 'St Thomas' Rest Park: Self-Guided Walking Tour Notes', North Sydney Council website, 2013, <www.northsydney.nsw.gov. au/files/868eb0d4-3da4-48d8-b0aa-a13a010abf43/StThomasRestParkBroch_Jan2013.pdf>.
- EJ Lea-Scarlett, *Saint Thomas's Church of England, North Sydney: Monumental Inscription in the Cemetery*, Society of Australian Genealogists, Sydney, 1963.
- Chris Morgan, *Life and Death on the North Side: a history of St Thomas' Church and Cemetery, North Sydney*, Stanton Library, North Sydney Municipal Council, 1988.

NORTH

GORE HILL MEMORIAL CEMETERY, ST LEONARDS

WESTBOURNE STREET, CORNER PACIFIC HIGHWAY, ST LEONARDS

Burials: 1877–1974

The North Shore did not get a large general cemetery until the late 1870s, but it was worth the wait. Gore Hill Cemetery evolved into a beauty, filled with quality memorials and vaults. A fine example of a landscaped public cemetery from the late Victorian / Edwardian era, this is a must-see Sydney cemetery. But don't go alone: the cemetery's forlorn, overgrown state evokes shivers of haunted memories and also legitimate primal fears of isolation. Best go with a friend to visit this State Heritage-listed cemetery.

Agitation for a general cemetery on the North Shore began in 1867, the same year that the Necropolis at Haslem's Creek opened and the borough of St Leonards was incorporated. William Tunks, the first mayor of St Leonards, spearheaded the initial effort.

While 5.5 hectares of land was

dedicated in May 1868 it took nearly another ten years for denominational trustees to be gazetted and the cemetery to open for burials. In the interim, burials continued at St Thomas' Church of England Cemetery, the recently established Roman Catholic Cemetery at Chatswood (1865–1907), and the Wesleyan Cemetery at South Chatswood (established 1871).

The local borough councils of St Leonards, East St Leonards, North Willoughby and Victoria were initially appointed trustees. This is another unusual example of how cemetery management evolved and changed in Sydney. The councils fenced the cemetery and tried to protect the site. Denominational trustees, each responsible for their own areas, were not appointed until October 1875.

The first confirmed burial in Gore Hill Cemetery was Elizabeth Dalton in the old Catholic section, who died 22 February 1877. Demand for burials was initially slow. William Tunks (d.1883), who had spearheaded the campaign for the cemetery, was the first burial in the Church of England section, at its entrance. The majority of the 14,456 burials at Gore Hill were between 1900 and 1930 and the last was in 1974 when the *Gore Hill Cemetery Act 1974* facilitated the potential conversion of the cemetery into a rest park and garden. The Act closed the cemetery and transferred control to Willoughby Council. Fortunately, Gore Hill was never

cleared or converted, like many other cemeteries, thanks to the Friends of Gore Hill Cemetery which formed in 1975 to lobby for its preservation. The *Gore Hill Memorial Cemetery Act 1986* was passed to revoke the option to make the site a public park and instead direct the preservation and management of the cemetery as a historic cemetery. Today Gore Hill is under the administration of the Northern Cemeteries Trust.

A central avenue, known as The Carriageway, defines the cemetery landscape. Each of the denominational areas is accessed from The Carriageway. The design of the cemetery was based upon the surveyor-general's standard plan for general cemeteries, but adapted in size and layout for the site.

Gore Hill is special as it retains many landscape features such as its original carriageway, gates and piers, sexton's cottage (constructed 1886), cabbage tree palm avenue plantings, a lychgate leading into the old Catholic section, an Arts and Crafts–style robing room in the new Catholic section, a basic federation style storage shed in the Methodist section, a shelter shed in the Congregationalist section by the carriageway and a stone arch entrance to the Baptist section.

The cemetery is laid out on a grid pattern with brick paths. Both the Roman Catholic and Church of England sections utilise paths and palms to define vistas to prominent memorials: the octagonal Jesuit plot

Left Cornwell family vault

and the Hordern plot respectively. There are several fine vaults including the Dalton vault and the Cornwell vault. At least 20 memorials were transferred from the Devonshire Street Cemeteries in 1901. Esther Wilshire (d.1836), wife of James Wilshire (1771–1840), public servant, tanner and manufacturer, has the memorial with the earliest death date.

There are many notables buried here and the Friends of Gore Hill Cemetery have done a remarkable job researching biographies of many of the cemetery's residents. The funeral of champion swimmer Barney Kieran (d.1905), whose talented career came to an abrupt end after a fatal bout of appendicitis, attracted 30,000 mourners. The most famous resident is no longer there: St Mary MacKillop (d.1909) was exhumed in 1914 and reinterred in the Mary MacKillop Memorial Chapel at the Josephite convent in North Sydney. The chapel has become a place of pilgrimage since her beatification in 1995 (she was canonised in 2010). Many other Sisters of St Joseph of the Sacred Heart are buried at Gore Hill.

Gore Hill Memorial Cemetery has a wonderful gothic atmosphere created by its overgrown vegetation. Don't start writing letters of protest. The cemetery is no longer neglected; the trustees have a deliberate low-level regime of vegetation management in place known as 'controlled overgrowth'. A visit in springtime will reward you with coreopsis and other flowering bulbs and perennials.

Opposite Avenue planting of cabbage tree palms

NORTH

Left Architect Walter Liberty Vernon's (d.1914) memorial

NOTABLE BURIALS

- William A Tunks (1816–1883), politician and founding mayor of St Leonards
- Sir Edward Strickland (1821–1889), army officer
- William Wilkinson Wardell (1823–1899), architect and civil servant, designed St Mary's Cathedral, Sydney and St Patrick's Cathedral, Melbourne
- Thomas Dalton (1829–1901), importer, merchant and politician
- Bernard Bede (Barney) Kieran (1886–1905), champion swimmer
- Walter Liberty Vernon (1846–1914), colonial architect and soldier, designed Art Gallery NSW, Mitchell wing of State Library NSW, and Central Station
- John Charles Ludowici (1836–1916), tanner, founder of JC Ludowici & Son Ltd, major leather manufacturers
- Louisa King (1883–1919), first woman pharmacist in Sydney
- Sir John Sulman (1849–1934), architect, commemorated by the Sir John Sulman Art Prize and the Sulman Architectural Medal
- Cornwell vault, brewers and maltsters, family established Cornwell's Vinegar

Left Sisters of Mercy memorial

MORE INFORMATION

- Gore Hill, Northern Cemeteries Trust website, 2016, <northerncemeteries.com. au/gore-hill>.
- Willoughby City Council Library, 'Gore Hill Cemetery', Willoughby City Council website, 2016, <www.willoughby.nsw.gov.au/library/history-at-willoughby/gore-hill-cemetery>.
- Nick Vine Hall (ed.), *Gore Hill Cemetery Transcripts*, vols 1 & 2, Royal Australian Historical Society & Society of Australian Genealogists, Sydney, 1976–77.
- Edith A Sims, *Gore Hill Cemetery 1868–1974*, The Friends of Gore Hill Cemetery, Lindfield, 1985.
- J Adams, L Thomas & W Adams (eds), *Gore Hill Memorial Cemetery Biographies*, vols 1 & 2, The Friends of Gore Hill Cemetery, Lindfield, 1994 & 2001.
- Heritage Office, 'Gore Hill Memorial Cemetery', State Heritage Register listing ID 5051524, NSW Office of Environment and Heritage website, 2016, <www.environment.nsw.gov.au/heritageapp/ViewHeritageItemDetails. aspx?ID=5051524>.
- Friends of Gore Hill Cemetery website, 2016 <friendsofgorehillcemetery.com>.

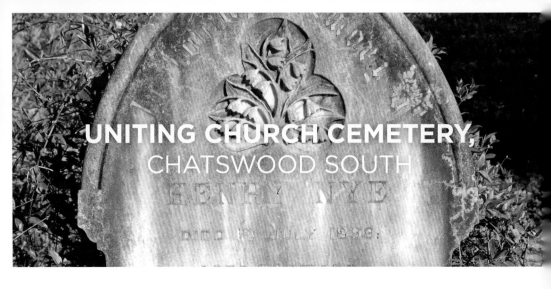

UNITING CHURCH CEMETERY,
CHATSWOOD SOUTH

581 PACIFIC HIGHWAY, CORNER MOWBRAY ROAD, CHATSWOOD SOUTH

Burials: 1871–1924 (converted 1984)

The quaint little Wesleyan church and cemetery has been a district landmark for over 140 years. Prominent architect Thomas Rowe designed the sandstone Gothic church, and North Sydney contractor John Jago built it. This is one of just two surviving churchyards along the North Shore, the other being St John's at Gordon. But the 21st century is not being kind. The church and cemetery look set to be sold off and incorporated into residential development.

There are only about 65 memorials in the cemetery, dating from the 1870s to 1924, although the *Sydney Morning Herald* noted in 1929 that families with existing burial rights could still be buried in this little cemetery. The churchyard was handed over to Lane Cove Council in 1982 and rededicated in 1984 as a Pioneers' Memorial Reserve. The majority of headstones suffered from regular vandalism in the 20th-century. This was one of the first sites where the National Trust Cemeteries Committee partnered with the local council to restore many of the smashed headstones to demonstrate cemetery conservation practices. A number of headstone fragments are attached to a wall on the western boundary.

A camellia bush smothers the sandstone headstone of William Bryson (d.1873) in the north-west corner. Bryson, the youngest son of prominent church members John and Mary Ann Bryson, died tragically at the age of 19 years and 4 months when he was thrown from his horse while on his way to visit his fiancée. Local histories record the romance of the camellia bush that sprung from his grave after the grieving family or the fiancée buried the camellia from his buttonhole there.

Many of the headstones are quite plain, although you can find symbols of roses, passionflowers, doves and downturned torches. George Jones' (d.1911) marble headstone includes a simple lead line drawing of a watering can, shovel and rake, hinting at his occupation as a gardener. Seek out the fine rendition of the Lily of the Valley that adorns the Nye and Bowen family headstone.

Go visit this cemetery in late winter when the snowdrops, daffodils and jonquils are blooming.

NOTABLE BURIALS

- Reverend William Hill (c.1832–1899), Wesleyan minister for 45 years

MORE INFORMATION

- Heritage Office, 'Chatswood South Uniting Church and Cemetery', State Heritage Register listing ID 5045420, NSW Office of Environment and Heritage website, 2016, <www.environment.nsw.gov.au/heritageapp/ViewHeritageItemDetails.aspx?ID=5045420>.
- 'Chatswood Methodists', *Sydney Morning Herald*, 18 November 1929, p. 17. Retrieved 16 May 2016, <nla.gov.au/nla.news-article16602767>.

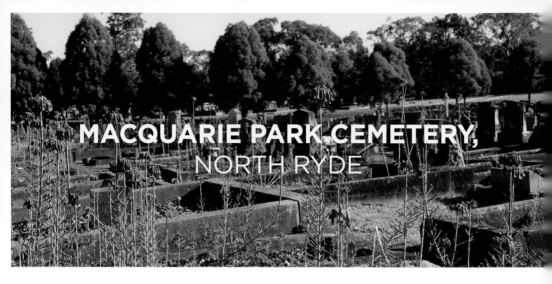

MACQUARIE PARK CEMETERY, NORTH RYDE

PLASSEY ROAD, CORNER DELHI ROAD, NORTH RYDE

Burials: 1922–present

Macquarie Park Cemetery and Crematorium, the largest cemetery on the North Shore, was dedicated on 9 July 1902 as the Northern Suburbs General Cemetery. The name changed in 2004, when the cemetery trustees introduced their own crematorium and chapels, thereby avoiding confusion with the Northern Suburbs Crematorium (constructed 1933) down the road.

The government set aside the cemetery just a few years after Field of Mars Cemetery opened, but the first burial did not take place until 20 April 1922. Dressed stone piers and an ironwork gate mark the original entrance way on Delhi Road. An avenue led past the caretaker's lodge and little brick office into a curvilinear landscape. The mature landscape, a fine example of interwar garden design, offers a haven for birdlife.

The cemetery has expanded and evolved over the 20th-century, gradually developing its 59 hectares. In 1954, Northern Suburbs Cemetery was the second Sydney cemetery to introduce lawn burials; it was pipped at the post by Woronora whose lawn cemetery area was gazetted late in 1953. Crypts were introduced in 1986 to cater for some European burial practices, and a large mausoleum containing 200 crypts was constructed in 1999. There is a Stations of the Cross. The Armenian portion has a striking memorial to the Martyrs of the 1915 holocaust that makes one pause and reflect. The cemetery has been transcribed and you can search the names register online.

Like Eastern Suburbs Memorial Park to the south, the graves at Macquarie Park Cemetery are a rollcall of modern Sydney. Many well-connected, cashed-up businessmen and women who lived on the North Shore found their last resting place here.

NOTABLE BURIALS

- Robert Rowan Purdon Hickson (1842–1923), civil engineer and first president of Sydney Harbour Trust, namesake of Hickson Road, Millers Point
- Louisa Margaret Dunkley (1866–1927), union leader and feminist
- William Morris (Billy) Hughes (1862–1952), Australian prime minister 1915–1923
- Walter Magnus (1903–1954), restaurateur, founder and partner of the fashionable Savarin restaurant (1946), among others
- Johnny O'Keefe (1935–1978), Australian rock'n'roll singer
- Francis John Nugan (1942–1980), lawyer and merchant banker, embroiled in the Nugan Hand bank scandal

MORE INFORMATION

- Macquarie Park, Northern Cemeteries Trust website, 2016, <northerncemeteries. com.au/macquarie-park>.
- *Macquarie Park Cemetery Transcriptions: Formerly Northern Suburbs Cemetery*, CD-ROM, Society of Australian Genealogists, Sydney, 2003.
- Local Government, 'Macquarie Park Cemetery and Crematoria', Heritage Inventory listing ID 2340201, NSW Office of Environment and Heritage website, 2016, <www.environment.nsw.gov.au/heritageapp/ViewHeritageItemDetails. aspx?ID=2340201>.

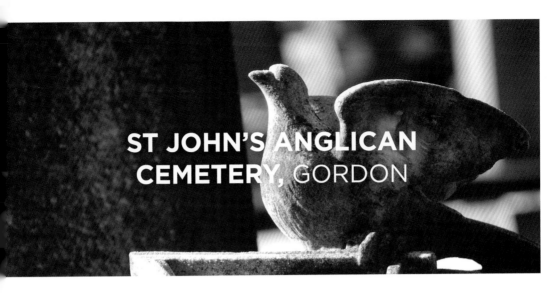

ST JOHN'S ANGLICAN CEMETERY, GORDON

750-754 PACIFIC HIGHWAY, GORDON (ENTER THE CAR PARK FROM ST JOHN'S AVENUE)

Burials: 1867–present (existing burial rights)

St John's Church Cemetery is a small, Anglican cemetery located down the slope to the west of the Edmund Blacket–designed church.

The earliest burial is Mary Britton, aged 27, on 8 May 1867. The cemetery's heyday was the period from 1900 to 1920, reflecting the growth of the district as a middle-class suburb. The overall tone of the cemetery is modest, but there are some substantial memorials and many prominent people who have shaped the North Shore and Sydney are buried here.

The oldest headstone in the cemetery comes from Devonshire Street, moved to Gordon by the McIntosh family in 1901. It commemorates Ellen McIntosh (d.1826) and her husband Robert McIntosh (d.1829), bandmaster of HM 46th Regiment. The McIntosh family are well represented in the cemetery, being early orchardists in the Gordon area. Robert

McIntosh Jnr's Gordondale Estate forms the centre of today's Gordon.

A severe red granite obelisk, erected by the New South Wales government, marks the grave of Edwin Stuart Hickey, Sergeant of Police at Pymble, who died while on duty 17 May 1913. Hickey was trying to serve a warrant when he was shot by orchardist Thomas Brown at St Ives. He died before reaching hospital and was bestowed a funeral with full police honours. Brown also managed to shoot his own son, who survived.

The grave of young mother Jane Swarzas is marked by a fine mourning widow sitting under a willow tree carved in bas-relief by the monumental mason John Roseby. Jane died in childbirth in 1875; her child died two weeks later.

There are over 1800 burials and cremated remains. The cemetery is well maintained by the local parish, and is still in use with a columbarium wall and rose garden dedicated in 2001.

NOTABLE BURIALS

- Joseph Henry Maiden (1859–1925), botanist, director Royal Botanic Gardens Sydney
- James George Edwards (c.1843–1927), real estate agent and alderman, the 'Father of Killara'.
- Sir Alfred Livingston Parker, (1875–1935) lawyer and lord mayor of Sydney
- John Job Crew Bradfield (1867–1943), engineer, 'designer' of the Sydney Harbour Bridge

MORE INFORMATION

- Jill Lyons, *Pioneers at Peace: The story of St John's Cemetery, Gordon*, Spurwood Press, Sydney, 1994.
- Berenice Hill, *St John's Cemetery Gordon*, self-published, Normanhurst, 1988.

Opposite A fine red granite obelisk marks the grave of Edwin Stuart Hickey (d.1913), a policeman killed on duty

THIS MONUMENT
WAS ERECTED BY
THE GOVERNMENT OF
NEW SOUTH WALES
TO THE MEMORY OF
EDWIN STUART HICKEY
AGED 52
SERGEANT OF POLICE AT PYMBLE
WHO WAS SHOT IN THE EXECUTION
OF HIS DUTY 1ST MAY 1913
DYING SAME DAY.

ALSO HIS DEAR WIFE
MARY ANN
PASSED AWAY 26TH APRIL 1955
AGED 88 YEARS.

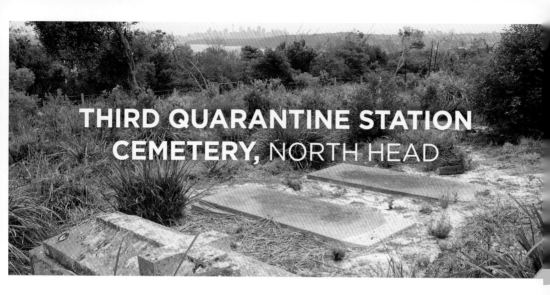

THIRD QUARANTINE STATION CEMETERY, NORTH HEAD

NORTH HEAD SANCTUARY, MANLY

Burials: 1881–1925

There is a melancholy loneliness to this cemetery nestled within the North Head Sanctuary. Deliberately set away from the Quarantine Station down at Spring Cove, this was the third cemetery to serve Sydney's main isolation hospital for immigrants and residents. Despite panoramic views of the harbour and today's modern city from the headland, the encroaching bushland and, paradoxically, the vistas reinforce the secluded, remote atmosphere of this burial ground.

The North Head Quarantine Station was established in 1832 to deal with sick passengers and crew arriving by ship, to isolate disease and prevent the spread of epidemics. The quarantine station closed in 1984. Thousands of people were quarantined during that time; around 570 people died there. The first graveyard, down among the station near Quarantine Beach, was in use from 1837 to 1853 and contained an estimated 228 burials.

The cemetery was later cleared and only a handful of headstones survive. The second cemetery, with 102 interments over the period 1853–81, was out of sight, behind the third-class accommodation. The second quarantine cemetery still exists, but is overgrown and inaccessible to the public.

The Third Quarantine Cemetery contains 241 burials from 1881 to 1925. The register of burials is preserved by the National Archives of Australia. The cemetery contains victims of three key epidemics that hit Sydney: a smallpox epidemic in 1881, the bubonic plague outbreak of 1900 and its subsequent emergences, and the influenza outbreak in the wake of the First World War. During the plague epidemic, many sufferers and their contacts, mainly family and other householders, were sent to the Quarantine Station. After 1925, the Quarantine Station did not have its own burial ground.

The wind-whipped cemetery is enclosed by a fence and overgrown with scrub. Small sandy pathways wend their way to various memorials scattered around the site. The cemetery is the last resting places of passengers, crew, hospital staff and their families, Sydney residents, and soldiers. Only a small proportion of the burials are marked. The largest memorial is a marble obelisk to Private Hector Fraser Hicks, an 18-year-old soldier who died from the Spanish flu. A marble cross with Madonna lilies and a ribbon bearing the epitaph 'Thy Will Be Done' was erected by the grieving widow of John Daniel Madden, who died of the bubonic plague on 5 March 1900. A second epitaph on the ledger stone speaks of the sadness at having to leave loved ones buried here:

By the sad and mournful sea
The dearest one that was to me
Lies sleeping here, eternal rest
His soul is numbered with the blest

A contemplative walk around the cemetery reveals a range of headstones: some to Chinese residents who died of the plague; to William Hay, a quarantine officer for 20 years who (the burial register records) shot himself in 1902; and to a nurse who died of the Spanish flu, along with many soldiers.

The cemetery is a short walk from the North Fort visitor centre (parking access is via North Head Scenic Drive) or a slightly longer walk from the Barracks Precinct. Either way you will be rewarded by the stunning bushland of the Eastern Suburbs banksia scrub, birds and wildflowers.

While you are here, call in at the

Q Station where you can view the headstones from the first cemetery in the museum at the Visitor Centre down by the water. There are about a dozen headstones on display dating from the 1830s to the 1850s. Many are quite effusive in the description of their origins, the ship that brought them here and their illnesses.

TIPS

There are café restaurants at both the North Head Sanctuary and the Q Station, but they get very busy, particularly on weekends, so you're advised to make a booking. Otherwise pack a picnic and make a day of it.

For the ultimate spooky experience, book a ghost tour of the Quarantine Station. There are adults-only and family-friendly versions!

MORE INFORMATION
- The Quarantine Station website, 2016, <quarantinestation.com.au>.
- Brett Miller & Paul Fitzgerald, 'Manly Quarantine Station 3 Cemetery', *Australian Cemeteries Index website*, 2014, <austcemindex.com/cemetery.php?id=1739>.
- 'Register of Deaths at Quarantine Station', digital copy, National Archives of Australia website, 2016, <recordsearch.naa.gov.au/SearchNRetrieve/Interface/ViewImage.aspx?B=314138&S=1>.

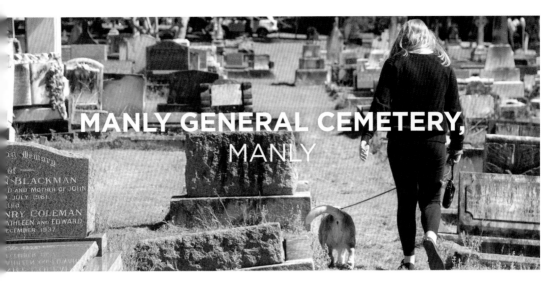

MANLY GENERAL CEMETERY, MANLY

GRIFFITHS STREET, MANLY

Burials: 1863–present

Manly General Cemetery is a welcoming and well-tended suburban cemetery. When it was established in the 1860s Manly was isolated, quiet and agricultural, with a dairy and market gardens nearby. As late as 1911 stock owners were grazing their cattle in the cemetery, to the detriment of the tombs and floral tributes. Now the cemetery is surrounded by residential houses and flats; not a cow to be seen.

With a park and children's playground at one end and the primary school situated at the other, the cemetery forms a connecting space for passive recreation. The cemetery is well-used and appreciated by dog walkers, mums with prams, joggers, along with locals taking a shortcut.

The site is quite open and two swales cut through the undulating cemetery, so it can be a little wet underfoot after rain.

The cemetery is divided into three denominational areas: Anglican,

Catholic and general. The earliest burial is Jane McLean, who died on 4 February 1863, and records show the Church of England section was consecrated in 1865. There are around 6000 discernible burial plots. Two local monumental masons used to operate beside the cemetery: George Watters on the corner of Griffiths and Hill streets from the 1920s and Harold Pickworth in Harland Street from the 1930s. Both have shut up shop.

As one of the earliest burial grounds for the northern beaches, Manly Cemetery features the graves of the district's early settlers from Mosman, Manly, Fairlight, Brookvale, Collaroy and Narrabeen. Civic service is well represented with 11 Manly mayors and a further 22 aldermen buried here.

Some notable achievers can be found here, alongside Manly characters such as The Corso carousel operator William 'Sovereign' Smith (d.1922) and Ellen 'Sweet Nell' Sullivan (d.1933) who sold confectionery in the 1920s and 1930s from her cart on Ocean Beach, The Corso and Manly Wharf.

While it is pleasant to walk around the cemetery as magpies warble and blue-tongue lizards scurry among the graves, there are few standout headstones to draw the eye. An exception is the large art deco trachyte monument to politician William Scott Fell (d.1930).

TIPS

Download the self-guided walk from the Manly Council website to make the most of your wanderings.

The burial registers have been transcribed and are available online for searching.

NOTABLE BURIALS

- Charles Hadley Hayes (1841–1924), established Ivanhoe Park, three times Manly mayor
- Millicent Maude Bryant (1878–1927), first woman to gain a private pilot's licence in Australia in 1927; she died later that year in the 'Greycliffe' ferry disaster. Her funeral featured a five-plane fly-over.
- Emmeline Freda Du Faur (1882–1935), first woman to climb Mount Cook, New Zealand in 1910

NORTH

- Thomas James (Tom) 'Rusty' Richards (1882–1935), rugby player, Olympian and First World War soldier
- Charles David Bryant (1883–1937), official First World War artist with AIF (Australian Imperial Force)

MORE INFORMATION

- Manly Council, 'Manly Cemetery', Manly Council website, 2016, <www.manly. nsw.gov.au/planning-and-development/heritage/manly-cemetery-heritage>.
- Nick Vine Hall, *Manly Cemetery Transcripts: 1845–1993*, Scriptorium Family History Centre, Albert Park, 1993.

Left Austere art deco trachyte monument to politician William Scott Fell (d.1930) and his wife Emma (d.1919)

FRENCHS FOREST BUSHLAND CEMETERY, DAVIDSON

1 HAKEA AVENUE, DAVIDSON

Burials: 1940–present

Frenchs Forest Bushland Cemetery is a thoroughly modern 20th-century cemetery. The 22 hectare site was set apart by the government in 1932, but the first burial did not take place for another eight years, on 24 April 1940 in the Church of England monumental section. Things moved slowly. The Jewish portion was consecrated on 12 September 1943, but the Anglican portion was only consecrated by Anglican Archbishop HWK Mowll on 20 February 1955.

There are four distinct burial approaches or sections in the cemetery. The main entrance leads to the earliest monumental sections, with 20th-century grave markers. Eucalypts and Christmas Bush line the main avenues between sections.

The earliest lawn cemetery section, with simple plaques set in the lawn, can be found towards the rear of the monumental sections. This was established in the 1960s, the first burial being in the Catholic lawn.

A large family vault and crypt section can be found behind the chapel and administration building. There are a few early red-brick vaults dating from the 1950s, before the dominant black granite family vaults take over.

The most recent section is the Bushland Memorial Gardens which are located on a hillock to the north-east of the site off Darwinia Drive. The memorial gardens are more informal in their enclosing landscaping, taking advantage of the indigenous vegetation, but still offer clearly defined lawn, monumental and cremation areas. The name of the cemetery was changed from Frenchs Forest General Cemetery to Frenchs Forest Bushland Cemetery in 1990 to reflect this new landscaping approach.

The many trees encourage an abundance of birdlife and the rainforest gully running beside Kanooka Way attracts water dragons.

TIP

To help you explore, pick up a map from dispensers around the cemetery or download it from the website. You can also do a name search on the cemetery website.

NOTABLE BURIALS

- John Albert (Jack) Beasley (1895–1949), trade unionist and politician, High Commissioner for Australia in London
- Mary Ann Josephine Lindsay (1892–1975), circus and trapeze artiste, Sole Bros Circus
- Kenneth Bernard Cook (1929–1987), novelist and filmmaker, author of *Wake in Fright*

MORE INFORMATION

- Frenchs Forest, Northern Cemeteries Trust website, 2016, <northerncemeteries.com.au/frenchs-forest>.
- Bob Pauling, *Frenchs Forest Cemetery* [transcription], CD, n.d.
- Beth Robertson, 'Frenchs Forest Cemetery', *Trove*, 2016 <trove.nla.gov.au/list?id=58354>.

NORTH

Early brick family mausoleums with unusual domed roofs

MONA VALE GENERAL CEMETERY, MONA VALE

107 MONA VALE ROAD (ENTRANCE FAZZOLARI AVENUE), MONA VALE

Burials: 1914–present

Mona Vale General Cemetery is a simple 20th-century cemetery on the northern peninsula that packs some surprises. The cemetery has a peaceful bushland atmosphere, and although the monumentation is low and simple, the observant visitor can pick out some interesting monuments.

Four and a half hectares of land was set apart in 1905 with trustees subsequently appointed for the different denominational areas. The cemetery was originally known as Turimetta cemetery, but in 1929 Warringah Council officially named it Mona Vale General Cemetery. The earliest burial recorded on a headstone is of the infant Percy Johnson, buried in the Anglican section, who died in 1914 aged 2 years and 9 months. His grave marker is a small marble headstone within a cast-iron surround. The earliest burials in the Anglican and

Methodist sections are easily picked out due to their headstone designs and irregular grave alignment.

The original landscaping was simple, with a central avenue from Mona Vale Road bisecting the cemetery. The original gate piers built by local stonemason James Booth can still be seen on the Mona Vale Road boundary, although the entrance is now via Fazzolari Avenue. The avenue, still lined by cypress trees, is now being infilled with graves, making the most of precious ground.

The cemetery sections have been redistributed among the faithful. One of the most interesting and unique features of this cemetery is the Bahá'í burial section, which services the nearby Bahá'í Temple at the top of the plateau.

The cemetery is still in use and managed by Pittwater Council. It has lawn sections, a cremation niche wall, and garden memorial sections for ashes, as well as monumental areas. Several people were tending to graves when we visited. The bird calls emanating from the tall gums made for a peaceful setting.

TIPS

You can search for grave locations on the cemetery's website.

The cemetery office has a mounted plan of the cemetery which shows sections and rows, and where the earliest burials are clustered.

Left Grave of Euphenia Eleanor Baker (d.1968), first Australian woman to convert to Bahá'í

NOTABLE BURIALS

- Euphemia Eleanor (Effie) Baker (1880–1968), photographer and first Australian woman to convert to Bahá'í
- William Albert Flick (1890–1980), pest exterminator, founder of WA Flick & Co
- Edward Richard Scarf (1908–1980), wrestler and butcher
- Francis Michael (Frank 'Bumper') Farrell (1916–1985), footballer and policeman
- Morris Langlo West (1916–1999), AO, novelist and playwright

MORE INFORMATION

- Mona Vale General Cemetery, Pittwater Council website, 2016, <www.pittwater. nsw.gov.au/cemetery>.
- Bob Pauling, 'History of Turimetta Cemetery, Mona Vale', *Manly Warringah and Pittwater Journal of Local History*, vol. 8, June 2004, pp. 14–23.

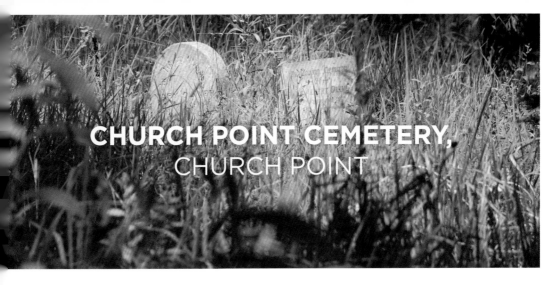

CHURCH POINT CEMETERY,
CHURCH POINT

Burials: 1882–1918

I have never been so disappointed by a cemetery. It promised so much: located on a rise at the very end of Church Point, I had envisaged Pittwater views, romantic melancholy. Instead I encountered weeds, lots of them. There is nothing so off-putting as having to wade through knee-high grass and weeds during snake season to try to read a few weathered headstones – even for a cemetery tragic like me! It hasn't always been like this. Back in 2014 when Brett Miller photographed and transcribed the cemetery the grass was much tamer. Perhaps I was just unlucky; maybe locals were going to mow it the next week.

The small cluster of headstones is all that is left of the little Methodist church and cemetery that gave its name to Church Point. There are 11 known burials between 1882 and 1918; nine memorials survive.

The earliest surviving gravestone fittingly memorialises William Oliver, who donated 4000 square metres of land for the Methodist church and burial ground back in 1871. Oliver died on 2 June 1882.

The burials here were all residents of the McCarrs Creek district. Thomas Oliver (d.1918), son of William, had lived his whole life at Broken Bay, a mariner on the Pittwater. Alfred Henry Turner (d.1892), who is buried in an unmarked grave, drowned while returning home to Stokes Point from Bayview. The residents here all relied upon water transport to get supplies from Sydney. This isolated little cemetery readily displays their remote existence in the late 19th century.

TIP

While you are up on the peninsula, take a look at a couple of gravestones associated with Barrenjoey Lighthouse. St John's Anglican Church, Mona Vale has an old headstone that commemorates William F Stark (d.1881), accidentally killed during the construction of the new lighthouse. The lone headstone of the first lighthouse keeper George Mulhall (d.1885) and his wife Mary (d.1886) is near the lighthouse on Barrenjoey headland.

MORE INFORMATION

- Brett Miller, 'Church Point Cemetery', Australian Cemeteries Index website, 2014, <austcemindex.com/cemetery?cemid=1266>.
- Peter Altona & Sue Gould, 'Church Point (NSW) History: Places, People and Activities. The Cemetery', Pittwater History website, 2011, <pittwaterhistory.files.wordpress.com/2012/08/111220-the-cemetery.pdf>.

BROOKLYN GENERAL CEMETERY, BROOKLYN

BROOKLYN ROAD, BROOKLYN

Burials: 1906–present

Brooklyn General Cemetery is a small general cemetery serving the local village of Brooklyn and the Peat and Milson Islands Mental Hospital. Located at the start of the road to Brooklyn, with large pine trees and screened by bushland, it appears a tranquil setting; until the weekend, that is, when motorbikes scream back and forth along the twisting Old Pacific Highway which borders the cemetery on one side.

The cemetery was dedicated in 1906 and is still in use. It hosts a diverse range of 20th-century slab and desk monuments and simpler vernacular timber crosses which cascade down the sloping site in neat rows. The majority of burials from the public institutions are in unmarked graves. A couple of large pine trees dominate the landscape. Most of the graves are clustered together at the northern end of the site, but there are a few outliers that probably belong to the smaller denominations. Be

careful where you walk in summer as spiders abound in this quiet little spot and their webs can startle the absorbed cemetery visitor.

The cemetery features many local families including the Buies, Greens, Coles and Hibbs families; some of whom are also represented within the earlier Bar Island Cemetery (see page 192). The first burial in the cemetery was Alice Maud Hibbs (d.1906), the infant daughter of William and Olive Emma Hibbs. An earlier death is recorded on the gravestone of the Jessups: James Jessup died in 1902 on Dangar Island.

The most fascinating inscription is on a fittingly red granite desk monument. It records that Robert Buie, a Lewis gunner in the First World War, had the distinction of shooting down Baron Von Richthofen, better known as the 'Red Baron'. Buie (who died on Anzac Day in 1964) is one of a few contenders for this title. He did not receive official recognition during his wartime service, that honour went to pilot Roy Brown, which may explain the lack of an official war graves headstone. Regardless, it is a fascinating brush with fame, also commemorated by a plaque in Brooklyn Park bearing a photo of Gunner Buie. The Buie family were well known in the Lower Hawkesbury as pioneers of the oyster industry in the district.

TIP

To fully appreciate the biker crowd and admire some of their finely tuned machines, call in at the Pie in the Sky for some sustenance.

NOTABLE BURIALS

- Robert Buie (1893–1964), oyster farmer and First World War gunner who is believed to have shot down the 'Red Baron'

MORE INFORMATION
- Roy Smith, 'Brooklyn Cemetery', Australian Cemeteries Index website, 2004, <austcemindex.com/cemetery?cemid=552>.
- Tom Richmond, *Brooklyn Underground: Transcriptions and family histories of Lower Hawkesbury burials*, Deerubbin Press, Berowra Heights, 2003.

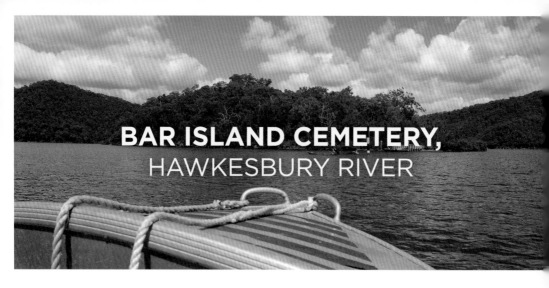

BAR ISLAND CEMETERY, HAWKESBURY RIVER

BAR ISLAND, HAWKESBURY RIVER

Burials: 1879–1906

This is the remotest cemetery in Sydney. The only way to get to this cemetery is by boat, but it is worth the effort. We hired a tinnie at Brooklyn and puttered our way out to the little island, pulling up at the jetty. Sandstone cliffs and bushland loom on either side as you travel along the river, transporting you back in time to when the Lower Hawkesbury was first settled. Scenes from Kate Grenville's novel, *The Secret River*, flash before your eyes; the isolation of this area envelops you like a cloak.

Bar Island is a small sandstone outcrop close to Fishermans Point, at the junction of Berowra and Marramarra creeks. The island is now uninhabited, fringed by saltmarsh and mangroves, and covered in bushland. A short trail with signposts leading from the jetty to the island summit introduces you to the Aboriginal and European history of this little island.

Aboriginal shell middens in the vicinity of the jetty show that

Aboriginal people have lived, foraged, fished and eaten here for thousands of years. Europeans began utilising the island in 1876, when they built a church and school. Only a sandstone fireplace and chimney remain. Beyond the church ruins is the cemetery.

The Reverend Henry Britten lobbied to have an Anglican cemetery dedicated at Bar Island; the government reluctantly agreed. Prior to this the locals were buried on private property or further up the river at Wisemans Ferry. The first burial in the cemetery was a child, Caroline Mary Banks, who died on 20 August 1879; she lies in an unmarked grave. The cemetery was in use until at least 1906, housing about 50 burials. Local Aboriginal elder Sarah Lewis Ferdinand (Biddy Lewis) is buried here in an unmarked grave. Signs also tell the story of little Maude Lloyd, about whom Henry Kendall penned some verses.

Only 14 memorials survive; some have been broken and vandalised over the years, but recent efforts to reconstruct and conserve the monuments have paid dividends. Ann Elizabeth Milson and Robert Milson of Milson Island, who died within a week of each other in 1886, are commemorated here. The grave of master mariner Charles F Brown (d.1901) is marked by an unusual sandstone rusticated headstone with obelisk inscription panel. An anchor is carved on the obelisk. My favourite is the diminutive headstone to six-year-old Francis J Byrnes (d.1887) which features the

crown of victory. There are many unmarked graves and no complete burial register. Local historian Tom Richmond has been painstakingly reconstructing a burial list for this cemetery. The marble and sandstone headstones stand silent witness to the Lower Hawkesbury community.

Make sure you climb up to the summit of the island where a large cross and memorial commemorates two Outward Bound instructors who tragically drowned in the Hawkesbury in 1963 while trying to save students. There are pretty river views through the trees.

Look out for Glossy Black cockatoos that feed on seeds of the forest oak (*Allocasuarina torulosa*) or the whistling kite that sometimes circles the island. We did not see either, but we were serenaded by a warbling magpie. There are a couple of seats along the short trail, so you could take a picnic. But it would be equally pleasant to drop anchor near shore under the majestic sandstone cliffs that line the river.

TIP

You can download a guide and map to Bar Island from Hornsby Council's website.

NOTABLE BURIALS

- Sarah Lewis Ferdinand (1803–1880), Aboriginal elder, later known as Biddy Lewis and Granny Lewis (unmarked)

MORE INFORMATION

- Tom Richmond, *Brooklyn Underground: Transcriptions and family histories of Lower Hawkesbury burials*, Deerubbin Press, Berowra Heights, 2003.
- Hornsby Shire Council, 'A guided walk around Bar Island', Hornsby Shire Council website, 2016, <www.hornsby.nsw.gov.au/media/documents/recreation-and-facilities/bushwalking/Bar-Island-Walk.pdf>.

TOP 5

CEMETERIES FOR SERAPHS
AND ANGELS

Waverley Cemetery, Bronte, *especially the Fiaschi monument*

South Head General Cemetery, Vaucluse, *especially the Wheeler monument*

Rookwood Necropolis, *especially the Dixson monument*

Castlereagh Cemetery, *especially for seraphs*

St Patrick's Catholic Cemetery, North Parramatta, *especially the Rispin headstone which depicts Thorvaldsen's 'Night with her children, sleep and death'*

Art deco angel headstone executed by sculptor Rayner Hoff, South Head General Cemetery

Dural

OLD NORTHERN ROAD

Glenhaven

GILBERT ROAD

Hornsby

PACIFIC HIGHWAY

PACIFIC MOTORWAY

Wahroonga

Thornleigh

NEW LINE ROAD

SHOWGROUND ROAD

Castle Hill

Cherrybrook

BOUNDARY ROAD

OLD NORTHERN ROAD

PENNANT HILLS ROAD

PACIFIC HIGHWAY

West Pennant
Hills

Pymble

WINDSOR ROAD

Beecroft

M2 MOTORWAY

Baulkham
Hills

M2 MOTORWAY

NORTH ROCKS RD

Epping

NORTH ROCKS RD

Carlingford

NORTH ROCKS RD

PENNANT HILLS ROAD

JAMES RUSE DRIVE

LANE COVE ROAD

North
Parramatta

West Ryde

SILVERWATER ROAD

VICTORIA ROAD

Ryde

LANE COVE ROAD

East Ryde

Parramatta

PITTWATER ROAD

Opposite Detail from lichen-covered headstone, Uniting Church Cemetery, Cherrybrook

NORTH
WEST

IN

EMORY OF

OMAS THOMP

D JUNE 7TH 18

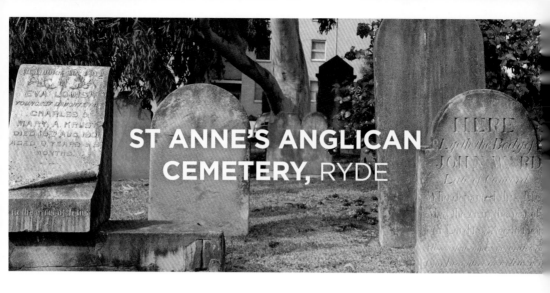

ST ANNE'S ANGLICAN CEMETERY, RYDE

Burials: 1826–1916

This is a gorgeous little cemetery which, despite having its perimeter shaved by Victoria Road, retains its English churchyard feel. It was the first cemetery established for the fruit-growing district of Kissing Point. About 280 grave markers fill up the ground to the north and south of the sandstone church.

Given the early establishment date of this cemetery, you will not be surprised to learn that there are at least five First Fleeters buried here:

James Bradley (d.1838), Edward Goodin (d.1839), Joseph Hatton (d.1828), Ann Smith (Colpitts) (d.1832) and John Small (d.1850). Look out for the little plaques added by the Fellowship of the First Fleeters. The first burial in the churchyard was Anthony Bergin, who died on 16 September 1826.

There are many interesting early sandstone headstones. My personal favourite is the spooky winged seraph to Richard and Mary Porter on the northern side of the churchyard near Church Lane. The most outstanding carved symbolism can be found on the headstone to George Spurway (d.1883). It features a carved winged hourglass and a broken chain with the broken links placed at the bottom of the headstone. The former is a symbol of the passage of time, and thus serves as a memento mori, and the latter the breaking of ties or relationships.

The grave of 'Granny' Smith (d.1870) features a switch of oak leaves, a symbol of strength, glory and honour, and the prominent ball-flowers that border the semicircular headstone could almost be mistaken for apples! The most unusual and striking grave marker in St Anne's is a terracotta surround featuring nuts, ivy and oak leaves for Amy McMaster and Agnes Irene Chisholm Ross, both of whom died 1889. There is nothing like it in any other cemetery in Sydney.

The cemetery has suffered from vandalism over the years and headstones have been removed for pathways, church extensions and road widening. For those undertaking family history, it is worthwhile checking the parish registers as well as different editions of monumental inscriptions to cross-check information and inscriptions.

St Anne's Church was built in 1826 and extended in 1861–62

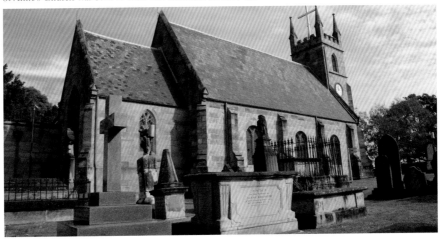

NOTABLE BURIALS

- Maria Ann 'Granny' Smith (1799–1870), orchardist, of apple fame
- William Forster (1818–1882), pastoralist, man of letters and politician, NSW premier
- James Squire Farnell (1825–1888), politician, NSW premier and grandson of James Squire the brewer
- Lady Eleanor Parkes (1857–1895), second wife of Sir Henry Parkes, NSW premier
- Edward Terry (1840–1907), hunting and racing enthusiast, politician and Ryde's first mayor

MORE INFORMATION

- St Anne's Anglican Church Ryde, 'History of St Anne's', St Anne's Ryde website, 2016, <www.stannes.org.au/History.html>.
- Michael Brookhouse, 'Ryde Anglican Cemetery', Australian Cemeteries Index website, 2011 <austcemindex.com/cemetery?cemid=837>.
- Kevin Shaw (ed.), *Historic Ryde: A Guide to Some Significant Heritage Sites in the City of Ryde*, Ryde District Historical Society, Ryde, 2002.

A unique Arts and Crafts terracotta grave surround

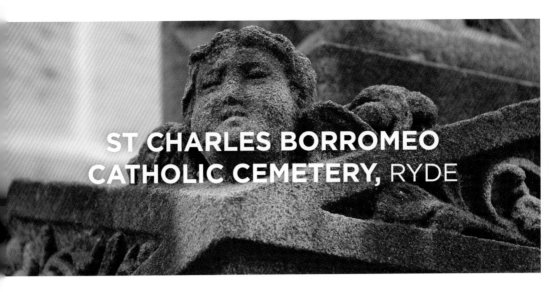

ST CHARLES BORROMEO CATHOLIC CEMETERY, RYDE

VICTORIA ROAD, CORNER CHARLES STREET, RYDE

Burials: 1856–1920

St Charles Borromeo is an early Catholic churchyard in the Ryde district, with burials from 1856 to 1920. It is a neat little cemetery; headstones surround the church on three sides. Conservation works in 1996 resulted in some rearrangement of the headstones. The church has also been rearranged. The original 1857 church was built to designs Archbishop Polding acquired from English architect AWN Pugin. At its dedication on 8 December 1857 the *Freeman's Journal* described it as 'the neatest and prettiest country church which we have seen'. In 1934 the church was enlarged, using much of the original stone; only the lovely western side with its belfry remains from Pugin's original concept.

The first burial was Father Charles Mattieu on 24 May 1856. The Society of Mary originally managed the parish church. The churchyard contains the earliest burials of the Marist brothers in

the district, 1878–91, with nine Marist brothers commemorated by a modern memorial. Other early Marist brothers are buried in the Villa Maria church grounds at Hunters Hill (which are not publicly accessible). Sisters of St Joseph of the Sacred Heart are also buried here. Another notable burial in the churchyard was Flora H MacKillop, mother of Mary MacKillop, who drowned in the wreck of the SS *Ly-Ee-Moon*, 30 May 1886. Her remains were exhumed and reinterred in the Nuns' Lawn Section of Macquarie Park Cemetery in 1973. And in a strange twist of fate, the Reverend Thomas Cooper Makinson, who helped design St Thomas' Anglican Church at Mulgoa, converted to Catholicism and is buried here with his wife.

Religious burials aside, there are some interesting sandstone monuments and headstones in the cemetery. Check out the large sandstone pedestal topped with a Celtic cross to the west of the church which commemorates the Kernahan family. It has chubby little seraph faces carved in the corners, and different floral symbolism carved on each face of the pedestal: passionflower, rose, shamrock, and a laurel wreath with a cross pattée, also known as St Andrew's Cross. A solid Gothic headstone to the rear of the church remembers John Crotty (d.1859), the local stonemason who built the original church. An exquisite rose with broken stem is carved on the headstone of Andrew Spring (d.1882).

The cemetery was officially

Left Headstone for stonemason John Crotty (d.1859)

closed in 1900 with the opening of the Field of Mars General Cemetery, but a few surreptitious burials happened up until 1920, with the undertakers incurring fines issued by Ryde Council.

NOTABLE BURIALS

- John Crotty (c.1810–1859), local stonemason and mast builder
- Didier Numa Joubert (1816–1881), French merchant, businessman and local politician, first mayor of Hunters Hill
- Charles d'Apice (Caroli Francisci Ludovici d'Apice) (1817–1888), professor of music, composer and pianist

MORE INFORMATION

- Michael Brookhouse, 'Ryde Catholic Cemetery', Australian Cemeteries Index website, 2011, <austcemindex.com/cemetery?cemid=838>.
- MCI Levy, *Wallumetta: A History of Ryde and its District, 1792 to 1945*, Ryde Municipal Council, Ryde, 1947.
- Kevin Shaw (ed.), *Historic Ryde: A Guide to Some Significant Heritage Sites in the City of Ryde*, Ryde District Historical Society, Ryde, 2002.

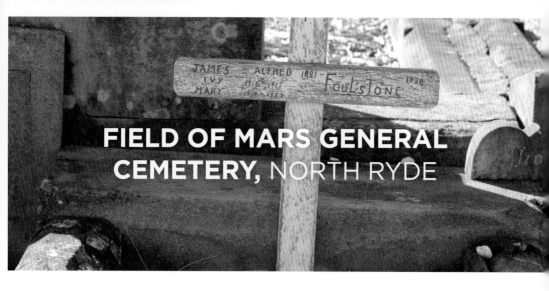

FIELD OF MARS GENERAL CEMETERY, NORTH RYDE

Burials: 1890–present

The government reserved land for a general cemetery at Ryde in 1884, but the Field of Mars General Cemetery did not come into use until 1890. The cemetery was originally divided into eight denominational areas and had a gardenesque layout with curving roads and burial areas. The date palms which line the main avenue show the original ambitions for this cemetery landscape. While the key roads still wend their way around the cemetery, many of the smaller ornate plots have been lost, taken over by graves and utilitarian planning.

The first burials took place in 1890 in the Catholic, Presbyterian and Church of England sections. Ryde Council passed by-laws in 1900 closing the Catholic and Anglican churchyards of the district, with all burials directed to the new cemetery. By 1915 the locals were concerned that the cemetery was filling up too quickly and the Gladesville Progress Association discussed whether they should ban burials from Drummoyne, Balmain and Leichhardt. They need not have worried. The Northern Suburbs General Cemetery (now Macquarie Park Cemetery) opened in 1922.

On first appearances, this cemetery does not particularly impress. There is a bleakness to the early 20th-century areas which are all paved with gravel or concrete; in some places grass is sadly lacking. But as you explore the earlier sections some interesting monuments emerge from amongst the lower monumentation: section B of the Anglican and Catholic areas are worth a closer look. A circular section in the Catholic area has burials of priests and there is a large burial plot for the Sisters of the Little Company of Mary. The Presbyterian section still has a rotunda making this area a nice place for a picnic.

There are a few estrays in Field of Mars. The cemetery includes a couple of headstones transferred from the Devonshire Street Cemetery,

including the Reverend John Ham (d.1852), a pastor of the Baptist Church Sydney. His headstone made its way into the Church of England section B. The graves at St Anne's Anglican Cemetery, Ryde affected by the widening of Victoria Road were reinterred in the 1950s. The headstones of John Small (d.1850) First Fleeter and his descendants were removed from St Anne's in 1976 and are now located near the old cemetery office.

The cemetery is still in use and there are low monumental and lawn areas, baby lawns, and areas for vaults and crypts, reflecting the differing burial preferences of the European communities.

NORTH WEST

NOTABLE BURIALS

- William Charles Piguenit (1836–1914), artist
- John Storey (1869–1921), boilermaker and NSW premier
- Henry Deane Walsh (1853–1921), engineer, namesake of Walsh Bay
- James (Jim) Stanbury (1868–1945), world champion sculler
- Selina Sarah Elizabeth Anderson (1878–1964), parliamentary candidate and trade unionist

MORE INFORMATION

- Field of Mars, Northern Cemeteries Trust website, 2016, <northerncemeteries. com.au/field-of-mars>.
- *Field of Mars, Ryde, inscriptions*, microfiche, Society of Australian Genealogists, Sydney, 1994.
- 'Field of Mars Cemetery', Australian Cemeteries Index website, 2013, <austcemindex.com/cemetery?cemid=1435>.
- MCI Levy, *Wallumetta: a history of Ryde and its district, 1792 to 1945*, Ryde Municipal Council, Ryde, 1947.

ST PAUL'S ANGLICAN CEMETERY, CARLINGFORD

OFF MARSDEN ROAD, CARLINGFORD

Burials: 1851–1984

This is a cemetery only locals would know about. It is not visible from Marsden Road and a driveway next to the nursery is the only indication of the access pathway that leads to this early cemetery. It is much easier to access the cemetery from behind through the residential streets.

William Mobbs junior donated 4000 square metres of land in 1847 for an Anglican church and burial ground on Mobbs Hill for the burghers in the Pennant Hills district (now Carlingford). Unfortunately, the land around the church proved unsuitable for burials – it was shale and too difficult to dig – so another piece of land, about 5000 square metres, was selected further down the road. His father, William Mobbs senior, had received one of the early land grants in the district and St Paul's Cemetery primarily served the fruit-growing community around Mobbs Hill.

The first burial was in fact William

Rare cross with ribbon inscription

undertaker had to give the cemetery manager at least 12 hours notice of intention to bury. Permission to erect a head- or footstone cost 10 shillings each. Permission to erect a stone covering over a grave, as Mobbs had, was double – £1. A vault cost £1 10s per person it held. Bad luck if you were not pious; double rates were charged for non-parishioners.

The cemetery is sparsely attended to – the grass was quite long when I visited and I was more than a little nervous about snakes – and so it has an air of romantic, perhaps even gothic, neglect. Headstones are broken and lean at odd angles, but it is a cemetery suffused in local history. At least 40 descendants of the Mobbs family are buried here. Other families that shaped the district, and are commemorated through the names of local streets and parks, as well as being chiselled in stone, include Aiken, Cox, Midson, Keeler, Spurway, Bellamy, Hockley, Wilkinson and Moseley. Over 1500 people were buried in the cemetery before it closed in 1984.

Mobbs junior himself. He died on 14 July 1851 at the age of 60 and was laid in the earth two days later. The cemetery has suffered vandalism over the years, but the grave marker of the cemetery's founder has endured: a large sandstone ledger stone upon which the inscription is barely visible.

The 'Rules and Regulations of St Paul's Cemetery', dating from 1896, survive. From them we glean that a basic grave of 8 foot x 3 foot (2.5 metres x 0.9 metre) cost 15 shillings. The fee for interment was £1 and the

TIP

Park in Kay Street and walk through Simpson Reserve to the cemetery.

NOTABLE BURIALS

- Susan Bell McGahey (1862–1919), hospital matron and reformer
- Charles Frederick Cox (1863–1944), CB, CMG, DSO, soldier, railway auditor and politician

MORE INFORMATION

- Michael Brookhouse, 'Carlingford Anglican Cemetery', Australian Cemeteries Index website, 2011, <austcemindex.com/cemetery?cemid=747>.
- Carl Hammond & Helen E Craig, *Time will tell: a century and a half at Carlingford: a history celebrating the sesquicentenary of St Paul's Anglican Church, Carlingford, 1850– 2000*, St Paul's Anglican Church, Carlingford, 2000.

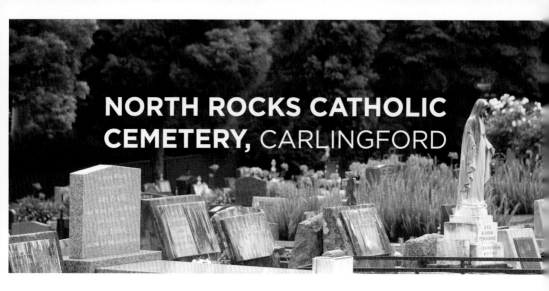

NORTH ROCKS CATHOLIC CEMETERY, CARLINGFORD

NORTH ROCKS ROAD, CORNER
PARMA PLACE, CARLINGFORD

Burials: 1891–present

North Rocks Catholic Cemetery is an undistinguished 20th-century cemetery that is still in use. The landscape is sparse and the uniform graves in the rectangular site suggest a monotony to eternity.

There are over 3000 people buried in this cemetery but few standout memorials. The largest monument in the cemetery is a tall marble Celtic cross which marks the family grave of Matthew Hayden who died in

Parramatta in 1905. There are both monumental and lawn sections. The majority of the lawn sections are dedicated to the Sisters of Mercy and the Benedictine Nuns.

The land, originally about 1.6 hectares in extent, was set aside for a Catholic burial ground by local Pennant Hills resident Edward James Maher in about 1884. Consequently, the burial ground was early on referred to as Maher's Cemetery.

The earliest marked grave that I spotted when I visited was James Allen (Maher's stepbrother) who died on 5 September 1894. However funeral notices in the newspapers suggest this cemetery was in use from 1891. Bishop Higgins was due to consecrate the cemetery in September 1896, but the ceremony was unavoidably delayed. It is not clear when the cemetery was finally dedicated.

NOTABLE BURIALS

- Edward James Maher (c.1832–1894), orchardist and founder of North Rocks Catholic Cemetery
- Reverend Father Michael MacNamara (1858–1939), priest
- Patrick Joseph Hartigan (1878–1952), priest and poet
- John Lawrence Tierney (1892–1972), schoolteacher and author

MORE INFORMATION

- *North Rocks Cemetery cnr. North Rocks Road & Palma Place, Sydney: headstone transcriptions*, microform, Society of Australian Genealogists, Sydney, 1996.
- Michael Brookhouse, 'North Rocks Catholic Cemetery', Australian Cemeteries Index website, 2011, <austcemindex.com/cemetery?cemid=840>.

Nuns' burial area

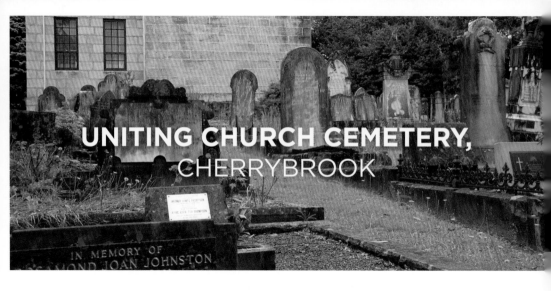

UNITING CHURCH CEMETERY,
CHERRYBROOK

134 NEW LINE ROAD, CHERRYBROOK

Burials: 1846–present

Blink and you would miss this once rural churchyard as you motor along the New Line Road. The little yard, tucked away behind a low sandstone wall, crowds around the old Wesleyan Chapel that was established for the Pennant Hills district in 1845. John and Mary Pogson, donated the land and both were subsequently interred in the cemetery (they died 1867 and 1856 respectively). As the area developed the church became known as the West Pennant Hills Methodist Church and more recently the Cherrybrook Uniting Church. The late Victorian Gothic-style church was built in 1888.

This churchyard is a well-kept secret and contains some early headstones from the mid-1840s and 1850s. Red lichen grows on many of the earliest sandstone headstones, making them very photogenic but which is detrimental to the reading of weathered inscriptions. One of the earliest headstones that I spotted was to Jane Waddell who died in 1849 aged 19 years. Her three-year-old brother Robert (d.1846) is also listed on the headstone but does not appear in the burial register. A spectacular sandstone carved post and iron rod fence encloses the Dale family plot. This is an elaborate variation on the tapering post and chain fence that can be found in other early cemeteries such as St John's at Campbelltown and St Stephen the Martyr at Penrith.

Prominent Wesleyan families with generations represented in the cemetery include the Thompsons, Pogsons, Harrisons, Harveys, Shields, Allsops and Booths. There are some historical family connections between this cemetery and the Uniting Church Cemetery in Dural.

Walking through this cemetery is like walking through a timeline of headstone designs from the 1840s to the 1990s. There are not any substantial monuments here, such as obelisks or draped urn pedestals, but the headstones are all finely carved.

TIP

Park in the church car park down the hill from the church.

NOTABLE BURIALS

* John Pogson (1794–1867), convict, donated church land
* Edward Purser (1803–1888), orchardist, tanner and schoolmaster Castle Hill Church of England

MORE INFORMATION

* Cherrybrook Uniting Church, 'Our Heritage', Cherrybrook Uniting Church website, 2016, <www.cherrybrookuc.org.au/our-heritage>.
* Michael Brookhouse, 'Cherrybrook Uniting Church Cemetery', Australian Cemeteries Index website, 2009, <austcemindex.com/cemetery?cemid=443>.
* Helen Barker & Ralph Hawkins, *Early Wesleyans of Pennant Hills*, Hornsby Shire Historical Society, Hornsby, 1983.

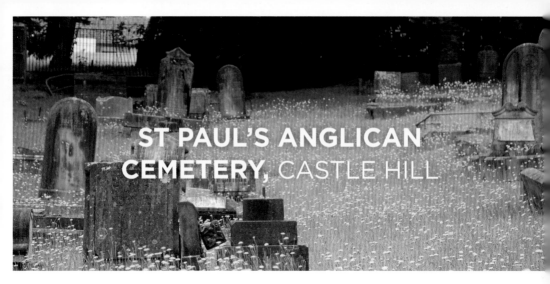

ST PAUL'S ANGLICAN CEMETERY, CASTLE HILL

245A OLD NORTHERN ROAD, CASTLE HILL

Burials: 1864–1994

This is the earliest cemetery surviving in Castle Hill. You have to know this cemetery exists as you won't see it from the street. It sits behind the Castle Hill Bible Education Centre and is hidden by a tall timber fence. The cemetery is closed to burials, but still administered by St Paul's Anglican Church at Castle Hill. Dandelions have overtaken the cemetery, their yellow flowers forming a cheery carpet.

This once rural cemetery is now surrounded by residential development and has suffered from neglect and vandalism over the years. Nevertheless, you can still admire some finely carved late 19th-century headstones here. Some notable symbols include seraphs, doves and the hand of God. Unexpectedly for an Anglican cemetery, there is a marble Celtic cross, a symbol normally associated with Irish Catholics. Also of note are some fine cast-iron surrounds.

A sandstone headstone with finely carved flowers and leaves marks the grave of Elizabeth and John Kentwell. They came to Castle Hill in 1821 and established an orchard. They had ten children, some of whom also became fruit growers.

The earliest death mentioned on a headstone is John Thomas Black, son of Henry George and Mary Black, who died 22 May 1864.

TIP

Park in the car park of 245 Old Northern Road, the Castle Hill Bible Education Centre.

NOTABLE BURIALS

- Elizabeth Kentwell (1810–1885) and John Kentwell (1804–1897), orchardists

MORE INFORMATION

- Jim Jones & Doreen Jones, *St Pauls Church of England, Castle Hill: monumental inscriptions*, Nepean Family History Society, Emu Plains, 1994.
- Michael Brookhouse, 'Castle Hill Anglican Cemetery', Australian Cemeteries Index, 2011, <austcemindex.com/cemetery?cemid=733>.

NORTH WEST

CASTLE HILL GENERAL CEMETERY, CASTLE HILL

GILBERT ROAD, CASTLE HILL

Burials: 1914–present

Castle Hill General Cemetery is a modern general cemetery surrounded by bushland. A central avenue runs through the long rectangular site. The cemetery covers 8.2 hectares but only a small proportion has been cleared and developed for burials, so it is possible to wander around the site and take in the different areas.

The government dedicated the land for the cemetery as far back as 1881 and the site was shown on an 1897 parish map.

However it seems that trustees were not appointed until 1902.

The cemetery was originally divided into four main areas: Church of England, Roman Catholic, Presbyterian and a general section. However, it became apparent that these simplistic religious divides would not serve the diverse 20th-century community of Castle Hill. In 1915, as the cemetery was finally beginning to be used, the area was rededicated with the

Opposite Unique crucifix on the Haddad family grave

following denominations: general, Baptist, Jewish, Independent, Methodist, Presbyterian, Catholic, Anglican and Seventh Day Adventist. Since then a Coptic Orthodox area has been added.

The first burial took place in 1914; a little boy aged 3 years, 11 months. But as the site was unfenced, George Phillip Fitzroy was simply buried beside the cemetery road. The first burial in the established, fenced and cleared cemetery was in the Anglican monumental section: Robert James McKay, who died on 17 February 1918, aged 2 years and 6 months.

Styles of burials have changed over the years with the cemetery now offering lawn burials, vaults and mausoleums, as well as a columbarium niche wall and gardens. There is also a lawn burial ground for Benedictine Fathers and Sisters. It is a peaceful cemetery to wander around. Look out for the funky ironwork crucifix that marks the Haddad family plot in the Catholic section.

TIP

A cemetery map is available from The Hills Council website, along with a virtual tour and biographies.

NOTABLE BURIALS

- George Kentwell (1851–1930), orchardist, born and bred in Castle Hill, son of Elizabeth and John buried in Castle Hill's St Paul's Anglican Cemetery
- Ernest Mark Baldwin (1892–1970), founder EM Baldwin & Sons, engineering company, largest employer in Castle Hill 1968–85
- Frederick Douglas Claude Caterson (1919–2000), politician and co-founder of The Hills District Historical Society

MORE INFORMATION
- The Hills Shire Council, 'Castle Hill Cemetery', The Hills Shire Council website, 2014, <www.thehills.nsw.gov.au/Services/Our-Community/Castle-Hill-Cemetery>.
- Michael Brookhouse, 'Castle Hill Cemetery', Australian Cemeteries Index website, 2011, <austcemindex.com/cemetery.php?id=814>.
- Hills Voices Online, 'Cemeteries: History of Local Cemeteries', The Hills Shire Council website, 2011, <www.bhsc.nsw.gov.au/external/hillsvoices/cemeteries.htm>.

ST JUDE'S ANGLICAN CEMETERY, DURAL

Burials: 1876–present

The Anglican cemetery at Dural is situated 500 metres down the road from St Jude's Anglican Church. The small cemetery is on a sloping site with its back to the now busy Old Northern Road, opposite Hargraves Nurseryland. A decorative garden entrance gate stands in the southern corner fronting the Old Northern Road, but you'll find it easier to park beside the cemetery at the squash courts. The graves face east overlooking a Christmas tree farm.

The cemetery retains a rural feel, although the sound of constant traffic disturbs the tranquillity.

Eleanor Wingate, third child of the Rouses of Rouse Hill, along with the Hawkins and Moore families sold the land for the burial ground to Bishop Barker for a song in August 1876. Sadly, the first burial in the cemetery was the infant son of William and Ruth Hawkins. Little Darcy died on 3 November 1876, aged just 20 months. His monument is by the roadside perimeter fence, an elaborate yet squat sandstone pedestal with garlands of flowers, surmounted by a draped urn.

The cemetery was not consecrated until 6 September 1884, when Bishop Barker also consecrated St Jude's Church.

There are a handful of 19th-century memorials, but St Jude's is mainly a 20th-century cemetery, which is still in use. Burial registers reveal that a high proportion of graves are unmarked: at least 10 per cent. There are a few interesting modern memorials. A sandstone headstone commemorating Captain Philip Thomas Addington Love (d.1995) is executed in a mid-19th–century style with cutaway shoulders; whereas the grave to John Saxon is a modern piece of slate with finely incised lettering, and a matching footstone. A number of graves of the Garemyn family, long-time residents of Dural, are simply marked with timber pegs and crosses beneath the large eucalyptus tree in the middle of the cemetery.

TIPS

After visiting this cemetery, stop at the roadside Dural Kiosk to pick up some local produce.

A spreadsheet of burials is available on the church website.

NOTABLE BURIALS

- Sir Wilmot Hudson-Fysh (1895–1974), soldier, aviator, businessman and co-founder of Qantas

MORE INFORMATION

- Dural District Anglican Churches, 'History: St Jude's Cemetery', Dural District Anglican Churches website, 2016, <www.ddac.org.au/st-judes-dural-cemetery-records>.
- June Roughley & Pauline Corthorn (eds), *Cemetery transcriptions: St Jude's, Old Northern Road, Dural*, Dural & District Historical Society, Dural, 1996.
- Michael Brookhouse & Toni Drake, 'Dural Anglican Cemetery', Australian Cemeteries Index website, 2009–12, <austcemindex.com/cemetery.php?id=730>.

Opposite Unusual modern memorial to John Saxton (d.2005

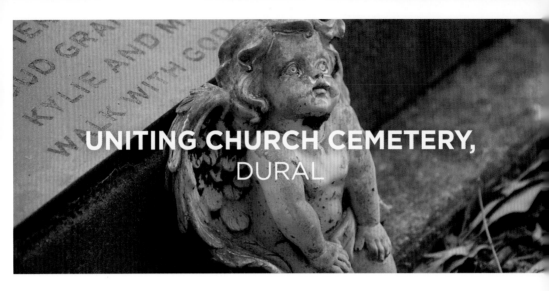

UNITING CHURCH CEMETERY,
DURAL

DERRIWONG ROAD, DURAL

Burials: 1865–present

The calls of bell miners, whipbirds, parrots and wrens greet you as you step out of the car, encouraging a contemplative wander through this otherwise quiet rural cemetery. Bushland surrounds the cemetery on two sides and large angophoras mark its roadside corners.

Methodism was active in the fruit-growing district of Dural from the 1840s. Thomas Williams sold the land for the burial ground to the trustees of the Wesleyan Methodist Church for a nominal sum in 1857.

The first burial in the cemetery was the former convict and fruit grower William Hunt who died on 9 January 1865. A simple semicircular sandstone headstone marks his grave. Another early memorial is a small sandstone headstone with a seraph carved at the top which marks the grave of infant Elizabeth Maria Cusbert, who was just 6 months old when she died in December 1865. The earliest burials are on the western side of the cemetery and are easily spotted due to their irregular alignment.

The cemetery hosts the graves of several generations of Dural families, particularly the Roughleys, Cusberts, Mobbs, Fagans and Hunts, all fruit growers and farmers.

The cemetery is still in use. A lawn cemetery was established in the 1980s along with a columbarium.

NOTABLE BURIALS

- Edgar GS Moulds (1878–1905), Boer war soldier
- John Charles Hunt (1856–1930), grazier, orchardist and politician, inaugural Hornsby Shire president

MORE INFORMATION

- June Roughley (ed.), *Cemetery Transcriptions: Uniting Church, Derriwong Road, Dural*, rev. edn, Dural & District Historical Society, Dural, 1991.
- Michael Brookhouse, 'Dural Uniting Church Cemetery', Australian Cemeteries Index website, 2009, <austcemindex.com/cemetery?cemid=444>.

SYMBOLIC GESTURES:
THE HIDDEN MEANINGS OF HEADSTONES

Funerary monuments are part of a long architectural tradition of ornamental decoration and embellishment. The shapes and symbols used on monuments convey certain attitudes and beliefs. People deliberately choose a memorial design as a personal, yet public, expression of their values, religious beliefs and social aspirations.

The architectural style and ornamentation of sepulchral designs in 19th-century Sydney can be divided into two broad categories: neoclassicism and Gothicism.

NEOCLASSICISM

The Classical Revival, or neoclassicism (also known as Greek Revivalism or Italianate), developed in late 18th-century Britain and was well established by the 1850s. The revival was inspired by archaeological discoveries in Greece and Italy, and the pillaging of ancient ruins. The Elgin Marbles, for example, were brought to Britain from the Parthenon in Athens in 1812. Interest in classical art also reflected a belief that ancient Greece and Rome were enlightened civilisations worth emulating.

Classic styling in sepulchral design produced headstones with architectural elements such as pediments, pilasters, columns and pedestals. The classical style was popular because it was easily referenced by such stylised motifs. Classicism also influenced decorative embellishments such as dentils, the egg and dart motif, acanthus leaves, wreaths, shells, garlands and urns. An interest in ancient Egyptian motifs and forms, stimulated by important excavations in Egypt in the 19th century, also found its expression in Sydney's cemeteries, most commonly in the form of obelisks.

GOTHICISM

The main alternative to neoclassicism was Gothicism. The Gothic Revival of the 19th century evolved from the serious study of the art and architecture of the Middle Ages, and was inspired by religious, patriotic, ethical and aesthetic principles. The work of John Ruskin, AWN Pugin and the Camden Society fuelled the moral side of the stylistic debate between classical and Gothic architecture in Britain. The Camden Society stridently proclaimed that 'Gothic is the only true Christian Architecture' which embodied Christian principles such as sacrifice, truth and beauty. Gothic headstones and monuments, inspired by the traditional medieval churches, featured spires, pointed arches, decorative tracery, corbels and crockets.

The relative popularity of neoclassical and Gothic styles waxed and waned throughout the 19th century, and their expression also changed. By 1860, the expansion and specialisation of the monumental masonry trade, and the wider availability of pattern books, helped to conventionalise each style and they were often fused together.

Left Neoclassical headstone with masonic symbols, Liverpool Pioneers Memorial Park *Centre* Gothic headstone with tracery, Woronora General Cemetery *Right* Gothic spire on pedestal, St Anne's Anglican Cemetery, Ryde

Left Gothic headstone with corbels and angel, Gore Hill Memorial Cemetery   *Centre* Neoclassical headstone with draped sarcophagus and garland, St John's Anglican Cemetery, Ashfield   *Right* Cross with passionflowers, Catholic Cemetery, Greenda...

STYLISTIC RULES, SPOKEN AND UNSPOKEN

Each denomination had its own ideas about what was appropriate in the eyes of God, reflecting the theology and social composition of the churches. You can discern distinctions among the various religious groups both in the design of memorials and their inscriptions. Roman Catholic monuments up until the 1880s were predominantly Gothic, often featuring a cross. Seraphs and angels were also common. Protestants shunned the Gothic, preferring the neoclassical style, and rejected the cross as too popish and iconographic. Angels and weeping widows are found on Church of England headstones, but figurative sculpture was less popular among nonconformists such as the Presbyterians, Wesleyans and Independents (Congregationalists). This reflects the doctrinal impact of the Reformation. Obelisks and pedestals with draped urns were popular for large monuments, particularly with Anglicans and Presbyterians.

Nineteenth-century Jewish graves are particularly interesting in symbolic representation. They function as a foil to Christian developments in monument design. Jewish orthodox teaching held that God should not be represented symbolically and limited the use of symbols on headstones to such things as the blessing hands, the seven-branched candlestick or menorah, the Star of David and the jug. Up until the 1870s in Australia, many Jewish monuments exhibited a liberalism contrary to this teaching. As the Jewish faith became more firmly established in the latter half of the 19th century, however, symbolic representations on monuments became sparser. So while the general trend in the late 19th century was for highly ornate monuments with many types of symbolism, Jewish grave markers became simpler.

That aside, by the 1870s, major denominational distinctions in memorial style and symbolism were starting to disappear and fashion was more likely to influence monument choice. In the late 19th century, everyone wanted to raise a monument in remembrance of their loved ones, with an emphasis on individual sentimental remembrance and respectability.

Clergy and cemetery trustees were anxious to ensure monuments were 'chaste' and appropriate, but were forced to do so at the cemetery, the end of the design process. Most cemeteries in Sydney regulated that monument designs be submitted for approval before work commenced onsite. Some denominational trustees even kept registers of designs and inscriptions. At Camperdown Cemetery, for example, the regulations stipulated that the chaplain inspect this register regularly to identify and prohibit 'any memorial, emblem or inscription proposed to be erected of immoral, irreligious, or unbecoming character or tendency'.

Unfortunately, none of these monument registers survive. A close reading of the minute books of cemetery trustees, however, suggests that censorship was a regular occurrence. Materials, designs and inscriptions were monitored with an eye to keeping 'order and uniformity'. Monumental masons consistently challenged the regulations, offering new headstone designs and tomb railings. To avoid problems and delays, some submitted their new designs for approval by the trustees prior to offering them to clients.

SYMBOLS AND MOTIFS

Monumental masons sometimes included a list of symbolic meanings at the back of their catalogues to help their customers choose a motif. There are four essential categories of symbols found on Sydney headstones up to the early 20th-century: mortality, religious faith, remembrance and floral.

MORTALITY

The cinerary urn was the most popular motif on classical-style monuments, appearing on headstones in Sydney from the 1840s and remaining popular for the rest of the century. Cinerary urns derived from the ancient Romans who placed the ashes in them after cremating human remains. The urn itself was thus a symbol of mortality and, typically, they were partially covered with mourning drapery or a pall. Embraced for its classical allusions, the urn replaced more traditional symbols of death such as the skull and cross bones or winged death's head. The inconsistency of Christians placing a cinerary urn (with its implied endorsement of cremation) above buried remains was not lost on 19th-century critics who variously described the 'repetitious' use of urns as 'offensive', 'Pagan' and 'utterly inappropriate'. Such criticisms, however, did little to damage the popularity of draped urns for headstones and monuments. The sarcophagus or tomb was also depicted in classical terms, another literal representation of the grave which acted as a memento mori.

Other symbols of mortality included the downturned torch and the winged hourglass. Both symbols were part of a long tradition of memento mori emblems acting as a reminder of one's own mortality. The downturned torch, frequently used in conjunction with cinerary urns, suggests a life extinguished. In art, an hourglass is often carried by personifications of Death or Time. A winged hourglass emphasises the swift passing of time. It was a common motif on 18th-century tombstones in England and America, and could be found in Sydney throughout the 19th century.

The broken column and the broken flower were sentimental favourites, expressing the idea of death cutting life off in its prime. A broken bud or young flower for children and young adults told of a life nipped in the bud.

RELIGIOUS FAITH

Symbols of Christian faith include the cross, the angelic hierarchy and tenets of the faith. The cross was seen as a particularly admirable funerary monument by fans of the Gothic Revival, a clear symbol of Christian hope in the Resurrection. Initially crosses were more the domain of Roman Catholics, but by the late 1870s they became popular across all denominations in Sydney. No doubt protestant hymns like 'Rock of Ages' which proclaimed the cross as a symbol of salvation, encouraged this popularity.

Angels were a messenger from the Lord and a symbol of divine communication, sent to encourage, guide and console. Two common angels in Sydney cemeteries are the Resurrection Angel pointing to heaven and the consoling, flower-dropping angel. The angelic hierarchy also includes seraphs, with just a face and wings to represent the soul; and cherubs, an integral part of classical ornamentation.

A single hand denotes the hand of God. The tradition derives from 16th- and

17th-century emblem books, when it was considered sacrilegious to personify God. The right hand is usually depicted, often emerging from a cloud and holding a scroll.

The dove, in Christian iconography, represents the Holy Spirit, and is an emblem of the soul while signifying purity of heart. A dove with an olive branch in its beak brings peace and good tidings, just as the dove with the fresh olive leaf in the Old Testament story of Noah's Ark showed that the floods were receding.

The anchor was a traditional symbol of hope that also represented patience and steadfastness. An anchor was often combined with an allegorical female figure, an emblem of hope and a classicised version of an angel.

Shells were another traditional form of Christian iconography, representing pilgrimage. The motif usually depicted is a scallop shell (semicircular, ribbed form), the martyr's emblem, that originated in the 12th century when pilgrims travelling to the shrine of St James at Santiago de Compostela in Spain wore it on their clothing. The scallop remains a symbol on the Camino de Santiago today.

Christians also took up the crown, a secular symbol of sovereignty and power, as an emblem of martyrdom, symbolising the victory of Christian faith over worldly sins, temptations and persecutions. The palm was another symbol of victory. The wreath is a variation on this theme, being a crown or garland of leaves, usually laurel, oak or olive. In ancient Greece and Rome it honoured emperors, heroes, athletes and poets. The wreath often appears in neoclassical funerary ornaments as a symbol of victory over death. The allegorical figure of grief is depicted holding a wreath.

Left Crown, St Paul's Anglican Cemetery, Cobbitty   *Centre* Dove with olive branch, St Mary the Virgin Memorial Chapel and Cemetery, Denham Court   *Right* Hand of God holding scroll, Uniting Church Cemetery, Cherrybrook

Left Broken flower stem, Catholic Cemetery, Windsor   *Centre* Flowers and garlands, St Peter's Anglican Cemetery, Richmond
Right Weeping widow, St John's Anglican Cemetery, Gordon

The passionflower symbolised faith and the Passion of Christ. An open book often represented the Bible, but could also be the book of life to record a person's virtues and deeds, much like the scroll held by the hand of God. The grapevine is often depicted with grapes, a symbol of the Eucharist, as is wheat, the chalice and the host.

REMEMBRANCE

Some symbols of faith and mortality came to be associated with remembrance. The weeping widow motif – a mourning widow either sitting beside or leaning over an urn – is a neoclassical motif popular in Sydney throughout the 19th century. The weeping widow is sometimes framed by a willow, a symbol of bereavement, lamentation and mourning. Goethe's novel *The Sorrows of Young Werther* (1774) popularised this theme: the much-illustrated scene of Charlotte mourning at the tomb of Werther even appears on Leeds and Staffordshire jugs and mugs. The death of Princess Charlotte (daughter of the Prince of Wales, later King George IV), who died in childbirth in 1817, provoked the production of prodigious quantities of ceramics ornamented with this weeping-at-the-tomb style of decoration. In Sydney cemeteries, it was popular as a pediment bas-relief carving from the 1840s until the late 1870s, and had become conventionalised as a three-dimensional sculpture by the 1880s. A symbol of remembrance as well as faith, it represented the idea of the grave as a site of personal meditation and consolation, and marks a shift away from memento mori symbols to personal remembrance. It became popular just as women's role in mourning culture was escalating, focusing on the mourner and her role (the mourner was invariably female) in perpetuating the memory of the deceased.

Clasped hands were a common emblem of union, friendship or affection. On cemetery memorials it may be a sign of farewell or, acknowledging heaven and the Resurrection, reunion. The clothing of the carved hands often ascribes masculine and feminine attributes, suggesting the hands of husband and wife. This symbolic representation has an associated consolation, that death has not severed the feeling of affection, love and friendship, because the pair will be reunited in heaven.

FLORAL

Flowers, fruit and leaves are common decorative elements on funerary monuments. They may be simply ornamental, gathered in garlands or festoons, but in some cases they take on a specific symbolic meaning. These meanings became increasingly elaborate with the publication of several books in France and Victorian England on 'The Language of Flowers'. The symbolic language was promoted through guides and manuals, and reproduced by monumental masons in catalogues to help customers choose decoration for their tombstones.

The Madonna lily (*Lilium candidum*) gets its common name from the fact it appeared in Christian art illustrating the Virgin Mary, particularly at the Annunciation. It is a symbol of purity, chastity and virginity. Other lilies such as arum lily and lily of the valley are also symbols of purity, piety and humility.

The poppy, a well-known opiate from classical times, was the attribute of Hypnos, god of sleep, and Morpheus, god of dreams and of night. Poppy flowers and seed pods were particularly popular for the decoration of bedrooms, beds and tombs. On a headstone the poppy denoted death or sleep, and its associated consolation of rest and peace.

The rose, thistle and shamrock are used as national symbols for England, Scotland and Ireland. The shamrock can also represent the Trinity while the rose is associated in Christian iconography with the Virgin Mary, particularly a rose without thorns. The rose also came to represent superlative beauty and perfection, and so illustrated a beautiful life, a beautiful person or love.

Other flowers that are sometimes represented are convolvulus (commonly bindweed, and thus representing bonds), tulip (charity), snowdrop (hope and consolation) and pansy (remembrance, thinking of you).

The oak and acorn are sometimes used as signs of strength and endurance. The acorn was also widely used in Celtic and Scandinavian art as a symbol of life, fecundity and immortality.

Ivy is an evergreen vine with a clinging quality that symbolises friendship, fidelity, faithfulness (due to its clinging quality) as well as memory, immortality and eternal life (due to its evergreen characteristic). Ivy is common on marble headstones as a decorative border.

TOOLS OF TRADE, OCCUPATIONS AND SOCIETIES

While wandering through cemeteries look out for symbols representing tools of trade, occupations and societies: cogs for an engineer, plumbline for a builder, an anchor, propeller or boat wheel for mariners, an anvil for a blacksmith, a rifle or slouch hat for soldiers, a set square and compass for freemasons. I've listed a few of my favourites in a top five (see page 61).

The design and symbolism on headstones were considered pieces of art chosen by relatives and friends to represent the deceased, their virtues and characteristics. Many cemetery visitors in the 19th century would have understood the symbolism and found consolation in it, while being encouraged to emulate these virtues. Such messages were not considered depressing rather they were a practical reminder of how one should live one's life. Even today, reading the headstones and pondering upon lives long and short, it is hard not to take away the memento mori message. And armed with this knowledge of symbolic motifs, the carvings on cemetery headstones take on a whole new meaning.

Anvil, Castlereagh Cemetery

TOP 5
CEMETERIES FOR BIRDWATCHING

BLACK COCKATOOS	**Randwick General Cemetery**
KESTRELS	**South Head General Cemetery, Vaucluse / Waverley Cemetery, Bronte**
BELLBIRDS, FINCHES	**St Thomas' Anglican Cemetery, Mulgoa**
BLUE WRENS	**Uniting Church Cemetery, Upper Castlereagh**
YOU NAME IT, IT'S PROBABLY THERE!	**Rookwood Necropolis**

Yellow-tailed black cockatoo (*Calyptorhynchus funereus*), Randwick General Cemetery

Opposite Rouse Hill Cemetery

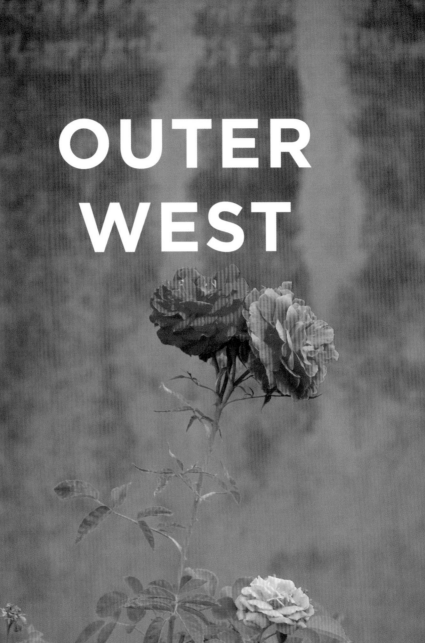

OUTER WEST

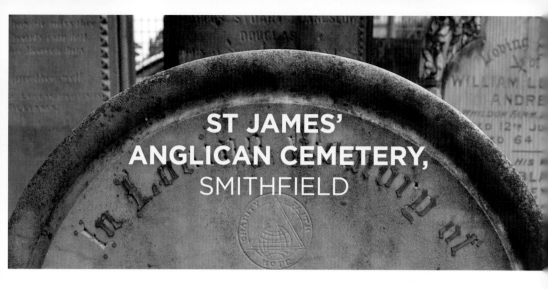

ST JAMES'
ANGLICAN CEMETERY,
SMITHFIELD

700 THE HORSLEY DRIVE, CORNER JUSTIN STREET, SMITHFIELD

Burials: 1861–1950s (converted c.1969)

St James Anglican Church at Smithfield is a neat little sandstock brick church that marks the core of the old village of Smithfield. The church was designed by architect Alfred Cook and built by the local parishioners in 1857–58.

The church and parish hall were once a hub of the local community. Fairfield Municipal Council held its meetings in the original weatherboard parish hall from its inauguration in 1888 until 1913.

The first burial in St James churchyard was Samuel Sidney Smith, the headmaster of the National School at Smithfield, who died on 15 April 1861. His headstone, if he had one, no longer survives.

The little churchyard has been destroyed. Originally the graves stretched behind the church, but the cemetery was cleared in the late 1960s. It is heartbreaking to see what

were once fine headstones redolent in symbolism and memories removed from their graves and shoved into a corner. The earliest dated headstone that has survived the drastic relocation is Jeremiah L Jones (d.1866). Even some of the marble inscription tablets from early 20th-century desk monuments have been mounted on a concrete wall, a mocking shadow of church memorial tablets. Just two graves remain in situ: John Braid (d.1902) and Arthur Ash (d.1912).

It seems that the churchyard has always been a bit neglected. In 1905 the *Cumberland Argus and Fruitgrowers Advocate* praised local resident Mr G Hillsden for cleaning up the graves and pathways and 'generally putting the cemetery in order … entirely at his own expense, and of his own volition'. William Freame, writing in 1918, described the little cemetery as 'overcrowded', with 'broken down picket fences', 'long grass' and 'little grey mounds (some holding up a jam jar or glass vase)'. He concluded it was 'rather depressing, practically it has no flowers or green trees'.

TIP

There is little to recommend visiting this cemetery. Combine it with a visit to the other cemeteries in Smithfield and go have a delicious lunch at one of the many restaurants in Fairfield. I recommend the Iraqi restaurant, Kebab Abu Ali.

MORE INFORMATION

- Ruth King, 'Smithfield Anglican Cemetery', Australian Cemeteries Index website, 2009, <austcemindex.com/cemetery?cemid=483>.

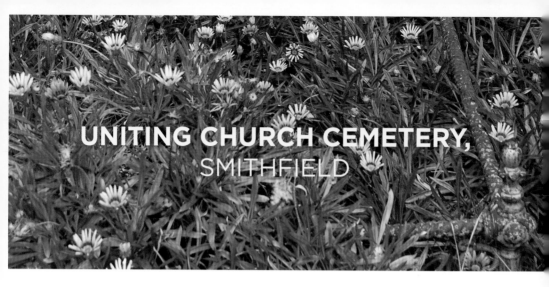

UNITING CHURCH CEMETERY, SMITHFIELD

711 THE HORSLEY DRIVE, SMITHFIELD

Burials: 1869–present

The Methodist Church and Cemetery was established in the late 1860s. It is located just down the road from St James Anglican Church and cemetery, and before the Baptist Church. Smithfield was once the religious centre for Smithfield and Fairfield. Fairfield did not become the main town centre until later.

This is a modest cemetery, complemented by the simple weatherboard church. The oldest graves are located to the left of the church and the churchyard continues behind it.

The earliest marked grave, surrounded by a high ornate iron palisade fence, is to Joseph John Watts, who died on 17 December 1873, and his wife Jane Watts, who died in 1888. The Watts helped to establish the first Wesleyan religious services in the district. Another early headstone memorialises Mary Ann Critchley (d.1874) and her husband the tanner Samuel Critchley (d.1888).

Trees smother both their graves.

There is an impressive black granite headstone to Cecil Ralph Bull. The date of death, 1914, and the crossed rifles, leads you to speculate that he was an early casualty of the First World War. In fact, the only son of Mr JG Bull died suddenly of appendicitis, 'cut off in the prime of his youth', as the *Cumberland Argus* reported.

The cemetery is still in use and contemporary gravestones illustrate the changing demographics of the area. The most recent burials are immigrants from Sudan.

MORE INFORMATION

- Jim Jones & Doreen Jones, *Smithfield Methodist Cemetery: monumental inscriptions old section – new section and mixed section old and new*, Nepean Family History Society, Emu Plains, 1994.
- Ruth King, 'Smithfield Uniting Church Cemetery', Australian Cemeteries Index website, 2009, <austcemindex.com/cemetery?cemid=512>.

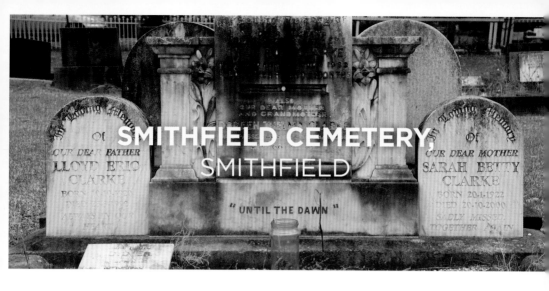

SMITHFIELD CEMETERY, SMITHFIELD

"UNTIL THE DAWN"

Burials: 1877–present

The Smithfield Cemetery was originally established as the second burial ground for the Baptist community. The cemetery was in use from the 1870s. As the nearby St James Anglican Cemetery became crowded, the congregation began to avail themselves of space in the Baptist Cemetery. By the 1970s the cemetery was being used by the whole community.

The earliest marked grave is Mary Ann Hollier, who died on 14 March 1877. Mary and her husband George Hollier were foundation members of the Smithfield Baptist Chapel. Mary's memorial is part of a set of sandstone headstones with matching footstones within a low cast-iron surround. Some of the other headstones are broken, including that of Mary's husband George. Another early headstone close by is to Ann Lewry, who died on 8 June 1878, aged 78.

Despite the cemetery being in use from the 1870s, it does not feel like a Victorian-era cemetery but more a down-at-heel 20th-century one, dominated by low monumentation. The site is long and narrow with the main entrance gates leading from the centre of Dublin Street.

The most striking feature of the cemetery is the large number of memorials to returned servicemen, with at least 35 headstones and memorial plaques to war veterans. Also of interest is the headstone of Minnie Giddings (d.1920), a bespoke carved low marble headstone on a three-step base bearing her initials as well as a spray of flowers.

The cemetery has an estimated 1300 marked graves and is still active. Previously managed by the Baptists, in 2016 the responsible authority is now the Syrian Orthodox Archdiocese of Australia & New Zealand.

TIP

There have been Baptists in the Smithfield area since the 1840s. A couple of gravestones also survive from their first burial ground in the grounds of the Baptist Chapel down the road.

MORE INFORMATION

- Jim Jones & Doreen Jones, *Smithfield General Cemetery: monumental inscriptions*, Nepean Family History Society, Emu Plains, 1997.
- Ruth King, 'Smithfield General Cemetery', Australian Cemeteries Index website, 2009, <austcemindex.com/cemetery?cemid=482>.

PINEGROVE MEMORIAL PARK, MINCHINBURY

Burials: 1962–present

The Pinegrove Cremation Society founded Pinegrove Memorial Park in 1962 as a modern way of burial and cremation. The 73 hectares, also called the Eastern Creek Cemetery, was Sydney's first major private lawn cemetery. It promised 'gently sloping lawns' and 'everlasting beauty, dignity and serenity' that would be 'maintained forever'. Given the neglected state of many church and general cemeteries at this time, such marketing would have appealed to many modern families.

Forest Lawn Memorial Park at Leppington was established in the same year. Pinegrove differentiated itself by emphasising the company was run by Australian businessmen, unlike the American-inspired Forest Lawn Cemetery. While Pinegrove Memorial Park still celebrates its Australian ownership, it is now part of the international funeral service

corporation InvoCare Australia Pty Limited, which also manages Forest Lawn, as well as cemeteries, crematoria and funeral services across Australia, New Zealand and Singapore. In 2015 it expanded into the United States of America.

The memorial park incorporates a cemetery and crematorium with chapels. There are lawn burial areas, monumental burial areas, a crypt area, as well as family vaults and mausoleums. The crematorium is an integral part of the cemetery landscape. Inurnment areas for cremated ashes include niche walls and traditional rose gardens, as well as a memorial pool. There are rock gardens, too, and it's possible to establish a family rock garden estate.

The cemetery has a distinct area for Chinese burials, with a lake and formal entrance flanked by dragons. The Lung Po Shan Chinese Memorial Gardens have been landscaped to meet the religious customs and requirements of Sydney's Chinese Buddhist, Christian and non-denominational communities. There are pagodas and space for large ceremonial practices.

This highly landscaped memorial park is a surprise for the sheer variety of memorialisation and the many personalised touches families place even within the lawn cemetery: flags, whirligigs, photos, flowers, toys, beads and bottles. On a sunny day it is peaceful and colourful. Look out for groups of apostlebirds which graze on grass seeds in the lawns.

NOTABLE BURIALS

- Kevin Arthur Wheatley (1937–1965), soldier, VC
- Sir Bertram Sydney Barnsdale Stevens (1889–1973), accountant and NSW premier
- Roy Howard Taffs (1919–1974) founder and co-managing director Pinegrove Cremation Society, endowed the Roy H Taffs Contemporary Art Society Award
- Alfred Percival Bullen (1896–1974), circus proprietor
- Anita Lorraine Cobby (1959–1986), nurse, murder victim
- Robert Trimbole (1931–1987), motor mechanic, illicit drugs wholesaler and racing identity

MORE INFORMATION

- Pinegrove Memorial Park website, 2015, <www.pinegrovecrem.com.au>.

ST BARTHOLOMEW'S ANGLICAN CEMETERY, PROSPECT

PONDS ROAD, PROSPECT

Burials: 1841–1992 (existing burial rights)

This is the slightly spooky cemetery you may have spotted while zipping along the Western Motorway. You've never stopped, right? Well you should. St Bartholomew's Church and Cemetery is a historic spot listed on the State Heritage Register and it is worth the visit. The church and original graveyard sit atop Prospect Hill and, even with maturing vegetation, encroaching development and massive power lines, the hill lives up to its name, offering views of

the city and the Blue Mountains.

The church was built by James Atkinson, who also built St Thomas' at Mulgoa, St Mary Magdalene at St Marys and St Peter's at Richmond, all churches with fascinating cemeteries. St Bartholomew's Church was completed and consecrated by May 1841. The first burials in the churchyard were two children of the Goodin family on 18 July 1841.

The earliest graves and most impressive vaults and monuments

Lawson family vaults

surround the church. The cemetery continued to be used throughout most of the 20th-century, closing in 1992 except for those with burial rights. The slab and desk monuments, which all face east, tumble down Prospect Hill. A central grassed avenue connects the cemetery and church.

The most famous resident in the cemetery is William Lawson, one of the trio who crossed the Blue Mountains. His companions are buried at Vaucluse (Wentworth) and Parramatta (Blaxland). Lawson had a large property and house 'Veterans Hall' at Prospect; his son Nelson built 'Greysteynes'. William Lawson can be found within a large family vault marked by an altar tomb. More

of the Lawson family, including Nelson Simmons Lawson, are in the severe classical monument topped by a sarcophagus. Originally classical urns surmounted the two pedestals that flanked the main monument.

Equally important, but less well known, is Maria Lock, daughter of Aboriginal elder Yarramundi. Educated through the Native Institution set up by Governor Macquarie, she married convict carpenter Robert Lock in 1823; it was the first officially sanctioned marriage between a convict and an Aboriginal woman. Maria used her education to secure a land grant for her family at Liverpool and then successfully petitioned for the transfer of her deceased brother Colebee's 12 hectare grant at Blacktown. Her land was divided between her surviving children when she died in 1878, only to be revoked by the Aborigines Protection Board in the 1920s.

The modern section is also worthy of attention. Seek out the grave of Freda Elizabeth Robertson (d.1978) whose gravestone records she was a 'bespoke tailoress, metal turner, socialist, peace movement activist'. There are at least three parish ministers buried here: Reverend George Middleton (d.1915), Reverend William Knox (d.1916) and Reverend Frederick Jones (d.1939).

Sadly, the church was gutted by fire in 1989, but a painstaking restoration has taken place. The fire also prompted the creation of the Friends of St Bartholomew's to encourage community values. A high cyclone fence has been erected around the church and some of the older graves. This is a terrible eyesore, but it protects the out-of-the-way church from further vandalism.

> **TIP**
>
> To get up close and personal with Lawson's vault, which is within the cyclone fence, contact Blacktown City Council for access or organise a group tour with the Friends of St Bartholomew's.

NOTABLE BURIALS

- William Lawson (1774–1850), explorer and pastoralist
- Maria Lock (c.1805–1878), Aboriginal landowner
- Freda Elizabeth Robertson (1924–1978), bespoke tailoress, metal turner, socialist and peace movement activist

MORE INFORMATION

- *Cemetery inscriptions from St. Bartholomews Church of England, at Prospect NSW,* Nepean Family History Society, South Penrith, 1983.
- Heritage Office, 'St. Bartholomew's Anglican Church (former) and Cemetery', State Heritage Register listing ID 5045521, NSW Office of Environment and Heritage website, 2016, <www.environment.nsw.gov.au/heritageapp/ViewHeritageItemDetails.aspx?ID=5045521>.
- Friends of St Bartholomew's website, 2016, <www.stbartholomewsprospect.org>.

CASTLEBROOK MEMORIAL PARK, ROUSE HILL

712-746 WINDSOR ROAD, ROUSE HILL

Burials: 1960s–present

Castlebrook Memorial Park is a private lawn cemetery and crematorium established in the early 1960s as the Australian Memorial Park of Sydney Pty Ltd. It was part of the new trend in Sydney for lawn cemeteries, forming a triplet with Forest Lawn and Pinegrove cemeteries. The chapel and crematorium were both commissioned in 1973.

The 73 hectare site is an undulating park-like cemetery that is kept in immaculate condition. Much of the cemetery is traditional lawn burials, with no kerbing or monumentation just plaques set into the lawn, however one section, 'Heritage Hill', provides more traditional monumentation with manicured family plots of shining granite, clipped shrubbery and roses.

An historic feature within the cemetery is the Battle of Vinegar Hill Monument. It stands on the highest hill in the cemetery and affords pleasing vistas of the district.

The monument commemorates the Castle Hill convict uprising and the subsequent battle with the New South Wales Corps on 5 March 1804. The uprising was symptomatic of ongoing Irish nationalist ructions in the colony and had its antecedents in the 1798 rebellion in Ireland. Fifteen convicts were killed in 1804, over 300 convicts captured including the uprising's leader Phillip Cunningham, a former United Irish captain and recruiting officer. He was hung immediately for treason, along with five other ringleaders.

The monument was a bicentennial project of Blacktown City Council, supported by the local historical society, and designed by sculptors Tom Sitta and Ivan Polak. A plethora of plaques document the official opening and meaning of the monument. You can pick up a brochure at the cemetery office that explains more of the uprising's history.

TIP

For the Irish nationalist double, you should also visit the 1798 Irish Monument at Waverley Cemetery.

NOTABLE BURIALS

- Galliano Eugenio Melocco (1897–1971), marble, scagliola and terrazzo mosaic manufacturer

MORE INFORMATION
- Castlebrook Memorial Park website, 2016, <www.castlebrook.com.au>.
- Anne-Maree Whitaker, 'Castle Hill convict rebellion 1804', Dictionary of Sydney website, 2009, <dictionaryofsydney.org/entry/castle_hill_convict_rebellion_1804>.

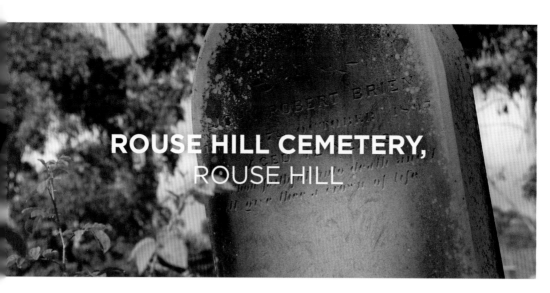

ROUSE HILL CEMETERY,
ROUSE HILL

10–12 ABERDOUR AVENUE, ROUSE HILL

Burials: 1874–2000

Despite its name, you will only find one of the Rouses of Rouse Hill buried in this cemetery. The majority are all to be found at St Peter's Anglican Cemetery at Richmond. Nevertheless, Rouse Hill Cemetery is a fascinating rural cemetery with a curious elliptical layout of graves. It was established in the 1870s and was associated with Christ Church Anglican Church on Mile End Road. The cemetery retained its rural character and attractive vistas into the 1980s. Today it is totally hemmed in by houses.

It is unclear exactly when the cemetery was established, or precisely when the first burial took place, as church registers only survive from 1886. The oldest headstone commemorates Grace Schofield, wife of Samuel Schofield. She died (possibly from the complications of childbirth) on 20 July 1874 at her home 'Melrose', on the Windsor Road, aged 36 years. Her husband must have struggled to look

Grave offerings

after their eleven children. Sadly their youngest infant son, Raymond Richard Schofield, died the following year on 27 November 1875, just 16 months old. His gravestone, which stands beside Grace's broken memorial, is carved with a seraph in the clouds.

Rouse Hill Cemetery possesses a number of interesting features. Aside from the rare elliptical arrangement of the graves and former carriageway, there are two large family plots where the marble headstones bear inscriptions on both sides of the headstones. Such arrangements were common for monuments such as pedestals and obelisks, but I don't recall seeing the idea applied to a headstone anywhere else.

Generations of established local families are represented in the cemetery, including Schofield, Sherwood, Pearce, Roughley, Rumery and Terry. There are many finely carved sandstone headstones featuring a range of symbolism including seraphs, angels, wreaths, broken flowers and diving doves. Look out in particular for the unusual carving of double laurel wreaths on William Rose's 1886 gravestone; the Horsley family plot covered with roses and with a rose carved on the memorial; and the downcast angel with exquisite wings on the headstone of Charlotte Smith (d.1911).

TIP

Go visit the extraordinary Rouse Hill House up the road, where six generations of the Rouse and Terry families lived. It's a living and layered time capsule for a colonial family and farming life.

NOTABLE BURIALS

- Nina Beatrice Terry (1875–1968), daughter of ES Rouse of Rouse Hill House and 'Guntawang'
- Constance Moulds (1897–1972), pioneering female trotting trainer

MORE INFORMATION

- Jim Jones & Doreen Jones, *Rouse Hill Cemetery: Mile End Road, Rouse Hill, Monumental Inscriptions*, Nepean Family History Society, Emu Plains, 1993.
- Jonathan Auld & Michelle Nichols, 'Rouse Hill Cemetery, Rouse Hill', Hawkesbury on the Net Cemetery Register website, 2009, <www.hawkesbury.net.au/cemetery/rouse_hill>.

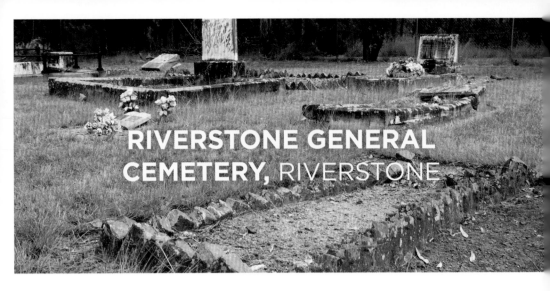

RIVERSTONE GENERAL CEMETERY, RIVERSTONE

Burials: 1894–present

Riverstone General Cemetery was dedicated 8 October 1892. Plenty of land was dedicated back in the day and the large rectangular open space is still sparsely populated. The land has been further divided and reallocated to accommodate more recent religious community groups. There are three distinct Islamic areas reflecting different ethnic communities: a Muslim section that faces Mecca in the south-west corner, and in the north-east corner the Ahmadiyya Muslim Association and the Ahmadiyya Anjuman Isha'at-e-Islam Lahore both have separate sections.

The cemetery is located outside the town of Riverstone, over the railway line. A local resident who grew up in Riverstone remembers: 'As kids we used to go for a walk to the cemetery for something to do of a weekend. We'd collect wild orchids from the bush to put on the graves.' (*A History of the Riverstone*

Cemetery, p. 28.) The cemetery is now grassed and largely cleared of bush. A few eucalypts are dotted through the areas not yet utilised.

The first burial was Mercy Mary Nelson of Riverstone, wife of Andrew Nelson, aged just 35 years. She was buried in the new cemetery on Saturday 29 December 1894 in the Anglican section. The *Windsor and Richmond Gazette* reported on 5 January 1895 that her sudden death, 'caused much sympathy to be expressed by the residents'.

The oldest headstones date from 1898 and can be found at the rear of the Anglican, Catholic and Presbyterian sections. There are a number of vernacular styles found here. Particular to this cemetery is the distinctive use of angled bricks to enclose grave plots. A number of simple timber crosses mark more recent graves.

The most interesting and attractive part of the cemetery is the Muslim section at the rear of the cemetery. The graves are planted with shrubs and flowers – roses, lavender, basil, gardenias, agaves, yuccas, cycads – providing visual relief in the otherwise plainly grassed site. Plastic chairs are dotted throughout this section, testament to its regular visitors.

TIP

Download a cemetery map from Blacktown City Council's website.

MORE INFORMATION

- Blacktown City Council, 'Riverstone Cemetery', Blacktown City Council website, 2013, <www.blacktown.nsw. gov.au/People_and_Community/ Community_Services/Council_ Cemeteries/Riverstone_Cemetery>.
- *Riverstone General Cemetery: monumental inscriptions and data from the burial registers concerning unmarked graves*, 3 vols, Nepean Family History Society, Emu Plains, 1994.
- Rosemary Phillis & Winsome Phillis, *A History of the Riverstone Cemetery*, Riverstone & District Historical Society, Rouse Hill, 1998.

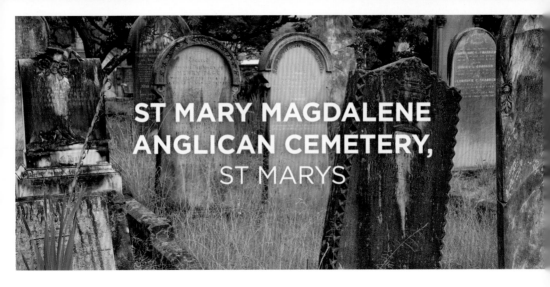

ST MARY MAGDALENE ANGLICAN CEMETERY, ST MARYS

Burials: 1840–present (existing burial rights)

Formerly known as South Creek, the suburb of St Marys gets its name from this simple Georgian church. It was completed in 1840, constructed by the local builder James Atkinson to a design by architect Francis Clarke. The first burial occurred that same year; an infant Thomas Revely, buried on 10 October.

The church and cemetery are situated on a rise above the South Creek crossing. The churchyard wraps around the east and south sides of the church. The neat cemetery is entered through a memorial gate for Timothy Ford, a young boy who drowned in 1956. The cemetery has a resident set of nesting plovers, so enter with caution during breeding season.

The cemetery's claim to fame is its association with Governor Philip Gidley King's family. The governor's son, Phillip Parker King, of 'Dunheved' estate, endowed the land for the church and the governor's widow, Anna Josepha King (d.1844)

is the earliest marked burial in the cemetery. The King family vault, containing the remains of Anna Josepha, is on the eastern border of the graveyard, surrounded by a high iron palisade fence. In 1988, descendants relocated the governor's memorial stone from St Nicholas Church in Tooting, England.

The cemetery features a small number of intriguing asymmetrical headstone designs dating from the 1860s, a particular design by a local mason. Look out for the graves of Peter Royal (d.1866) and Charles Quiney (d.1862). Similar headstones can be found in Emu Plains General Cemetery too. There are some fine examples of symbolic carving on headstone pediments, including grapes and wheat (for the Eucharist).

A marble broken column that commemorates the death of William Garner in 1888 bears the apt verse:

Tombs are but dust
and money vainly spent.
A man's good fame
Is his best monument.

Yet the Bennett family of 'Bronte', St Marys, like many of their generation, certainly felt the need to commemorate the death of their son Billie, an Anzac solider who died in Damascus in 1918.

The cemetery is still in use, with a cremation wall extending from the memorial gates.

NOTABLE BURIALS

- Philip Gidley King (1758–1808), NSW governor (relocated memorial)
- Anna Josepha King (1765–1844), wife of Governor Philip Gidley King
- Phillip Parker King (1791–1856), naval officer, hydrographer and company manager, endower of church and cemetery
- Robert Copeland Lethbridge (1798–1865), of 'Werrington'
- Philip Gidley King (1817–1904), pastoralist, son of Phillip Parker King
- Sapper Sydney William Bennett (1889–1918), Anzac Mounted Division AIF

MORE INFORMATION

- *St. Mary Magdalene Church of England, St. Marys, monumental inscriptions*, Nepean Family History Society, St Mary's, 1982.

Anna Josepha King (d.1844), wife of Governor Philip Gidley King

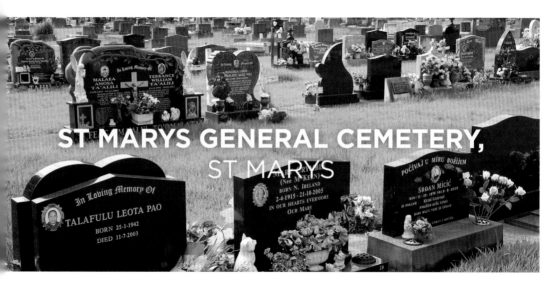

ST MARYS GENERAL CEMETERY, ST MARYS

Burials: 1890s–present

The early cemetery gate piers still stand sentinel on the Great Western Highway, but you now enter this thoroughly modern cemetery from Sydney Street. The original layout of the cemetery was a simple central avenue dividing the Anglican, Catholic and Presbyterian sections. The cemetery was dedicated in 1881 and within a decade was in 'a fearful state of disrepair' prompting calls to transfer control from the religious trustees to the local council. There were also protests that the cemetery, meant to serve the residents of Penrith, was located in St Marys.

The earliest graves, dating from the 1890s and executed in marble and occasionally sandstone, are highly visible in this predominantly 20th-century cemetery. A substantial granite obelisk with trachyte plinth and base sits beside the central avenue in the Presbyterian section, commemorating the Angus family. The patriarch, James Angus, was killed by a train at Rooty Hill Station in 1916.

A cast-iron grave marker known as an iron Etna is a rare survivor in the original Roman Catholic section. These low-cost memorials could be ordered through mail order catalogues such as Lassetters and the inscriptions were usually painted on a panel, fading and peeling over time; this one, however, has a cast bronze panel with art nouveau style lettering. A flower pinned to the cross indicates that the parishioners of St Marys Catholic Church at Prospect still respect the loss of their 15-year-old altar boy, Ernest Cooney, who died in 1916.

The modern graves in the Roman Catholic, Greek Orthodox, Independent and Coptic Orthodox sections provide a colourful and exuberant celebration of life and death, with artificial flowers, photographs and expansive epitaphs. When I visited, several families were tending graves and bubbles drifted across a child's grave.

TIP

A map of the cemetery can be downloaded from Penrith City Council's website.

NOTABLE BURIALS

- John Henry Smith Angus (1875–1937), businessman, grazier, Vice-President Royal Agricultural Society NSW, councillor and president Blacktown Shire

MORE INFORMATION
- Penrith City Council, 'Cemeteries', Penrith City Council website, 2016, <www.penrithcity.nsw.gov.au/services/other-services/cemeteries>.
- Jim Jones & Doreen Jones, *St Mary's General Cemetery: monumental inscriptions*, Nepean Family History Society, Emu Plains, 1995–96.

Rare iron 'Etna' memorial to Ernest Cooney (d.1916

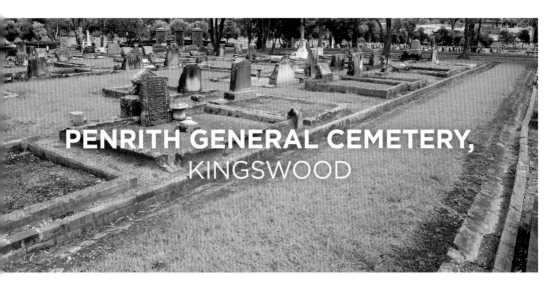

PENRITH GENERAL CEMETERY, KINGSWOOD

COX AVENUE, KINGSWOOD

Burials: 1910–present

Penrith General Cemetery is a large tranquil cemetery situated on a sloping site just north of Kingswood railway station. The weatherboard office stands near the entrance off Cox Avenue. The main avenue running east–west is lined with trees.

The search for an appropriate site for a general cemetery began in 1884, with various aldermen, clergymen and businessmen forming delegations and meeting with politicians, but Penrith's main cemetery was not finally gazetted until 12 September 1903.

Archbishop Wright consecrated the Anglican portion on 19 January 1910 and the first burial in the cemetery followed seven months later: Doris Vivian, a little girl just 5 years old. Sadly, her modest marble gravestone in the second row of the Anglican section has been damaged, but a plaque placed by Penrith City Council on the plot ensures 'Dear little Doris' is not overlooked.

Originally portions were set aside

for Church of England, Roman Catholic, Presbyterian, Methodist, Salvation Army and an unsectarian (or general) section. The unsectarian section has greatly expanded to include lawn sections and a children's garden for ashes and burials.

The Nepean Family History Society has transcribed the cemetery twice – in the early and late 1990s.

TIP

A map of the cemetery can be downloaded from Penrith City Council's website.

NOTABLE BURIALS

- Catherine Beatrice (Caddie) Edmonds (1900–1960), barmaid, author of *Caddie:*
- *A Sydney Barmaid*, later made into the feature film *Caddie*.
- John Wallace Metcalfe (1901–1982), state librarian

MORE INFORMATION

- Penrith City Council, 'Cemeteries', Penrith City Council website, 2016, <www.penrithcity.nsw.gov.au/services/other-services/cemeteries>.
- *Penrith General Cemetery: monumental inscriptions and burial register records*, 2nd edn, Nepean Family History Society, Emu Plains, 1998.

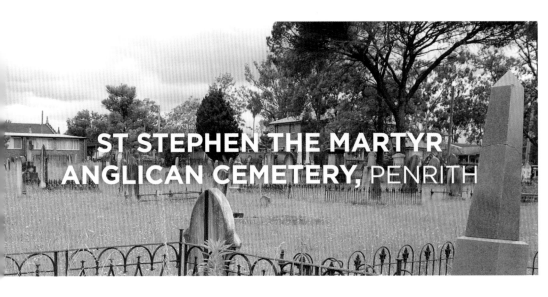

ST STEPHEN THE MARTYR ANGLICAN CEMETERY, PENRITH

FULTON LANE, PENRITH

Burials: 1838–1957

This gorgeous 19th-century cemetery is tucked away in the heart of Penrith. What a shame that the churchyard is now disconnected from St Stephen the Martyr Anglican Church, with a 1960s hall destroying the visual connection and a fence denying access. You now access the cemetery from Fulton Lane.

St Stephen the Martyr Anglican Church was built by James Atkinson, who also built the Anglican churches at Mulgoa and St Marys. Bishop Broughton consecrated the church and cemetery on 16 July 1839.

A grassed cruciform pathway that aligns with the church tower divides the cemetery, with monuments placed prominently along the north-south axis. The monuments face towards the path so cemetery visitors can easily read them. This avenue would have been the pre-eminent place to be buried within the churchyard.

The first recorded burial was Elizabeth Morkley on 23 July 1839;

however, William Martin's headstone states that he died on 25 December 1838. Church historian PW Gledhill reports that a young Aboriginal girl, Georgiana, was buried even earlier, on 7 September 1838.

The cemetery retains many early headstones, still legible, from the 1840s and 1850s. They are easy to spot with their footstones and sandstone post surrounds. St Stephen the Martyr Anglican Cemetery is enjoyable to wander around, with lots of old headstones executed by Sydney-based monumental masons as well as local ones, especially John Price and Son of Penrith. John Price, a prominent citizen who served as an alderman as well as Penrith's first council clerk, had a substantial business as a monumental mason and undertaker. Price and some of his family are buried here. The cemetery also has some fine examples of wrought-iron surrounds, such as around the tomb of Sir John Jamison.

Look out for James Perry's gravestone (d.1840): the letter cutter engraved the '4' back to front. George Dent's sandstone headstone (d.1862) is flanked by carved vine leaves and has a lovely rendition of a mourning widow with urn and willow in bas-relief. At the other end of the scale you will see the elaborately carved sandstone obelisk and pedestal to Emily Popplewell (d.1868), made by her husband and monumental mason, Joseph Popplewell. He carved many of the headstones that once stood in the Devonshire Street Cemeteries and also worked on the quadrangle at Sydney University.

NOTABLE BURIALS

- Sir John Jamison (1776–1844), of 'Regentville', physician, landowner and constitutional reformer
- Steevy (c.1805–1861), 'last of the Comleroy tribe of Aboriginals'
- James Beatty (c.1836–1890), Penrith police sergeant, killed on duty

MORE INFORMATION
- Jean McDowell Jones, *History in Stone, Penrith (New South Wales): a genealogical study of headstones, St Stephen the Martyr Church of England*, Sydney, 1976.

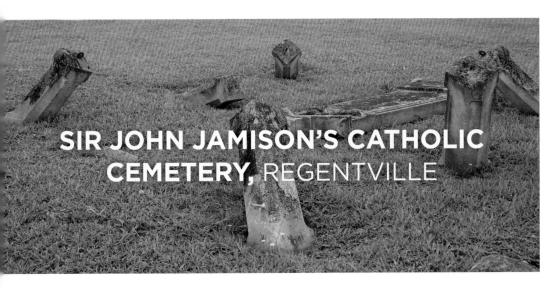

SIR JOHN JAMISON'S CATHOLIC CEMETERY, REGENTVILLE

LILAC PLACE, REGENTVILLE

Burials: 1834–1967

This burial ground on the estate of Sir John Jamison once had panoramic views. Now, suburban subdivision encases this historic relic and obliterates the original carriageway that wended its way up the hill from the old Mulgoa Road to the gate flanked by yew trees. Today a modern, rustic, timber post-and-rail fence encloses the cemetery.

The cemetery dates from the 1830s and was established by Jamison for his Irish convicts and workers.

Jamison himself was Anglican, and was buried in the St Stephen the Martyr Church Cemetery in Penrith. This Catholic cemetery and the McCarthy Cemetery at Cranebrook were the main Catholic cemeteries for the Penrith district until the 20th-century. The McCarthy Cemetery is within the Penrith Lakes Scheme and is currently inaccessible; although plans are afoot to reopen it to the public at some stage.

Graves are scattered over the open

grassed site and the old headstones tilt at crazy angles. Headstones from the 1830s and 1840s are still partially legible. The earliest I was able to discern was 1836. It is a simple sandstone headstone located near the fence line erected by Michael Moore to his father Laurence Moore. The letter carving exhibits a touching naivety in its execution. Another early headstone was for the infant John Stapleton who died in 1839 aged 3 years and 4 months.

The last burial in this cemetery was in 1967. The headstones have been transcribed numerous times. If you are particularly interested in who is buried here, I suggest you compare transcriptions as the cemetery has suffered neglect over the decades and many headstones have been damaged or have disappeared.

MORE INFORMATION

- Jean McDowell Jones, *Nepean District Cemetery Records, 1806–1976*, Sydney, 1977.
- Jim Jones & Doreen Jones, *Sir John Jamison's Roman Catholic Cemetery Regentville, Lilac Place, Jamisontown: heritage photographic collection with monumental inscriptions*, Nepean Family History Society, Emu Plains, 1994.

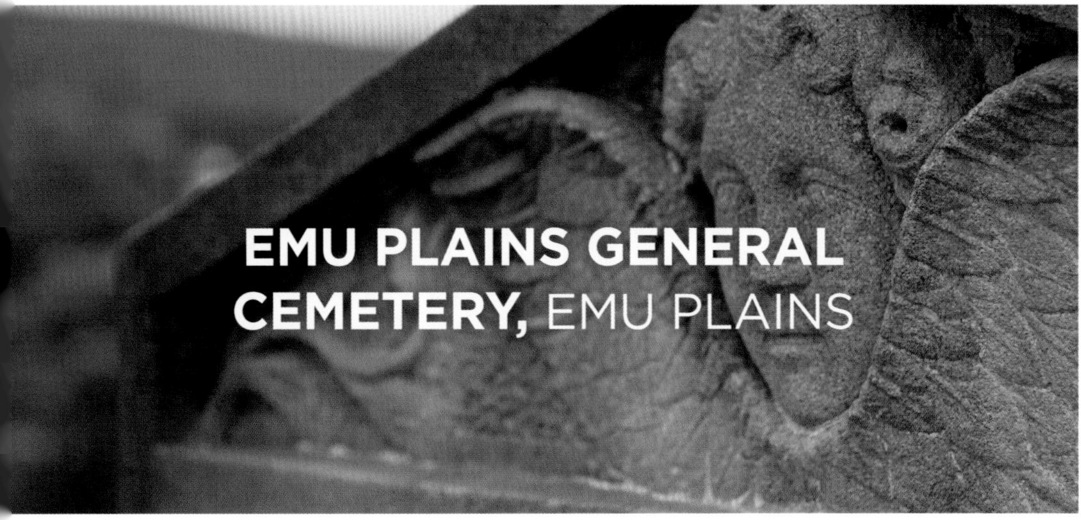

EMU PLAINS GENERAL CEMETERY, EMU PLAINS

SHORT STREET, EMU PLAINS

Burials: 1859–present

It was touch and go whether to include this cemetery (it is over the Nepean River, after all) but if you are out Penrith way it is certainly worth a visit. The cemetery is next to St Paul's Anglican Church (built 1848) and together they form a charming grouping. Some people refer to it as St Paul's Cemetery Emu Plains, however it was dedicated as a general cemetery. The first recorded burial was James Evans (d.1859) who is buried in a large altar tomb.

The Anglican section is the most impressive. Its central avenue draws the eye back to the church and the avenue is lined with large family vaults and monuments. An exquisite array of wrought-iron surrounds enclose these familial plots. A series of large white cedar trees, which once grew along the avenue and among the graves, were removed when they started causing serious damage to monuments; their stumps a silent warning of what

Left Fine tombs and wrought iron surrounds line the main avenue, Anglican section

happens when cemetery landscapes are allowed to grow unchecked.

There is an array of sandstone altar tombs, classical urns with pedestals, and finely carved monuments. A large sandstone pedestal with urn marks the family grave of the genial Toby Ryan of 'Emu Hall' (built 1852), which can be found on the Anglican avenue. Also look out for the red granite obelisk that marks the grave of politician Charles Moore (d.1895). Earlier graves in the Presbyterian and Methodist sections have headstones with matching footstones. Each area has its own character. In the Methodist section I encountered a memento mori inscription: 'Watch for ye know not when He cometh'.

Being located on the western railway line, the cemetery contains a number of burials connected with railway disasters, including Emu Plains 1878, Bell 1890, Granville 1977 and Glenbrook 1999. David Heron (d.1890), an engine driver on the western line, was killed in the spectacular railway accident at Bell. His grave can be found in the Presbyterian section.

Penrith City Council, who manages the cemetery, has erected some interpretive signage near the entrance to the Anglican section.

TIPS

Download a map of the cemetery from the Penrith City Council website.

While in the area, visit the Penrith Regional Gallery and the Lewers Bequest down by the river. Aside from changing exhibitions, there is a lovely garden and café.

OUTER WEST

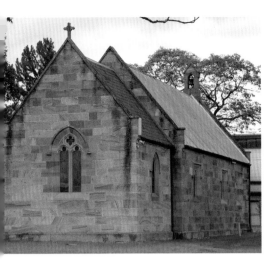

Left St Paul's Anglican Church dates from 1848   *Right* James Tobias Ryan's family grave

NOTABLE BURIALS

- Charles Moore (1820–1895), merchant, auctioneer and politician, mayor of Sydney
- James Tobias (Toby) Ryan (1818–1899), butcher, pastoralist, politician and sportsman, built 'Emu Hall'
- David McKee Wright (1869–1928), poet and journalist
- Zora Bernice May Cross (1890–1964), writer

MORE INFORMATION

- Penrith City Council, 'Cemeteries', Penrith City Council website, 2016, <www.penrithcity.nsw.gov.au/services/other-services/cemeteries>.
- Tania Smidt, 'Emu Plains Cemetery', Australian Cemeteries Index website, 2010 <austcemindex.com/cemetery?cemid=647>.
- *Emu Plains General Cemetery: short stories of the residents*, Nepean Family History Society, Emu Plains, 2013.

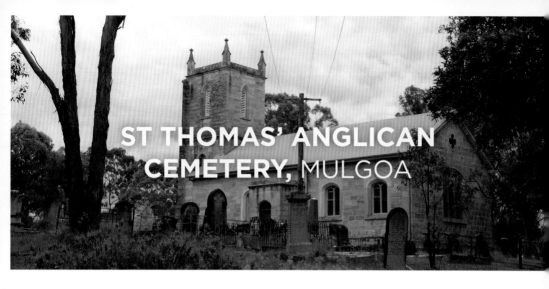

ST THOMAS' ANGLICAN CEMETERY, MULGOA

ST THOMAS ROAD, MULGOA

Burials: 1838–2004

Although a little off the beaten track, this picturesque church and cemetery on the outskirts of Mulgoa has a charming setting. Some claim St Thomas' Mulgoa is one of the most romantic rural churches in New South Wales; it certainly grabbed the attention of artists such as Hardy Wilson.

St Thomas' Anglican is a historic church and burial ground associated with the Cox family of Mulgoa. Edward Cox gave the land for the church, his brother George Cox of 'Winbourne' gave land for the rectory. The golden sandstone for the church was quarried nearby. Architect James Chadley and the Reverend Thomas Makinson designed the simple Gothic church. Built by James Atkinson between 1836 and 1838, St Thomas' Mulgoa was one of the first churches subsidised under Governor Bourke's Church Act and it remains one of Australia's earliest Gothic Revival churches. Atkinson went on to build the Anglican churches at St Marys and Penrith. Bishop Broughton consecrated the church on 13 September 1838.

There are a number of simple sandstone gravestones dating from the late 1830s and 1840s along the western perimeter of the cemetery, down the hill from the church tower. The area is a bit overgrown, so be careful. We encountered a snake during our late spring visit and you also need to dodge the ant nests.

Nathaniel Norton died in 1838; his headstone has been damaged. The earliest legible headstone I could find on my visit was Peter Brown, who died on 1 August 1839, aged 28 years. You can still see the lightly carved lines picked out to guide the stonemason with his letter cutting, and he managed to stuff up the spacing of the memento mori epitaph, running out of room on the first line and squeezing in the final word 'see' in small letters above:

All you that come my grave to ^{see}
Prepare yourselves to follow me
Repent in time make no delay
For I in haste was call'^d away.

Unusual wrought iron surround encloses the grave of Anne Maria Anshaw (d.1853)

There are some impressive wrought-iron grave surrounds in this cemetery. Look out for the barley twisted ironwork with Gothic crosses that encloses the grave of Anne Maria Anshaw (d.1853). She had quite the life: married, with child, and then died, all by the age of 17.

The most impressive monuments are the classical-style Cox family vaults and graves, which are to the north-west of the church. Also among them is an early headstone to Anna, the infant daughter of Henry and Frances Cox of 'Glenmore'. She died in 1827, aged 5 months 12 days. John Lowe (d.1849), 'an old and faithful servant of Fern Hill'

according to his headstone, is not buried in the Cox precinct but down the hill among the early graves.

The cemetery was closed in 2004. The site is now owned by Sydney Anglican Schools Corporation. The church still has services and its setting makes it popular for weddings. The church and cemetery grounds are usually open on Sundays, so plan your visit for the holy day.

TIP

Plans of the cemetery and a list of burials can be downloaded from the parish website.

NOTABLE BURIALS

- Alexander (Allaster) Grant Maclean (1824–1862), surveyor-general of NSW
- Edward Cox (1805–1868), of 'Fern Hill', Mulgoa, grazier
- George Cox (1795–1868), of 'Winbourne', Mulgoa, grazier and brother of Edward

MORE INFORMATION

- Anglican Parish of Mulgoa, 'Mulgoa Ministry Centre', Anglican Parish of Mulgoa website, 2016, <sites.google.com/site/anglicanparishmulgoa/st-thomas--mulgoa>.
- *St Thomas' Church of England Mulgoa: monumental inscriptions and burial register records*, Nepean Family History Society, 1997.
- Peter Robinson, *A Short History and Guide to St Thomas' Mulgoa*, 1988, reproduced on the parish website.

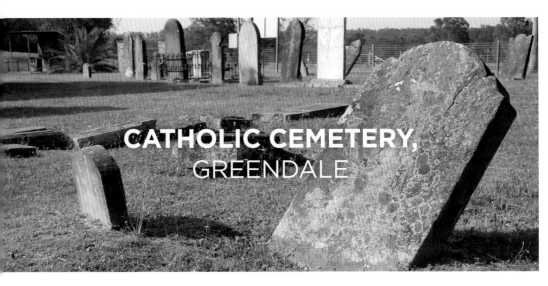

CATHOLIC CEMETERY, GREENDALE

946-984 GREENDALE ROAD, GREENDALE

Burials: 1844-present

Headstones leaning at precarious angles and footstones indicate some of the earliest graves in this small, but well-tended church cemetery. Green lichen grows on some of the stones though and, along with weathering, makes the inscriptions almost illegible.

Greendale was a flourishing farming community in the 1840s with a population of over 2000, but the arrival of leaf rust in the 1860s put an end to wheat growing in the area. George Wentworth gave the land for the Catholic church in 1818. A little timber church held regular services until 1893. Some of the earliest headstones in the cemetery commemorate the Dorahy family. William Dorahy and his wife arrived in Sydney from Tyrone, Ireland in 1837 and settled immediately in Greendale, where they farmed. They lost three children in 1844, 1845 and 1853. The Dorahys, the Lovats and the Anschaus families are all related through marriage. An unusual sandstone cambered headstone with cutaway shoulders marks the grave of Mary, young wife of Patrick Dorahy (d.1858).

This cemetery also contains 77 graves relocated from St Francis Xavier's Catholic Cemetery at Luddenham. These are located in a block in the western corner of the cemetery, with pebblecrete paths running between the graves. St Francis Xavier's Catholic Church was established in 1912 on land donated by the Anschau family. The federal government acquired the land from the church in 1990 for Sydney's proposed new airport and the church arranged for the graves to be relocated the following year. The St Francis Xavier Chapel that now stands in Greendale Cemetery is a replica of the original church at Luddenham, built by the Petith and Fordham families. The chapel opened on 4 November 1995.

The cemetery is still in use, along with a columbarium.

The chapel, built 1995, is a replica of the original church at Luddenham

TIP

While you are here, you might want to travel down the road towards Wallacia to see the Shadforth memorial. Lieutenant-Colonel Thomas Shadforth, formerly of HM 57th Regiment, who fought at the Battle of Waterloo, died on 4 August 1862. The obelisk was removed from St Mark's Anglican Cemetery at Greendale in 1980 by Liverpool Council and now sits down the hill beside the entrance to the Free Church of Tonga. It is the only reminder of St Mark's. The Edmund Blacket-designed church, which dates from 1849, had a turbulent history. It lost its roof in a furious storm in 1903 and its last service was in 1929. The church was sold in 1980 and is now a private residence; the surviving headstones from the burial ground are laid down flat. There is no public access.

MORE INFORMATION

- Jim Jones & Doreen Jones, *Heritage photographic collection Roman Catholic Cemetery Greendale: together with monumental inscriptions from St. Francis Xavier Catholic Cemetery Luddenham, graves relocated to Greendale*, Nepean Family History Society, Emu Plains, 1994.

KEMPS CREEK CEMETERY, KEMPS CREEK

230–260 WESTERN ROAD, KEMPS CREEK

Burials: 1965–present

This lawn cemetery, established in the mid-1960s, is on a gently sloping site with four main burial areas that look down on the chapel and dam. There is little to draw you here, unless you are a mourning relative; there is not a lot to see.

The most interesting feature is the St Francis Natural Burial Field, Sydney's first eco-burial area, which opened in 2010. A plot of ground in the back corner of the cemetery caters for natural or environmental burials, where the body is prepared without chemicals and buried in a biodegradable coffin. There is no lawn or monumentation in this part of the cemetery; a large sandstone rock just outside the burial ground allows for names to be inscribed on a communal memorial to those who are buried there.

Originally called the Sydney Catholic Lawn Cemetery the cemetery, although managed by the Catholic Cemeteries and

Crematoria Board, now apparently caters for all denominations.

Surprisingly for a modern cemetery, the Liverpool Genealogy Society has transcribed it: see 'More information' below or visit <www.lgs.org.au>.

MORE INFORMATION

- Sydney Natural Burial Park, Kemps Creek website, Catholic Cemeteries & Crematoria, 2016, <www.sydneynaturalburialparks.com.au>.
- Catholic Cemeteries & Crematoria, 'Kemps Creek Cemetery', Catholic Cemeteries & Crematoria website, 2013, <www.catholiccemeteries.com.au/cemeteries/kemps-creek>.
- *Transcriptions, burial register entries & photographs of Sydney Catholic Lawn Cemetery Kemps Creek, NSW*, CD-ROM, Liverpool Genealogy Society, 2005.

Memorial stone outside the Natural Burial Field

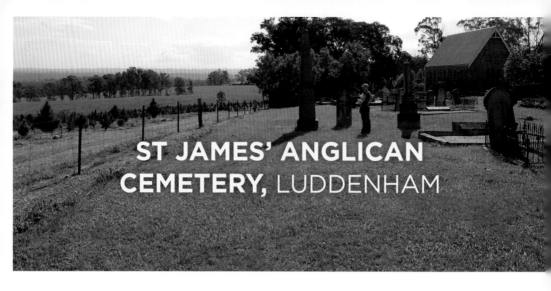

ST JAMES' ANGLICAN CEMETERY, LUDDENHAM

Burials: 1873–2006

This picturesque church and cemetery is located on a rise on the outskirts of the little township of Luddenham. Sir Charles Nicholson, physician and parliamentarian, donated the land. The church, built out of locally quarried basalt, was dedicated on St James' Day, 25 July 1871.

The earliest headstone is to Thomas Magee, who died of dysentery on 11 May 1873, aged 59 years. The Most Reverend Frederick Barker, Bishop of Sydney, consecrated

the cemetery soon after this burial, on 19 September 1873.

The earliest headstones dating from the 1870s and 1880s are easy to spot. They are all sandstone and clustered together at the southern end of the cemetery. The rest of the 19th-century headstones are marble and the graves wrap around the church with 20th-century desk monuments to the rear.

The two most substantial monuments in the cemetery, a sandstone obelisk and a tall sandstone pillar and pedestal with urn atop, mark the graves of the West family. The cemetery also affords bucolic vistas making for a pleasant visit.

MORE INFORMATION
- Jim Jones & Doreen Jones, *Cemeteries of St John's Church of England and Uniting Church, Badgery's Creek; St Mark's Church of England, Greendale; St James Church of England and Uniting Church, Luddenham: monumental inscriptions and burial register records*, 2nd edn, Nepean Family History Group, Emu Plains, 1998.

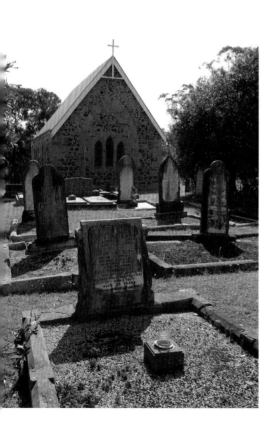

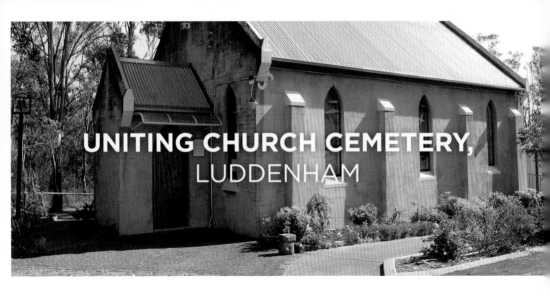

UNITING CHURCH CEMETERY,
LUDDENHAM

Burials: 1889-present

This modest little cemetery is on a sloping site tucked behind the rendered brick Uniting Church with simple buttressing and Gothic arch windows. The church dates from 1886, although Primitive Methodist church services had been happening in the district since 1855.

The majority of the graves date from the 20th-century. There are almost 50 marked graves and the cemetery is still in use. The earliest burials recorded on a headstone are for Annie Lucy Longley who died on 9 December 1890 and her three-year-old daughter Ivy V Longley, who died the previous year, on 18 December 1889.

Some active parishioners are buried here. William Bray (d.1928) and his wife Elizabeth Jane Bray (d.1937) were superintendents of the Methodist Sunday School at Luddenham from 1901 to 1937. Others were respected citizens of Luddenham village, such as Arthur

Sidney Herbert Willmington (d.1962), who lived all his life in the village and was the postmaster for 40 years. Arthur's mother, who is also buried here in an unmarked grave, was postmistress for 26 years prior to Arthur taking up the position.

The little church is worth a closer look. It has some colourful modern stained glass windows and a history of the church is posted up at the entrance way.

MORE INFORMATION
• Jim Jones & Doreen Jones, *Cemeteries of St John's Church of England and Uniting Church, Badgery's Creek; St Mark's Church of England, Greendale; St James Church of England and Uniting Church, Luddenham: monumental inscriptions and burial register records*, 2nd edn, Nepean Family History Group, Emu Plains, 1998.

OUTER WEST

A STROLL IN THE CEMETERY

Sydney's major cemeteries were once public recreational spaces which rivalled public parks and gardens. While we may baulk at this idea today, the *Sydney Morning Herald* in 1862 thought Sydney's cemeteries should be 'a place of festive or pensive resort as in many other countries' since 'an occasional stroll through the avenues of the well-kept cemetery will afford instruction without depression'.

Sydney's cemeteries are filled with monuments that celebrate exemplary deeds and Sydney's citizens once flocked to venerate and emulate the good and the virtuous. A well-tended grave was a public sign of remembrance and affection. Epitaphs on sepulchral memorials addressed passers-by, extolling virtues and acting as a memento mori. Pilgrimages to gravesites were an outward and public sign of faithfulness, respect and remembrance.

PUBLIC VENERATION

Hundreds of people attended the unveiling of monuments raised by public subscription to prominent persons – politicians, explorers, poets. Such enterprises were often a deliberate attempt by society's leaders to define the collective memory of Sydneysiders and celebrate what they deemed to be appropriate or noble achievements.

The memorial to the poet Henry Kendall in Waverley Cemetery is an example of public veneration. Kendall wrote the words for the Sydney International Exhibition opening cantata and several volumes of poetry. But his tumultuous personal life betrayed his success and poetic recognition and he died on 1 August 1882, in poverty and a drunkard. Nevertheless, obituaries described the 'lyre set in his soul' and lamented the fact that his death 'deprive[d] Australia of its sweetest singer'. From the tenor of the public obituaries, Kendall seems an ideal candidate for a state funeral. But he was not awarded this honour and his funeral was a modest affair with only the poet's closest friends in attendance.

The movement to raise funds for a more substantial memorial to Kendall was underway within two weeks of his burial. The *Sydney Mail* saw his death as an excellent opportunity to establish the country's literary merit. Not everyone was as enthusiastic about the memorial effort. The *Bulletin* scoffed on 8 May 1886 that after three years only £125 had been raised, most of which had come from 'foreigners'. 'Let Kendall, say we, continue to rest by the sea, in a grave decorated with sardine boxes and surmounted by a wooden cross with a tin label. The poet's best monument is his poetry. If *that* doesn't remind the world that he once lived, then let all that belongs to the poet fade and perish utterly.'

Despite the *Bulletin*'s scorn, the monument was unveiled four years after Kendall's death by the governor of the day, Lord Carrington. In their reports of the occasion, journalists emphasised the importance of remembrance as an expression of gratitude or atonement for past wrongs. Large crowds attended the ceremony, in striking contrast to the small attendance at his funeral. The new identity for Kendall as the admired poet was complete. He had a choice location 'high above the cliffs, looking far away out on the placid surface of the blue Pacific', an impressive Italian marble monument rising '25 feet above the adjacent pathway', and an inscription vouching for his many friends who 'loved and admired him'. The poet chosen to summarise the people's feelings was not Kendall himself but Shelley, and the words were appropriate for an alcoholic: 'Awake him not! Surely he takes his fill / Of deep and liquid rest, forgetful of all ill.' The monument and its unveiling was as much a public ceremony to draw attention to the philanthropic deeds of the city's movers

Unveiling the Kendall Memorial, 1886

and shakers, as it was a personal remembrance of Kendall himself. As the *Town and Country Journal* happily recorded on 4 December 1886, 'It will be remembered of the present generation that it did not leave unhonored the last resting place of its favourite poet'. There is possibly no clearer statement of how public memory and history are entwined in funerary monuments.

POLITICAL REMEMBRANCE

Funerary monuments can also make political statements. The Irish monument, also in Waverley Cemetery, commemorates the Irish Rebellion of 1798. The foundation stone was laid in 1898, the centenary of the rebellion, and the remains of Michael Dwyer, the 'Wicklow Chief' who was one of its prominent leaders, along with those of his wife, were transferred to the vault from the Catholic burial ground at Devonshire Street. This event was preceded by a two and a quarter hour funerary procession from St Mary's Cathedral to Waverley Cemetery, with over 4000 participants, and witnessed by 'tens of thousands' more along the streets. The 'immense gathering' took organisers by surprise. The *Daily Telegraph* reported on 23 May 1898 that although the Commemoration Committee had made arrangements to deal with a large concourse of spectators in the cemetery, 'few expected such a monster demonstration, and the result was an unfortunate scrimmage for a sight of the proceedings at the graveside'.

The vault was located prominently in the cemetery near the Pacific Ocean, where, according to the *Sydney Morning Herald*, 'the stillness of the sea lent a touch of natural solemnity to the proceedings'. The ceremony and speeches lasted till dusk. Jostling aside, organisers commended the large crowd of spectators for the 'orderly and decorous behaviour' which they believed 'reflected credit on themselves and on the people of Sydney'.

The memorial, designed by architects Sheerin and Hennessy, was unveiled two years later on 15 April 1900 in front of 'many hundreds of ladies and gentlemen' reported the *Sydney Morning Herald* the next day. Public remembrance is the central motif of the monument. The words 'Remember 98' are carved, in the form of a monogram intertwined with laurel and shamrocks, beneath a Celtic cross. The main inscription emphasises the importance of public memory and commemoration: 'Erected by the Irish People and Sympathisers in Australasia. In Loving Memory of all who Dared and Suffered for Ireland in 1798'. Beneath two

1798 Irish Memorial, Waverley Cemetery

Irish wolfhounds which flank the monument, another inscription exhorts readers not to forget the republican cause. The monument resonates with nationalistic symbolism: the Celtic cross and other Celtic interweavings, shamrocks, Irish harps, Irish wolfhounds and the Round Tower. Such patriotic symbols were fused in the public memory with the republican cause.

The chair of the commemorative committee Dr CW MacCarthy, who unveiled the monument, reminded the crowd of the important role of the monument in defining public memory. The memorial was both a sign of the public's admiration and a site of memory, pilgrimage and patriotism. The Irish Monument has remained a source of community strength, particularly for Irish Catholics, for years and regular commemorative services are still held at the monument.

A SUNDAY PROMENADE

People did not only visit cemeteries to see a particular grave or attend a specific ceremony. The attractive grounds and the prevailing positive attitude to rational recreation in the 19th century, enticed many casual cemetery visitors. Promenading in cemeteries and admiring the monuments became a popular pastime.

Rookwood Necropolis in particular was a favourite resort. Most tourist guidebooks of Sydney recommended Rookwood Necropolis as the principal cemetery, noting its location and size and providing information on the fares and number of funeral trains for the convenience of visitors. *Fuller's Sydney Hand-Book*, published in 1879 just 12 years after the cemetery opened, declared the Necropolis 'is daily becoming more and more worthy to compare with Kensal Green and Pere-Lachaise'. The embellished grounds were described by contemporary newspapers and tourist guidebooks as 'neat', 'tasteful', 'pleasing' and 'consoling' and were highly recommended 'from the mere horticultural standpoint'. But the Necropolis went beyond that. The landscape was 'abound[ing] in dear and high associations while silently preaching homilies which connect themselves with human dignity and pride'. It was, in other words, a sublime landscape not to be missed.

The weekends were particularly popular for cemetery visits. Sunday, being the Sabbath, was seen as an especially appropriate day for a cemetery visit. *Pfahlert's Hotel Visitors' Guide, or, How to Spend a Week in Sydney* (1879) encouraged visitors to join the locals for a Sunday stroll in the cemetery:

> To some people the Cemeteries are objects of interest, and it is no uncommon thing to see crowds thronging the Necropolis at Haslem's Creek, and the other 'Gardens of the Dead', which are so well taken care of, in the vicinity of the metropolis.

Cemeteries were also a favoured meeting place of courting couples. Camperdown Cemetery in Sydney was described as a 'favourite promenade for

Asters in full bloom beside an ornamental pond, 1930s; Rookwood's gardens were a significant drawcard for visitors

young people' on Sundays. Sometimes grave visitation and courtship went hand-in-hand, although not everyone regarded this as appropriate behaviour. In 1926 a man collapsed and died at Rookwood Necropolis after his proposal of marriage was refused. The *Cumberland Argus* reported the sensational news on 20 August 1926 with the headline: 'Drama at Graveside. Tragic Termination of Romantic Courtship'. The tragedy of the whole affair was that the woman intended to marry him. The *Cumberland Argus* continued:

> She did not accept him on the Saturday afternoon because she considered her brother's graveside was not the proper place for such a proposal. But, so far from rejecting him, it was her intention to accept him on the following Monday morning.

Sadly, the woman would now have the melancholy duty to visit two graves.

FACILITIES FOR 'THRONGING CROWDS'

Minutes and reports from cemetery trustees document the development of facilities for visitors. Trustees endeavoured to provide a 'supply of fresh water, places of shelter and sanitary accommodation for visitors'. Garden seats or benches were the simplest addition for the comfort of visitors. But some cemeteries also built summer houses or rest houses, often with small rainwater tanks attached to provide water.

The large number of visitors to cemeteries attracted commercial enterprise on a small and large scale. Local boys took the opportunity to earn a few bob helping visitors find a grave or fetching them water. Hawkers also canvassed for business, touting everything from tombstones to flowers. They pestered and annoyed visitors and disturbed the tranquillity of the cemetery grounds.

From its inception in 1867 Rookwood Necropolis provided lavatories and rest rooms for women as well as men, a telling factor about cemeteries. Public parks in Sydney were not nearly as advanced. In 1902, 34 years after the Necropolis had its first ladies' restroom, the Botanic Gardens was the only public park that provided 'special accommodation for women and children'. And the first female public conveniences on Sydney city streets did not arrive until 1906. In this respect, the cemetery was a public space which catered for the presence of women in a way that the public street and park did not. It demonstrates that large numbers of women visited cemeteries.

Florist and tea rooms at Rookwood Necropolis, 1933

Rookwood Necropolis had tea rooms by the early 20th-century to cater for the weekend crowds. They were a popular meeting place for locals as well as visitors. Today a few modern cemeteries are beginning to reintroduce cafés or tea rooms to provide refreshments for casual visitors as well as to cater for wakes. Such enterprises should not be dismissed as crass marketing; they join a long tradition in catering for cemetery visitors.

The utilisation of the cemetery in the 19th and early 20th-century for both mourning and promenading may seem incongruous to us today. However, this merely reflects our changing values to death, memory and the role of the cemetery as a public cultural institution. Cemeteries were once a place for courting as well as mourning, picnicking as well as weeping. Rookwood Necropolis has been trying to revive public appreciation and interest in their grounds. The cemetery hosts an annual sculpture exhibition, as well as an open day and monthly tours of the grounds hosted by the Friends of Rookwood. Many other cemeteries around Sydney have similarly established friends groups to promote awareness and appreciation of these amazing heritage landscapes. Part of the reason I wrote this book is to encourage people to visit Sydney's cemeteries once more. If you do, you'll be reviving a great Sydney tradition of cemetery tourism and promenading.

TOP 5

CHURCHYARDS

St Paul's Anglican Cemetery, Cobbitty

St Matthew's Anglican Cemetery, Windsor

Ebenezer Uniting Church Cemetery

St Anne's Anglican Cemetery, Ryde

St Thomas' Anglican Cemetery, Enfield

St Paul's Anglican Cemetery, Cobbitty

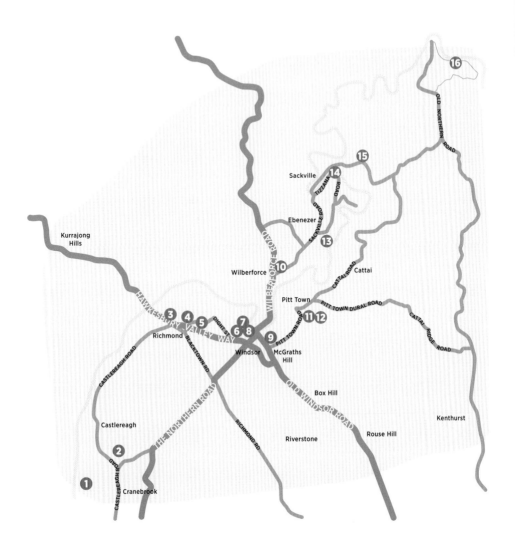

Opposite Castlereagh Cemetery

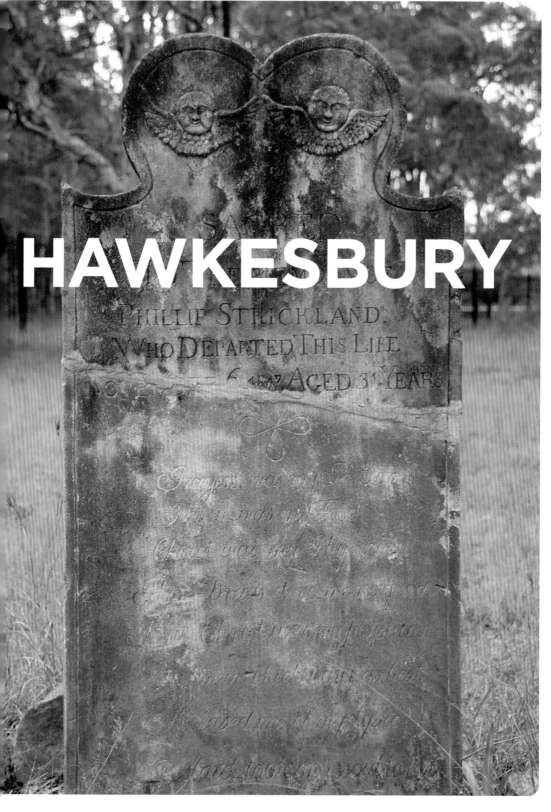

HAWKESBURY

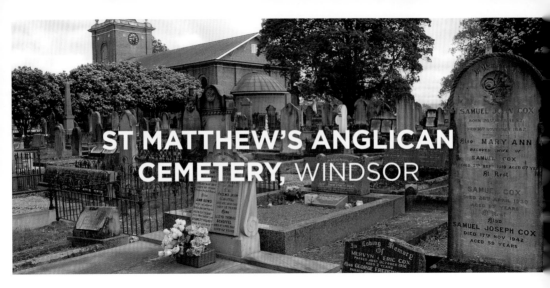

ST MATTHEW'S ANGLICAN CEMETERY, WINDSOR

MOSES STREET, CORNER GREENWAY CRESCENT, WINDSOR

Burials: 1810–1999

St Matthew's Anglican Cemetery is a well-known historic site. If you have not yet visited, you should add it to your cemeteries bucket list. Windsor, the administrative centre for this fertile agricultural region, is one of the five Hawkesbury towns established by Governor Lachlan Macquarie – the others are Richmond, Castlereagh, Pitt Town and Wilberforce. The cemetery's gravestones are like pages from a history book documenting our local and national history.

Macquarie granted land for the church and burial ground in 1810. The red brick Georgian church, designed by convict architect Francis Greenway was completed in 1820. Sitting on a rise overlooking McQuade Park, the church is a favourite of artists and acclaimed as one of the most beautiful in Australia. The gravestones envelop the church in true churchyard style. The early headstones are not located all together but can be found all around. You won't be surprised to learn that the church and cemetery are on the State Heritage Register.

The earliest marked burial is emancipist Andrew Thompson, who died on 22 October 1810 and the governor himself erected the ledger stone in 1813. An effusive inscription, some two long paragraphs, extolls the virtues of Thompson; unfortunately, these days it is almost impossible to read.

SACRED to the MEMORY

of

ANDREW THOMPSON ESQUIRE

Justice of the Peace and Chief Magistrate of
the Hawkesbury, a Native of Scotland
Who at the age of 17 Years was sent to this Country who
from the time of his arrival he distinguished himself by
the most persevering industry and diligent attention
to the commands of his Superiors. By these means he
raised himself to a state of respectability and affluence
which enabled him to indulge the generosity of his nature
in assisting his Fellow Creatures in distress more
particularly in the Calamitous Floods of the river
Hawkesbury in the Years 1806 and 1809 where at the
immediate risque of his life and permanent injury
of his health he exerted himself each time during
three successive Days and Nights in saving the lives
and Properties of numbers who but for him must
have perished.
Inconsequence of Mr. Thompson's
good Conduct Governor Macquarie appointed him
a Justice of the Peace. This act which restored him to
that rank in Society which he had lost made so deep
an impression on his grateful Heart as to induce him
to bequeath the Governor one-fourth of his Fortune.
This most useful and valuable Man closed his
Earthly career on the 22nd Day of October 1810, at His

House at Windsor of which he was the principal Founder
in the 37th Year of his age, with the Hope of Eternity.
From respect and esteem for the Memory
of the deceased,
this Monument is erected by
LACHLAN MACQUARIE GOVERNOR
of New South Wales
A.D. 1813.

There are at least a dozen people who came out on the First Fleet buried in the cemetery; their gravestones bear the distinctive little commemorative plaques of the Fellowship of the First Fleeters. Clergy, military, magistrates, farmers; all can be found in this historic spot.

An imposing marble monument, located within a circular garden bed and columbarium, dominates the southern side of the cemetery along Moses Street. Mayor McQuade erected it in 1882 to commemorate his daughter. The McQuades were a prominent family in Windsor and give their name to the large park opposite.

Look out for the large vault to famous star-gazer John Tebbutt (d.1916) and his family, which has marble celestial spheres depicting the celestial co-ordinates on all four corners of the vault. A marble cypress tree with a broken branch, surmounting a large marble pedestal, rich in symbolism, is one of the most unusual monuments in the cemetery. It commemorates the Pitman family.

The Greenway-designed church was completed in 1820

Violent deaths are also recorded, such as William Green (d.1826) who was 'barberrously Mur-dred in the Execution of his Duty as Cunstable' and George Spinks (d.1869) who was killed with an axe. His epitaph records 'His death was not in battle, Nor any lawful strife, But by a vile assassin, Deprived of his life'.

A fair amount of wrought-iron and cast-iron surrounds survive. Delicate wrought-iron arrows surround the rare sandstone cross and ribbon monument to the young child Mildred Fitzpatrick (d.1872). A tall wrought-iron fence and double gate protect the Terry family altar tomb.

NOTABLE BURIALS

- Andrew Thompson (c. 1773–1810), chief constable, farmer and businessman
- Thomas Arndell (1753–1821), First Fleet surgeon, magistrate and landholder
- William Cox (1764–1837), military officer, roadmaker and builder, namesake of Cox's River
- John Tebbutt (1834–1916), astronomer

MORE INFORMATION

- *St Matthews church of England Windsor, NSW, Parish register 1810 to 1856: A complete transcription*, Lake Macquarie Family History Group, Teralba, 2003.
- *St Matthews church of England Windsor, NSW, Parish register 1951 to 2000: baptisms & burials*, Lake Macquarie Family History Group, Teralba, 2009.
- Reverend LM Abbott, *St Matthew's Windsor: A Short Guide to the Church and its History*, The Church, Windsor, 2002.
- Ron Withington, *Dispatched Downunder: Tracing the Resting Places of the First Fleeters*, self-published, Wentworth Falls, 2013.
- Explore The Hawkesbury series, 'Hawkesbury Cemeteries', Hawkesbury City Council website, 2016, <www.hawkesbury.nsw.gov.au/__data/assets/pdf_file/0016/19303/Hawkesbury-Cemeteries.pdf>.

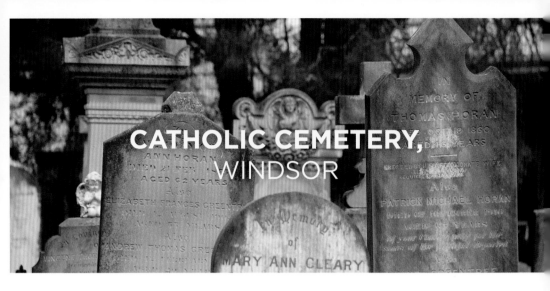

CATHOLIC CEMETERY,
WINDSOR

GEORGE STREET, CORNER HAWKESBURY
VALLEY WAY, WINDSOR

Burials: 1833–1970 (existing burial rights)

At the base of McQuade Park, bounded by a couple of busy roads, you can find one of the earliest surviving Catholic cemeteries in Sydney. This would once have been a prominent yet peaceful spot on the edge of the agricultural town of Windsor.

The earliest recorded burial is John Pendergast, who died on 27 January 1833 and was buried two days later. His inscription is recorded on the flat top ledger of an imposing sandstone altar tomb with marble inscription panels. An earlier gravestone to Patrick Cullen, who died in 1822, is a reinterment from 1840. There are many other headstones dating from the 1830s and 1840s dotted through the cemetery.

It is worthwhile wandering among the sandstone headstones for the excellent symbolic carvings, including the Madonna lily, seraphs, angels and cavalry crosses. An upright semicircular cast-iron stele with an ivy border is a rare survivor in a Sydney cemetery.

The local council was gazetted trustee of the cemetery in 1970 and proposed to convert the cemetery into a rest park in 1978, preserving a few headstones. Thank goodness opposition quashed this idea, so we can still ramble among the headstones and enjoy this early cemetery.

TIP

Make sure you pay a visit to the Hawkesbury Regional Museum while you are in Windsor. The modern, purpose-built museum features a range of permanent and temporary history exhibitions.

NOTABLE BURIALS

- James Augustine Cunneen (1826–1889), farmer, politician and land agent

MORE INFORMATION

- Jonathan Auld and Michelle Nichols, 'Windsor Catholic Cemetery', Hawkesbury on the Net: Cemetery Register website, 2006, <www.hawkesbury.net.au/cemetery/windsor_catholic>.
- Graham Wilson, *Windsor Roman Catholic Cemetery, Heritage Plan of Management*, Archaeological & Heritage Management Solutions, for NSW Roads & Traffic Authority, June 2006.

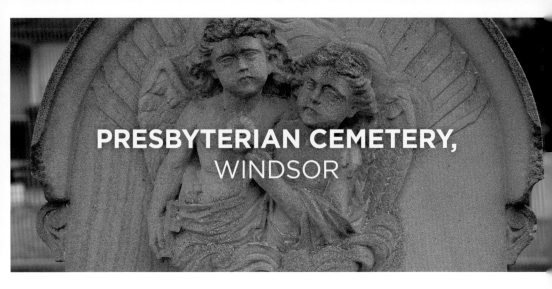

PRESBYTERIAN CEMETERY,
WINDSOR

8 CHURCH STREET, SOUTH WINDSOR

Burials: 1838–present

Windsor's Presbyterian Cemetery is tucked away beside the railway station. It has an unassuming air of forgetfulness, although the cemetery is still technically in use. A relatively small pocket of marked graves is clustered in ten rows near Church Street. The cemetery has been occasionally fenced in the past to protect it from the minister's grazing horse, but it is currently unfenced making it feel vulnerable to vandalism.

The cemetery, also known as the Scotch Cemetery, has been in use since the 1830s. The earliest burials were apparently made on the low ground near the road and many were unmarked. There are about 230 burials recorded on headstones, although there could be many more. Some of the earliest burials commemorated on a stone are to Robert Smith (d.1852) and his children Mary (d.1838) and James (d.1839). Robert's original headstone was replaced by a later marble headstone commemorating

James Smith (d.1907). In 2005 two early grave plots were discovered among the grass and shrubs near the railway line, away from the majority of marked graves: the Walker vault and a headstone to Henry McCourt (d.1858). Unfortunately, I missed these on my visit; don't you do the same.

There are several prominent Windsor families represented here, such as the Cadell, Cross, Dick and Walker families. Granite monuments mark a number of graves, including a grey granite obelisk to the Reverend Matthew Adam (d.1863). Look out for the pair of exquisitely carved angels holding a Madonna lily on the sandstone headstone to wife and husband, Isabella and William Nicholls.

The most outstanding monument is the cast-iron pedestal with urns and a thin column. The memorial marks the graves of Mary Ann Robertson (d.1895) and two of her sons, James (d.1885) and Donald (d.1889). This grave marker is one of a kind; I've not seen another in my Sydney cemetery visits. It was almost certainly made by Mary Ann's husband, Donald Robertson, who had an extensive blacksmiths and wheelwright business on George Street, Windsor. Robertson was probably also responsible for many of the iron surrounds that enclose the tombs in this modest but endearing cemetery.

NOTABLE BURIALS

- Robert Dick (1821–1898), Windsor's first mayor 1871
- John 'Jock' Stewart, junior (1831–1904), veterinary surgeon
- William Walker (1828–1908), solicitor and politician, founding president of the Windsor School of Arts 1861, inaugural alderman Windsor Council, mayor 1878

MORE INFORMATION
- Jonathan Auld & Michelle Nichols, 'Windsor Presbyterian Cemetery, Windsor', Hawkesbury on the Net: Cemetery Register website, 2005, <hawkesbury.net.au/cemetery/windsor_presbyterian>.

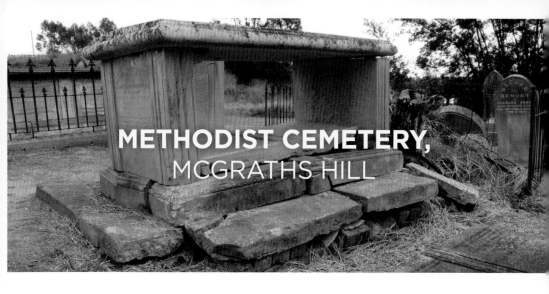

METHODIST CEMETERY,
MCGRATHS HILL

HIGH STREET, CORNER CHARLES STREET, MCGRATHS HILL

Burials: 1851–present

This tiny little cemetery tucked away off High Street is a remnant of the early settlement of McGraths Hill. It is on the edge of the plateau before crossing the South Creek flats to Windsor. The cemetery retains its rural setting and there are views west over paddocks to Windsor. Originally you could see the Methodist Church from the cemetery. Today traffic thunders along nearby Windsor Road.

Sandstone headstones that face east predominate. There are three altar tombs and only six marble headstones. The Wesleyan trustees were established in the 1850s and the first marked burial appears to be Rebecca Cavanough (d.1851). However there are a few memorial stones with death dates that predate the burial ground's establishment. This cemetery is one of the oldest surviving Wesleyan Methodist burial grounds in Australia; along with those in Cherrybrook and Upper Castlereagh.

Some of the inscriptions record

tragic deaths. George Frederick Robinson was just 20 years old when he 'drowned while bathing in the Hawkesbury' in November 1851. The Reverend Peter Turner, who was minister and missionary for some 40 years, is buried here.

NOTABLE BURIALS

- Reverend Peter Turner (c.1803–1873), minister and early missionary for the Wesleyan Methodist Missionary Society to Samoa and Tonga, 1831–1853
- William Farmer Linsley (c.1831–1903), soldier and mayor of Windsor

MORE INFORMATION

- Jonathan Auld, Michelle Nichols, Joyce Nichols & Dylan Lloyd, 'McGraths Hill Cemetery, McGraths Hill', Hawkesbury on the Net: Cemetery Register website, 2008, <www.hawkesbury.net.au/cemetery/mcgraths_hill>.

ST PETER'S ANGLICAN CEMETERY, RICHMOND

WINDSOR STREET, RICHMOND

Burials: 1811–present

The Anglican cemetery at Richmond, another Macquarie town, is located opposite St Peter's Anglican Church and on the edge of the ridge overlooking the lowlands. The central pathway of the cemetery aligns visually with the church door. This is another early church built in 1836 by local Penrith builder James Atkinson. Although relatively small, you will want at least an hour to explore this fascinating early cemetery. It is the second burial ground established in the Hawkesbury, after St Matthew's in Windsor.

The gravestones are densely packed together. The earlier headstones are generally to be found to the west of the pathway; modern memorials are further east. A memorial wall for cremated remains stands at the end of the central pathway. The most prominent monument in the cemetery is the marble angel on two pedestals that marks Edward Hordern senior's family grave plot.

The most unusual grave marker that I encountered was a glazed ceramic marker featuring a heart and arum lilies with a marble inscription panel; there was even ceramic grave furniture to match. The memorial is signed by Robert William Farlow, a local Richmond man, and commemorates his grandson Francis Robert Brazzale, who died in 1928 aged 4 months.

The cemetery was in use by 1811, but the earliest death recorded on a gravestone is George Rouse (d.1809), the five-year-old son of Richard Rouse. There are many people associated with the First and Second Fleets buried in St Peter's Cemetery.

Convict Margaret Catchpole is buried here, but her grave is unmarked.

The Hawkesbury was one of the earliest districts to be settled and some of the headstones record the violence experienced in this frontier place. Both Edward Pugh and Thomas Cheshire were murdered. Joseph Hobson 'lost his life on the 7th day of July / In the year of our Lord 1816 by the natives / or Aboregines of this colony / Aged 46 years'.

Although many of the inscriptions are weathered and difficult to read, there are many examples of early 19th-century epitaphs.

Unusual ceramic memorial to Francis Brazzale, designed by the infant's grandfather

NOTABLE BURIALS

- Margaret Catchpole (1762–1819), convict and pioneer (unmarked grave)
- Thomas Hobby (c.1776–1833), soldier, farmer settler and assistant on the Great Western Road
- William Faithful (1774–1847), soldier and settler
- Richard Rouse (1774–1852), public servant and settler, of Rouse Hill house and farm
- George Matcham Pitt (1814–1896), stock and station agent

MORE INFORMATION
- Yvonne Browning, *St Peter's Richmond: the early people and burials 1791–1855*, self-published, Mullion Creek, 1990.

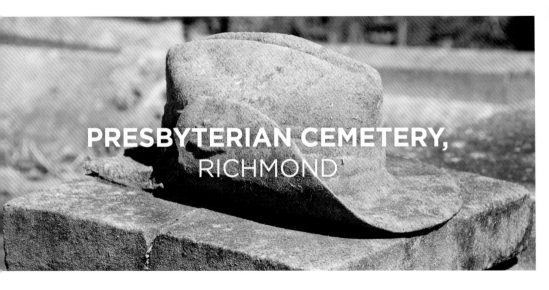

PRESBYTERIAN CEMETERY, RICHMOND

JERSEY STREET, INTERSECTION OF BOWMAN AND DIGHT STREETS, RICHMOND

Burials: 1863–present

This little Presbyterian cemetery on the outskirts of Richmond retains its rural setting with scenic views across Richmond Bottoms (the lowlands). The earliest marked burial is infant, Elizabeth Perry (d.1863). An impressive number of wrought and iron grave surrounds survive.

The most prominent memorial is the white painted Bowman vault. George Bowman (d.1878) was a prominent and faithful man in the district, who endowed the distinctive Presbyterian Free Church in West Market Street (constructed 1845). Generations of Bowmans have lived in Richmond and in the Hunter Valley.

Private family monuments commemorate two local recruits who fought and died at Gallipoli: Captain William Bowman Douglass and Corporal Maurice Cameron Fergusson. Look out for the slouch hat on Fergusson's memorial. Douglass is recorded on the lengthy trachyte scroll.

NOTABLE BURIALS

- George Bowman (1795–1878), landholder, politician and benefactor Richmond Presbyterian Church
- Reverend James Cameron (1826–1905), minister at St Andrew's Richmond for 50 years

MORE INFORMATION

- Jonathan Auld & Michelle Nichols, 'Richmond Presbyterian Cemetery – Richmond', Hawkesbury on the Net: Cemetery Register website, 2012, <www.hawkesbury.net.au/cemetery/richmond_presbyterian/index.html>.
- Linda Stubbs & Rex Stubbs (eds), *Gravestones of the Hawkesbury*, vol. 1, Pitt Town Research & Preservation Society, Windsor, 1982.

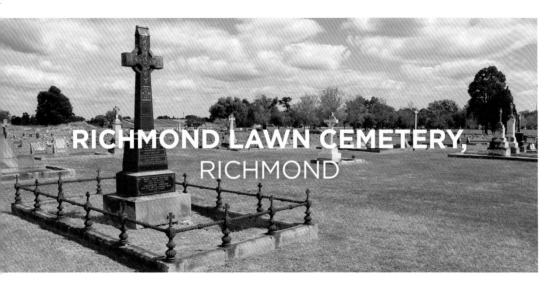

RICHMOND LAWN CEMETERY, RICHMOND

CLARENDON STREET, CORNER DIGHT STREET, RICHMOND

Burials: 1902–present

Richmond Lawn Cemetery is located on the outskirts of town next to the RAAF base. This is definitely the place to bury a plane-spotter. When drills are running, planes take off right beside it.

The 6.5 hectares of land was dedicated as a general cemetery in 1893 on the Clarendon common. Initially there was not much demand for burials and the cemetery was not fenced until 1902. The first burial recorded in the newspapers was 11-year-old Jane Williamson, who died of pneumonia, and was buried in the Catholic section on 11 October 1902, following a widely attended funeral. Archbishop Kelly subsequently blessed the Catholic section on 22 December 1902.

The oldest headstones in the cemetery, to be found in the Catholic and Methodist sections, are easy to spot as they stick out, literally. A marble Celtic cross with a three-step base marks the grave of parish priest Father O'Brien in the Catholic section. Father O'Brien's funeral attracted a large gathering, with the *Nepean Times* observing on 2 October 1915, that 'judging by the numbers present … all Richmond seemed to mourn the loss of a father and a friend'.

Some deaths recorded on headstones predate the cemetery, including teacher Thomas Sullivan (d.1873) and Richmond's first postmaster William Price (d.1877).

Overall the cemetery is remarkably plain. The most impressive monument is the black granite Celtic cross which marks the Waters family graves. Michael Waters (d.1906) was a farmer and horse breeder at Richmond Bottoms. The most poignant gravestone is to little Laurie Elizabeth Mahon (d.1920) who died just before her eighth birthday. Her innocence and purity is symbolised by the lily of the valley carved on her child-sized marble headstone.

The lawn areas are colourful as many of the plaques set in the ground are decorated with artificial flowers. Richmond Lawn Cemetery is still operational and is managed by Hawkesbury City Council.

A small section of the cemetery has been dedicated as a war cemetery. It is fully enclosed by a high brick pier and palisade fence with a separate entrance on the Dight Street perimeter. The war cemetery was established during the Second World War when the Richmond aerodrome was a major base for several squadrons of the Royal Australian Air Force (Numbers 3, 6, 9 and 22). It is a little oasis within Richmond Lawn Cemetery.

NOTABLE BURIALS

- William Price (1792–1877), first postmaster at Richmond
- William Sullivan (c.1830–1906), of 'Osier Bank', bootmaker, inaugural alderman Richmond Borough Council (1872), JP and magistrate
- Father Michael Edward O'Brien (1858–1915), parish priest of Richmond

MORE INFORMATION
- Jonathan Auld, 'Richmond War Cemetery', Register of War Memorials in NSW website, 2014, <www.warmemorialsregister.nsw.gov.au/content/richmond-war-cemetery>.

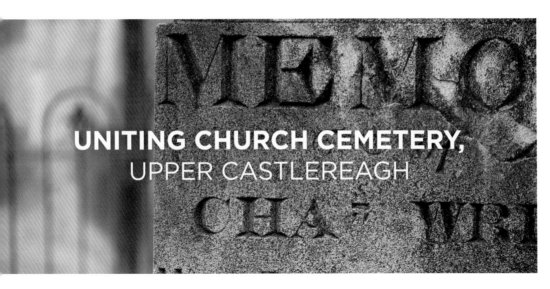

UNITING CHURCH CEMETERY,
UPPER CASTLEREAGH

297-305 OLD CASTLEREAGH ROAD, UPPER CASTLEREAGH

Burials: 1836–present

The first Wesleyan church in Australia was built here in 1817. The story goes that John Lees, a New South Wales Corps soldier and Castlereagh settler, built the chapel in thanksgiving after he survived a snake bite, using part of his 1804 land grant. The close shave with death apparently spurred him on to repent of his dissolute ways. A brick chapel replaced the original church in 1847, but this historic spot is a fragile reminder of early settlement in the Castlereagh area.

John Lees is buried in the cemetery south of the church beside the old schoolhouse. You can see his grave singled out near the gate entrance. His headstone records that he 'departed this life after seven years severe affliction' on 28 August 1836. Lees was originally buried in Castlereagh Cemetery; his remains were reinterred within the grounds of the chapel he founded on 15 October 1921.

This is a pleasant little church cemetery, which now sits beside the Penrith Lakes Scheme. It is quiet and idyllic, blue wrens twitter and flit among the hedges. There are a variety of sandstone headstones dating from the 19th century and granite slab and desk monuments up to the mid-20th-century. Unlike many early churchyards, the graves here face both east and west, no doubt an economical measure to squeeze as many burials as possible into the tiny ground. The earliest marked grave, aside from Lees the chapel founder, is Alfred, the infant son of Henry Gorman, who died in 1846.

Some of the inscriptions are dramatically designed with a large arching 'Sacred', such as (another) John Lees (d.1848), Sarah Lees (d.1855), Ann Elliott (d.1850) and Charles Wright (d.1852). A delicate widow weeping beside a classical urn and framed by a grapevine is subtly carved on the grave of Margaret Furness (d.1872) and Joseph Furness (d.1873). The local Colless and Parker families are well represented. Look out for the marble column commemorating John Rolston (d.1891) 'erected by his friends and fellow employees on the Western Line'.

NOTABLE BURIALS

- John Lees (1771–1836), benefactor of first Wesleyan Chapel in Australia

MORE INFORMATION
- Fay Woodgate & Kay Radford, *Heritage photographic collection, Upper Castlereagh Methodist Cemetery*, Nepean Family History Society, 1993.

Chapel builder John Lees' (d.1836) grave was moved here in 19

CASTLEREAGH CEMETERY, CASTLEREAGH

CHURCH LANE, CORNER WILCHARD ROAD, CASTLEREAGH

Burials: 1811–1973

Castlereagh is one of the five Macquarie towns. The cemetery, consecrated by 1811, is all that remains of the early town. There was little reason to come here in the early 19th century. Few took up their town blocks, even after the floods of 1811 and 1816, preferring to stay on their farms near the river. The church and schoolhouse, where local children were educated, and the burial ground were its only attractions. The cemetery has a forsaken atmosphere, the gravestones of early settlers scattered among the gums. It is appealing and picturesque.

The cemetery is revered for its associations with the early land grantees and residents of the failed township. The Friends of Castlereagh Cemetery have put a lot of effort over the last 20 years into restoring headstones and reclaiming the cemetery from the bush.

The cemetery was clearly in use from 1811. The 'Register Book for Burials at the Parish Church of Hawkesbury New South Wales', maintained by the Reverend Robert Cartwright at Windsor, records a handful of burials in 1811, 1812 and 1814. These graves are unmarked.

The earliest marked burial is 34-year-old Mary Ann Smith. The parish register at St Matthews Windsor records that she died suddenly 20 May 1814 and was buried two days later. Mary speaks to us through her epitaph, inscribed neatly on the wide sandstone headstone, a word of warning:

Good people all as you Pass by
As you are Now so once was I
And as I Am so must you be
Therefore Prepare to follow me

Plenty of convicts and former convicts were buried here; even the Reverend Henry Fulton came out as a convict, implicated in the Irish Rebellion of 1798 and charged with sedition. And yes, there are some First Fleeters; just look for the little plaques. Some prominent Castlereagh families buried here include the McHenrys, the Ryans, the Fields and the Tindales.

There are so many early headstones to be spotted. I was particularly taken with the pair of chubby-cheeked, mischievous seraphs that crown the headstone of Phillip Strickland (d.1817). Also look out for the headstone of Edward Field (d.1846), which is adorned with an anvil. Many of the graves are clustered in family groups, some with traditional grave fencing around the larger family plot.

A couple of early sandstone post-and-chain grave surrounds survive.

The cemetery was in use throughout the 19th and much of the 20th-century. It is now managed by Penrith City Council, but closed to burials.

NOTABLE BURIALS

- Reverend Henry Fulton (1761–1840), clergyman

MORE INFORMATION
- Penrith City Library, 'Castlereagh Cemetery', Penrith City Local History website, 2016, <penrithhistory.com/places/castlereagh-cemetery>.
- Kevin Lennox & Roma Waldron, 'Castlereagh Cemetery', Australian Cemeteries Index website, 2011, <austcemindex.com/cemetery?cemid=819>.
- *The Pioneers of Castlereagh Anglican Cemetery*, The Friends of Castlereagh Cemetery, Granville, 1995.

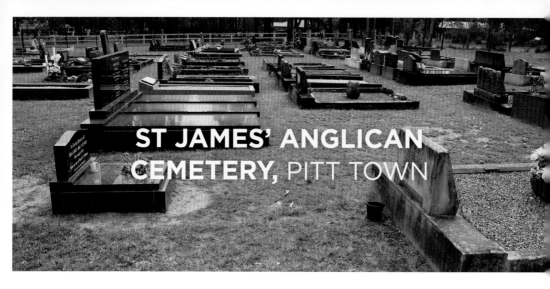

ST JAMES' ANGLICAN CEMETERY, PITT TOWN

OLD PITT TOWN ROAD, PITT TOWN

Burials: 1825–present

Governor Macquarie planned Pitt Town as the refuge town from the floods. The original site selected to the east on Nelson Common was too far from the farms on the river, however, and so in 1815 Macquarie relocated the town to its present site. It has remained a rural village since that time.

The evolution and early use of the Pitt Town burial grounds is a bit mysterious. The *Sydney Gazette* on 11 May 1811 reported that the cemetery at Pitt Town had been 'lately consecrated'. Where was this cemetery? Nobody knows, as no map survives of the town as originally laid out. A burial ground, about 4000 square metres in size, was included in the plan of new Pitt Town, on Eldon and Liverpool streets. Presumably it was in use from at least 1815 to 1828; stories of headstones being purloined and used in local gardens swirl around. By 1828 Surveyor E Knapp's plan of the township shows a 'new' burial ground, similar in size and orientation to the former one, immediately to the east of the Church of England glebe land. This is the site of the present St James' Anglican Cemetery.

There is a good selection of early headstones dating from the 1820s and 1830s. These are plain, with little ornamentation, but with interesting (and quirky) inscribed lettering. Most can be found on the western perimeter of the cemetery.

The earliest deaths recorded on a headstone that I found was a double headstone for infants John and Sarah Ryan (d.1823 and 1824). Five-year-old Elizabeth Fleming has a similar headstone with a Georgian fan motif and italicised script; she died in 1825. Whether these burials occurred in the cemetery or were moved from the old burial ground is difficult to determine. Regardless, they are a fascinating historic record of this peaceful district. The Hobbs, Jurd and Stubbs families are among the early settlers of the Hawkesbury buried here.

The headstone of Ann Smallwood (d.1838), closer to the centre of the cemetery, demonstrates the illiteracy and mixed skills of early stonemasons. The inscription and epitaph features uneven spacing of words, both upper and lower case lettering within the same word, a correction over-incised to insert a missed word and small letters snuck in to correct spelling mistakes. The epitaph features the young mother Ann speaking from the grave:

Smallwood (d.1838)

> Farewell dear friends
> Seven Babes adieu. My
> Soul I hope to heaven
> Has flew, where I hope
> We shall meet again,
> Where Christ for ever
> Lives and reigns.

A number of other inscriptions also demonstrate a level of inexperience and naivety, including the headstones of Daniel Jurd (d.1833), Daniel Buckridge (d.1834) and William Gyatt (d.1858). The guiding lines for lettering are clearly visible on Mary Payton's headstone (d.1837).

The cemetery is well cared for, has a modern entrance gateway and is still in use. It contains predominantly slab and desk monuments, reflecting closer residential subdivision in the 20th-century and Pitt Town's growing population. Residential development is starting to encroach on the rural setting of the cemetery, surrounded by eucalypts.

MORE INFORMATION

- Linda Stubbs & Rex Stubbs (eds), *Gravestones of the Hawkesbury*, vol. 1, Pitt Town Research & Preservation Society, Windsor, 1982.
- Explore The Hawkesbury series, 'Hawkesbury Cemeteries', Hawkesbury City Council website, 2016, <www.hawkesbury.nsw.gov.au/__data/assets/pdf_file/0016/19303/Hawkesbury-Cemeteries.pdf>.

Left Daniel Jurd (d.1833)

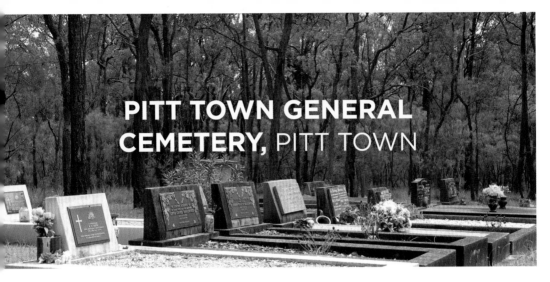

PITT TOWN GENERAL CEMETERY, PITT TOWN

524 OLD STOCK ROUTE ROAD, PITT TOWN

Burials: 1901–present

Pitt Town General Cemetery is located off the Old Stock Route Road. Surrounded by bushland, what appears to be a modest little cemetery, is actually a small portion of a much larger planned site.

Land for the general cemetery at Pitt Town was resumed in 1889 and, after some false starts and delay, dedicated on 27 November 1895. Nine hectares were set aside, divided up for Church of England, Roman Catholic, Jewish, Independent, Wesleyan, Presbyterian, Primitive Methodist and a general burial area. A central avenue was planned and land on either side of the denominational areas reserved for expansion.

Seemingly only the Wesleyan and Presbyterian areas have been cleared and used for burials. There are less than 50 burials in this rural cemetery and they all date from the 20th-century. The earliest marked burial is to Anna Pauline Hanckel. A simple red granite plaque on a desk and kerbstone records the 26-year-old's death on 25 August 1901. A columbarium has been added at the back of the cleared Presbyterian portion. The cemetery is still in use and much of the cemetery remains as bushland.

MORE INFORMATION

• Jonathan Auld & Carolyn Auld, 'Pitt Town Cemetery', Hawkesbury on the Net: Cemetery Register website, 2004, <www.hawkesbury.net.au/cemetery/pitt_town>.

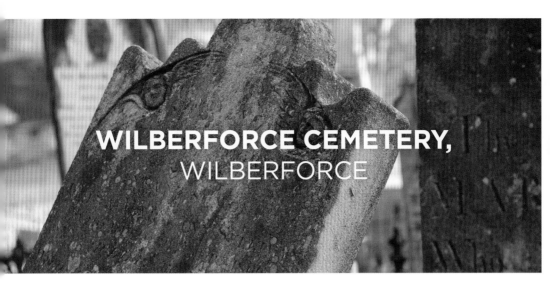

WILBERFORCE CEMETERY,
WILBERFORCE

OLD SACKVILLE ROAD, WILBERFORCE

Burials: 1811–present (existing burial rights)

This was one of the five burial grounds that Governor Macquarie established in the Hawkesbury in 1811. Wilberforce Cemetery is located on the outskirts of the town's original rectangular grid layout, next to the land dedicated for a church and school. The ground is sloping and gravestones tumble down the hillside, divided by a central avenue. There is much variation in the alignment of graves, an indication of the ad hoc manner in which

burials occurred for many years. This is part of the cemetery's charm.

The first three burials in the cemetery were a consequence of a triple drowning in the Hawkesbury River in December 1811: convict Joseph Ware, emancipist James Hamilton and soldier John Tunstal all lie in unmarked graves. The earliest marked burials are Margaret Chaseling (d.1815) listed on an altar tomb and Antony Richardson (d.1816) whose stone is the earliest

grave marker in its original position.

An amble around this cemetery reveals many early graves from the 1810s to the 1830s. The simple headstones with blacked incised lettering are signs of early craftsmanship with some lovely examples of typography and script. The cemetery has seven First Fleeters (arrived 1788), fifteen people who arrived on the Second Fleet (1790), and a further twelve from the Third Fleet (1791).

You can see a handful of altar tombs and a rare table top tomb on the verge of collapse here, and assorted family groupings. Seek out the four headstones of the Buttsworth family, each with different style and symbols: a pair of chubby seraphs, a broken flower, an open book, and Gothic pinnacles. The deep bas-relief carving of an angel on Sarah Turnbull's grave

(d.1886) is an impressive headstone that almost feels like a portrait.

The cemetery is still in use for those who have burial rights and is actually much more crowded than it looks. There are over 1300 known interments, at least a third of them are unmarked. The modern monumentation tends to be lower in style, slabs and desks. The once isolated cemetery is now surrounded by residential subdivision.

TIP

While you're here, wander across to St John's Church (1859) and school (1819), the Hawkesbury's oldest surviving schoolhouse. A single gravestone to John Howorth (d.1804) has been relocated here from the river bank.

NOTABLE BURIALS

- Matthew James Everingham (1768–1817), convict, settler and constable, drowned
- Thomas Rose (c.1754–1833), farmer and respected early settler of Wilberforce

MORE INFORMATION

- Cathy McHardy & Nicholas McHardy, *Sacred to the Memory: A study of Wilberforce Cemetery*, self-published, Kurrajong, 2003.
- *Wilberforce Cemetery Conservation Management Plan*, Hubert Architects and Ian Jack Heritage Consulting Pty Ltd, for Hawkesbury City Council, April 2008.
- Cathy McHardy & Nicholas McHardy, 'Wilberforce Cemetery, Wilberforce', Hawkesbury on the Net: Cemetery Register website, 2003, <www.hawkesbury. net.au/cemetery/wilberforce>.

SACKVILLE NORTH GENERAL CEMETERY, SACKVILLE NORTH

437 SACKVILLE FERRY ROAD, SACKVILLE NORTH

Burials: 1921–present

The government set aside Sackville North Cemetery on 2 December 1899. It is a modern 20th-century general cemetery and is also known as Maroota General Cemetery and Sackville Cemetery. About 1.6 hectares of land has been dedicated for burial purposes, with Anglicans, Wesleyans and Roman Catholics each allocated 4000 square metres, and the remainder split between Presbyterians and unsectarians. But only a small

proportion of the cemetery is in use; it currently has less than 50 burials and no denominational distinctions.

The graves are set back from the road and enclosed by eucalypts, reinforcing an isolated bushland atmosphere. A modern concrete fence imitates a timber post-and-rail fence to blend into the rural setting. The majority of grave markers are modest slab and desk memorials. There is some variation in the grave orientation suggesting earlier burials were ad hoc and the surveying of rows of grave plots came later.

The last burial was in 2001, and the cemetery is now the responsibility of the Hills Shire Council.

MORE INFORMATION
- Michael Brookhouse, 'Sackville Cemetery', Australian Cemeteries Index website, 2011, <austcemindex.com/cemetery?cemid=834>.

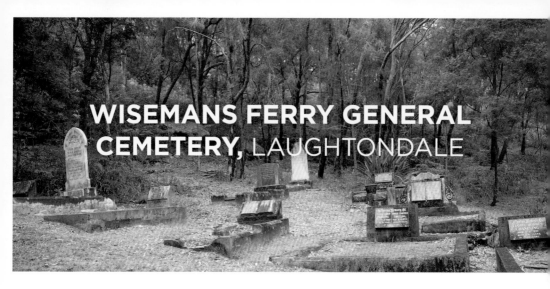

WISEMANS FERRY GENERAL CEMETERY, LAUGHTONDALE

SINGLETON ROAD, LAUGHTONDALE

Burials: 1826–present

Wisemans Ferry is named after Solomon Wiseman, one of the early Hawkesbury settlers, who came to the district in 1817. The area was originally known as Lower Portland Head. Laughtondale, named after another early settler, is downstream. This historic cemetery is approximately 3 kilometres east of Laughtondale village, close to the river.

The burial ground was informally established by 1826. When the ground was formally surveyed in 1833 it had already been fenced. Originally the Church of England managed the cemetery. At the end of the 19th century members of the local progress association lobbied the government for a general cemetery and the existing burial ground was extended to provide space for Catholics and Wesleyans, along with some unallotted ground. The cemetery was formally dedicated on 22 August 1900.

You need a sturdy pair of boots to explore this cemetery properly. When you first clap eyes on it, you see the original portion. Gates on either side of the cemetery indicate the roadway surveyed between sections, but it is unformed. Look up: above on the steep slope are the Catholic and Wesleyan burials. Go to the right and clamber up the hill to see these graves.

The earliest burials and headstones are found in the original part of the cemetery. The earliest burial date on a gravestone is Jane Wiseman, who died in 1821. However, Jane was originally buried near the Inn and the marble headstone dates from 1884 when she was reinterred here, along with her husband Solomon (d.1838). The earliest original gravestone you will find

commemorates the infant Mary Ann Rose, who died in 1828. The naively spaced, rickety lettering on this simple sandstone headstone, along with this early death, is a poignant reminder of the isolation of this early community, despite the river connections.

A number of gravestones document life on the river. William Henry McKay (d.1906) was 'Hawkesbury River's First Engineer' and his headstone features a ship's propeller. George Books (d.1934) is recorded as a 'Master Mariner' on the grey granite obelisk that marks his grave. His family were mariners and boat builders who ran a punt across the Macdonald River. John Laughton's marble headstone up in the Wesleyan

section has a ship's anchor prominently carved on the pediment; there are at least 20 Laughtons buried here.

This peaceful cemetery on the edge of Sydney has many intriguing memorials to make for an absorbing visit.

TIP

Make a day of it and go for a walk along part of the Great North Road or, for the less energetic, have some lunch at the Wisemans Ferry Inn.

NOTABLE BURIALS

- Solomon Wiseman (1777–1838), convict, merchant, publican and operator of Wisemans ferry
- Peter Hibbs (1761–1847), English sailor and naval master, seaman on the *Sirius* and later the *Norfolk* when Bass and Flinders circumnavigated Tasmania

MORE INFORMATION
- Diana Wood, *Not lost but gone before: Wisemans Ferry cemetery*, Dhurug and Lower Hawkesbury Historical Society, Wisemans Ferry, 2000.

Jane (d.1821) and Solomon Wiseman's (d.1838) remains were moved here in 1884

HAWKESBURY

ST THOMAS' ANGLICAN CEMETERY, SACKVILLE REACH

616 TIZZANA ROAD, SACKVILLE REACH

Burials: 1827–1987

This small rural cemetery close to the Hawkesbury River marks a second wave of burial grounds that were established as the Hawkesbury settlement consolidated. The earliest burial recorded on an inscription is on the Tuckerman family altar tomb. Little Emma Tuckerman died in 1827.

The cemetery contains many interesting graves, including some local Aboriginal people. Martha Everingham, a local elder, was 80 years of age when she died in 1926 and was buried here in an unmarked grave. Several of the Barber family are also memorialised. You'll spot the names of other well-known Hawkesbury settler families: Turnbull, Chaseling, Cavanough. First Fleeter Owen Cavanough (d.1841) was originally buried here; his headstone was later moved to Ebenezer Uniting Church Cemetery. The headstone of another First Fleeter Anne Huxley (d.1851) is still here.

The cemetery records river life

and tragic drownings. Richard Wall and his two young daughters Martha and Rachel were returning from Windsor on 20 January 1881 when they got caught in a squall and their boat overturned. All three drowned. When the bodies were recovered, the father was found clasping his youngest daughter Rachel.

The large family vault surmounted by a marble pedestal with draped urn and enclosed by an elaborate cast-iron fence houses the Manning family. Captain George Manning (d.1907), was one of the many river shipmasters that plied the Hawkesbury, transporting goods and passengers between Sydney and Windsor. His vessel the *Maid of Australia* was a popular passenger and cargo boat for Hawkesbury residents. His wife Elizabeth (d.1890) and members of their large family are also buried here.

This ground was also the site for the original St Thomas' Anglican Church (1833); an obelisk commemorates the site. The church got washed away in the flood of 1867 and was rebuilt down the road on higher ground. It is now privately owned.

NOTABLE BURIALS

- George Manning (1811–1907), river master
- Martha Everingham (1846–1926), local Aboriginal elder

MORE INFORMATION

- Local Government, 'St Thomas' Anglican Cemetery', Heritage Inventory listing ID 1740163, NSW Office of Environment and Heritage website, 2016, <www.environment.nsw.gov.au/heritageapp/ViewHeritageItemDetails. aspx?ID=1740163>.
- Jonathan Auld & Michelle Nichols, 'St Thomas' Cemetery, Sackville Reach', Hawkesbury on the Net: Cemetery Register website, 2003, <www.hawkesbury. net.au/cemetery/st_thomas/index.html>.

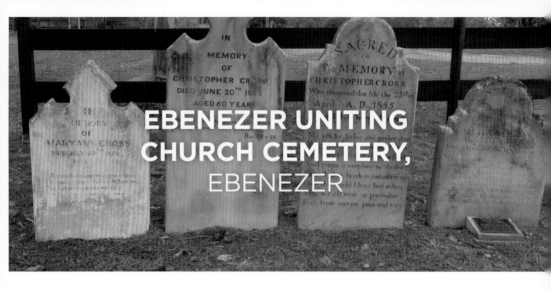

EBENEZER UNITING CHURCH CEMETERY, EBENEZER

COROMANDEL ROAD, EBENEZER

Burials: 1825–present

The church and churchyard at Ebenezer are deservedly famous. The sandstone church is celebrated as Sydney's first non-conformist and then Presbyterian Church and the oldest standing church in Australia. It's still in use. It is also on a well-worn path for tourists around the Hawkesbury and is listed on the State Heritage Register.

Ebenezer Church perches high on the bank above the Hawkesbury River. The cemetery wraps around the church and schoolmaster's residence on two sides. The road leading to the church pays homage to its origins. In 1802 the *Coromandel* carried eight families to colonial New South Wales – the Davisons, Halls, Howes, Johnstons, Johnstones, Meins, Stubbs and Turnbulls. They became founding families of Portland Head, settling on 40 hectares granted to them by Governor King. Other Hawkesbury families, including the Arndells, Bushells, Cavanoughs,

Ebenezer Church, established 1809, is Australia's oldest church

Gronos, Jacklins, Joneses and Suddis, joined them to form a little ecumenical congregation embracing Presbyterians, Anglicans, Methodists and Catholics. Owen Cavanough donated land for the church and the building was complete by 1809. James Mein, a Presbyterian lay preacher, led services for many years. The Ebenezer Chapel was formally established as a Presbyterian church in 1824.

It is difficult to determine exactly when burials commenced in the cemetery, as early church records were lost in the great flood of 1867. The dates of 1812 and 1813 are often cited; with infant Sarah Gilkerson gaining the honour of the earliest marked grave from the Ebenezer Church Trustees in 2006. But the little sandstone headstone is rather weathered and the spacing of the inscription suggests it could be 1843 rather than 1813.

Another contender is named by William Freame, who visited the cemetery in 1904 and penned an article in the *Windsor and Richmond Gazette* recording the earliest decipherable headstone as Richard Hayes, who died on 11 January 1812. This headstone can be found among the early crosses. But family genealogists now claim that Hayes died in 1842.

The story is further complicated by a contemporary account of James Mein's funeral, whose altar tomb can be found at the far left of the cemetery. On 9 July 1827 the *Sydney Gazette*, acknowledging Mein's important role in founding the little chapel, notes that 'his body is the first interred in the burial ground'.

Sacred
to
the MEMORY of
WILLIAM JACKLIN
Who Departed this Life
Jan'. 6. 1836. Aged 76 years

On swelling waves and da
ngerous seas
I toiled all my youthfull
days
But now I rest beneath the
ground
And waitthe trumpet Joy
full sound

Sacred
to
the MEMORY of
ELIZABETH JACKLIN
Who Departed this Life
Sep. 23rd. 1836. Aged 60
years

Impressive vaults and tombs line the churchyard in front of the church and schoolhouse. The Grono family have a prominent position. Captain John Grono RN was a naval captain, river master and boat builder. In 1813 he rescued five stranded crew of the whaling brig the *Scotch Lassy* from an uncharted island off the coast of New Zealand. Two of the men, Alexander Books and Robert McKenzie, subsequently married two of Grono's daughters. Robert McKenzie's inscription is particularly interesting as it reflects his seafaring life:

> Through blustery gales and
> poling waves
> I have been tossed to and fro
> Now at last by God's decree
> I have a Harbour here below.
> Now at Anchor here I lie
> With many of my Fleet
> But once again I will arise
> My Saviour Christ to meet.

But there are definitely earlier burials recorded on other gravestones.

The altar tomb to Robert McKenzie records his death as 19 February 1825, while the Hall family vault near the church door records that Mary Hall, wife of George, died 29 June 1827. In 2013 the Ebenezer Church Trustees settled upon Robert McKenzie as the oldest gravestone.

Leaving firsts and earliests aside, we can rightly say this is a very old cemetery. There are as many as six generations of the *Coromandel* settlers represented in the cemetery.

Hawkesbury settlers were firm supporters of Governor Bligh and many opposed the Rum Rebellion. The settlers' loyalty is reflected in local family names and thus headstone inscriptions. Andrew and Mary Johnston christened their youngest son James Bligh Johnston, a practice that has continued for

Opposite James Grono (d.1829) was the son of Captain John Grono (d.1847)

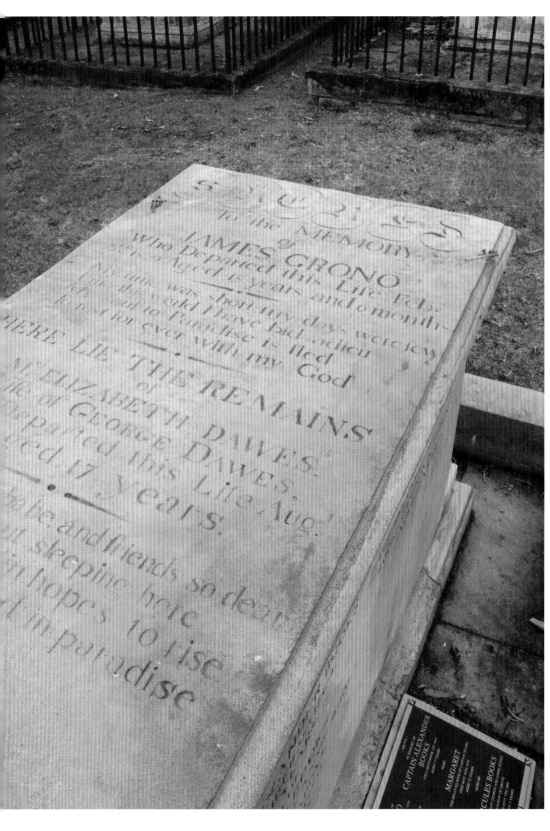

eight generations. Similarly, John and Ann Turnbull named their son William Bligh Turnbull and the Bligh naming tradition has continued for six generations.

There are monuments right through the 19th and 20th centuries. Look out for the fine sandstone headstones to Ann Logan (d.1853) and John Logan (d.1867) with the sheaf of wheat. They were removed here from the Devonshire Street Cemetery. Two rare table top tombs mark the graves of the local minister and schoolmaster.

TIP

This is a great cemetery for a picnic. It overlooks the river and there are picnic tables in the grounds. A little café serves Devonshire teas every day of the week.

NOTABLE BURIALS

- Robert McKenzie (c.1771–1825), mariner
- James Mein (1761–1827), *Coromandel* settler and devout Presbyterian
- Reverend John Cleland, AM (c.1793–1839), Presbyterian minister, Hawkesbury district
- John Grono (c.1767–1847), naval captain, river master and shipbuilder
- Andrew Johnston (1766–1849), *Coromandel* settler, farmer, orchardist and architect
- John Anderson (c.1793–1858), schoolmaster at Ebenezer for 34 years

MORE INFORMATION
- Ebenezer Uniting Church, *Historic Ebenezer Church – since 1809*, Ebenezer Uniting Church, 2016, <www.ebenezerchurch.org.au>.
- *A colonial churchyard: Ebenezer Church, Ebenezer, New South Wales*, compiled by Ebenezer Church Cemetery Trust, Ebenezer, 2006.
- Ebenezer Uniting Church, 'Ebenezer Uniting Church Cemetery Trust Register 1813 – 2005', Hawkesbury on the Net – Church Registers website, <www.hawkesbury.net.au/church/cemeteries/eucct2005.html>.

TOP 5
QUIRKY SPELLINGS AND MISTAKES

JAMES RUSE HEADSTONE	St John's Catholic Cemetery, Campbelltown *naive letter cutting and phonetic spellings: 'memrey', 'houre', 'natef', 'coleney', 'Forst Fleet'*
WILLIAM GREEN HEADSTONE	St Matthew's Anglican Cemetery, Windsor *'barberrously Mur-dred in the Execution of his Duty as Cunstable'*
ANN SMALLWOOD HEADSTONE	St James' Anglican Cemetery, Pitt Town *upper and lower case lettering within the same words and small letters snuck in to correct*
JAMES PERRY HEADSTONE	St Stephen the Martyr Anglican Cemetery, Penrith *4 in the death date 1840 is carved back to front*
PETER BROWN HEADSTONE	St Thomas' Anglican Cemetery, Mulgoa *lines to guide letter cutter visible and epitaph spacing all wrong with words squeezed in and above lines*

Epitaph of William Green (d.1826), St Matthew's Anglican Cemetery, Windsor

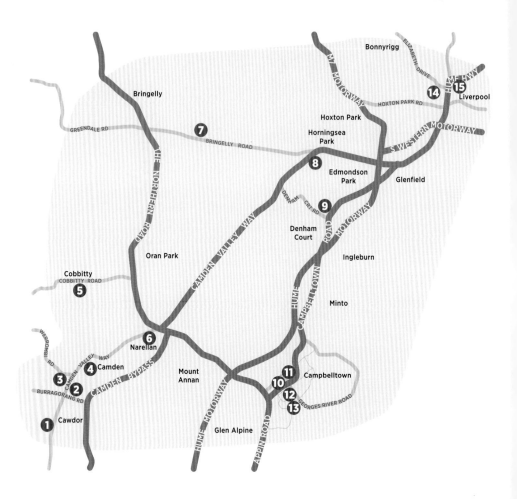

Opposite St Paul's Anglican Cemetery, Cobbitty

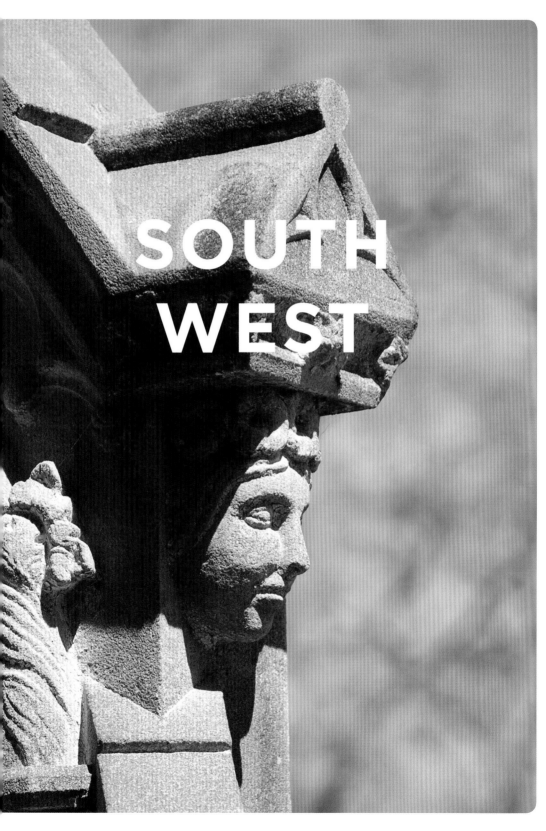

SOUTH
WEST

LIVERPOOL PIONEERS MEMORIAL PARK, LIVERPOOL

MACQUARIE STREET, CORNER CAMPBELL STREET, LIVERPOOL

Burials: 1821–1958 (converted 1970)

The Liverpool Pioneers Memorial Park is the site of the second cemetery for Liverpool. The first was located on Elizabeth Street, now the site of Apex Park which was consecrated in 1811. However, it was abandoned after about ten years when the land proved too boggy and close to the water table. No monuments survive in situ.

The second burial ground for Liverpool was selected two blocks north of St Luke's Church. Over the years many people have referred to this cemetery as St Luke's Cemetery, but, despite its proximity, there is no formal connection. It's hard to imagine the link now. The visual connection between the cemetery and the church has been broken by the intrusion of Westfield.

Liverpool Cemetery was active from 1821–1958. The first burial was Richard Guise, a farmer from

Casula, recorded on 16 April 1821. The cemetery was subdivided and extended over the 19th century. The Catholics were initially granted 4000 square metres in 1827, which was extended in the 1860s. The Wesleyans were given land for burials in 1863. A large area for Catholic asylum burials and paupers was dedicated at the northern end of the cemetery beyond Lachlan Street in 1884, along with a Presbyterian area. The evolution of Liverpool Cemetery shows how the government responded to burial needs of different denominations and grouped the burial areas together. Provision for the dead was ad hoc in the first half of the 19th century; the genesis of this cemetery predates the concept of the denominational general cemetery in Sydney.

The cemetery was handed over to Liverpool Council in 1970 who cleared the vegetation and converted it into a memorial park. Monuments were laid flat, removed from graves and placed cheek-by-jowl in walls. I was dreading my visit, as it is known among cemetery lovers as a depressing conversion. However, in the last few years Liverpool City Council has spent considerable time and money undoing the nasty conversion and reinstating the gravestones into a more regular cemetery layout.

The result is impressive; visitors can now enjoy the remnants of an early and historic cemetery.

The majority of the Liverpool asylum burials were unmarked. One of the most famous permanent residents here was William Francis King (1807–1873), the 'Flying Pieman'. He was a pedestrianist (competitive walker) and street character who performed many bizarre walking feats competing against the ferries and the mail coaches, while carrying animals for weights. He died in the Liverpool asylum, forgotten and a pauper.

There are a number of handsome headstones and altar tombs. Look out for the sandstone headstone of freemason Joseph Metcalfe (he was a brother of the Lodge Cosmopolitan, No. 16), which features fine Grecian details such as Doric pilasters and dentils, and matching masonic symbols of compass, set square and plumb. Metcalfe was engaged on the Sydney Waterworks in 1884 when he died suddenly, aged 27.

The gravestone of Charles Fortescue (d.1855) features a high bas-relief carving of Thorvaldsen's *Night with her children, sleep and death* framed by bold acanthus leaves; while Mary Barrett's headstone, located within a cluster of Catholic graves, features a Grecian woman with a scroll hovering above her – possibly a representation of the death scene. Matching headstones featuring large seraphs and drapery mark the child graves of Catherine Lane Sloane (d.1858) and Kate Charlotte Lane (d.1859). Coffin style kerbing connects up to the matching footstones. There is plenty of other symbolism represented on the 19th-century headstones, including pairs of angels, seraphs, scrolls and wreaths, draped urns, and even a cornucopia of fruit in a Grecian urn.

Some early headstones survive. The earliest I spotted was to John Fraser, who 'was Born a Native in the District of Concord' and died in 1823 aged 35 years. This puts him as one of the earliest births in the colony. Another early gravestone commemorates Sarah and Frederick Meredith. Frederick was a steward on the *Scarborough* in the First Fleet. He died in 1836 aged 73 years.

TIP

An early gravestone from the first burial ground memorialising ex-convict Nathaniel Lucas (d.1818) has been relocated to the nearby grounds of St Luke's Church in Elizabeth Street. Lucas, a master carpenter and builder, actually built the church.

Rare table top tomb

Left Children's graves of the Sloane and Lane families

NOTABLE BURIALS

- Charles Throsby (1777–1828), surgeon, settler and explorer
- Frederick Meredith (1763–1836), First Fleeter, sailor, constable and Liverpool's first postmaster
- Thomas Moore (1762–1840), sailor, farmer and philanthropist, endower of Moore Theological College
- William Francis King (1807–1873), pedestrianist and the 'Flying Pieman'

MORE INFORMATION

- *Liverpool Pioneers' Memorial Park*, Liverpool City Council, Liverpool, 1974.
- *Liverpool Pioneers' Memorial Park: headstone photographs and inscriptions*, Liverpool Genealogy Society, Liverpool, 2004.
- *Whispering Bones*, Liverpool Regional Museum, Liverpool, 2000.

LIVERPOOL GENERAL CEMETERY, LIVERPOOL

207 MOORE STREET, LIVERPOOL

Burials: 1894–present

Liverpool General Cemetery dates back to the late 19th century, but is a thoroughly modern cemetery. Set aside in 1892, it originally had Anglican, Catholic, Presbyterian, Jewish, Independent, Wesleyan, Primitive Methodist and general sections. Remnants of the original layout survive including a curving road that bisects the cemetery on the diagonal and parts of the radiating layout. But the central circle, originally dedicated for a mortuary chapel and plantation, is barely discernible; now it contains lines of vaults. The cemetery's denominational trustees were amalgamated in 2010 and the Catholic Metropolitan Cemeteries Trust and a general trust now manage the cemetery.

The first burial took place on 15 February 1894. Many early burials were from government institutions, such as the Liverpool Asylum and Liverpool Old Men's Home, as well as pauper burials and bodies from the University of Sydney medical school. Over 28,000 people are buried in the cemetery.

Despite some lawn burial areas, overall the cemetery is highly monumental, dominated by vaults and above-ground crypts. A flower and ornament policy curtails the vernacular decorative excesses seen in other cemeteries. All 'ornaments, photo frames, toys, windmills, flags, wind chimes, rosary beads, crosses, statues, figurines or the like' are banned from the cemetery lawn areas; decorative borders and crushed stone are not permitted in the monumental lawn area; and 'ornaments, figurines, balloons, and cards' are forbidden in the crypt complexes. But there is still plenty of fresh and artificial floral colour among the crypts and tombs. The cemetery features a modern two-storey mausoleum in the south-east corner of the cemetery, the St Padre Pio Garden Mausoleum. It has the external design, landscaping and bearing of a modern residential unit complex.

NOTABLE BURIALS

- Hubert Peter (Bert) Lazzarini (1884–1952), politician

MORE INFORMATION

- *Liverpool General Cemetery*, vols 1–6, Liverpool & District Family History Society, 1993–98.
- Rob McDonell, 'Liverpool Catholic Cemetery', Australian Cemeteries Index website, 2014, <austcemindex.com/cemetery?cemid=1703>.

FOREST LAWN MEMORIAL PARK, LEPPINGTON

1500–1600 CAMDEN VALLEY WAY, LEPPINGTON

Burials: 1964–present

American businessman James Keuger brought American lawn burial practices to Australia when his company Memorial Gardens Pty Ltd established the Forest Lawn Memorial Park in 1962. Keuger based the name and the concept on the famous American Forest Lawn Memorial Park at Glendale, California, the cemetery that inspired Evelyn Waugh's 1948 novel *The Loved One*. Originally Keuger planned to buy 67 hectares at Kellyville, but the community and Baulkham Hills Council rejected his ideas and so eventually he settled on 60 hectares at Leppington, just south of Liverpool.

The first burial took place on 29 December 1964. Initially it was all about lawn burials, but when the cremation of Sydneysiders tipped 60 per cent in the mid-1960s, Forest Lawn management installed a crematorium to penetrate this side of the market. The first cremation took place on 21 August 1968. It was a wise decision. Forest Lawn Memorial Park's website now boasts 'to date there have been over 30,000 cremation services and 11,500 burial services conducted at Forest Lawn'.

Forest Lawn is much smaller in extent than Pinegrove Memorial Park in Minchinbury, but its hilly site provides vistas and respite from the relentless run of lawn grave plaques. Forest Lawn Memorial Park also caters to the multicultural community with separate burial areas for the Chinese and the Vietnamese.

A funky 1960s sculpture figuration of a saint overlooks some crypts in Section U. There is also a cluster of crypts down near the dams. Watch out for the resident geese who rule the lawns near the dams and can be quite aggressive. Ducks and coots also paddle on the ponds.

Forest Lawn's company management was taken over by its rival Pinegrove in 1988. It was later subsumed within the behemoth funeral industry company Service Corporation International Australia, and subsequently by the Australian-based international funeral services company InvoCare Australia Pty Limited.

This modern lawn cemetery has yet to be transcribed.

NOTABLE BURIALS

* Lester (Charlie) Leon (1900–1982), Aboriginal activist
* Ralph Benson Marsh, OBE (1909–1989), trade unionist and politician

MORE INFORMATION
* Forest Lawn Memorial Park website, 2016, <www.forestlawn.com.au>.
* Pat Jalland, *Changing Ways of Death in Twentieth-century Australia: war, medicine and the funeral business*, UNSW Press, Sydney, 2006, pp. 316–21.

Left Ceramic saint overlooks crypts in Section U

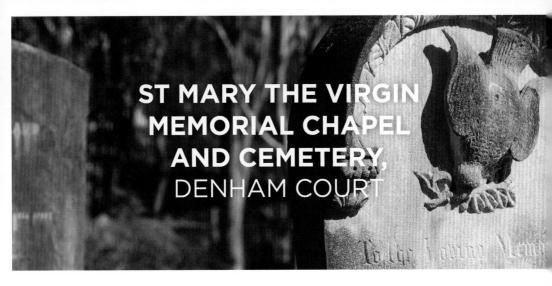

ST MARY THE VIRGIN MEMORIAL CHAPEL AND CEMETERY, DENHAM COURT

CHURCH ROAD, DENHAM COURT

Burials: 1833–present

St Mary the Virgin Church was originally built as a private memorial chapel to commemorate Captain Richard Brooks and his wife Christiana of 'Denham Court'. The design by architect John Verge in 1833–35 in the 'Picturesque Gothick' style, was a copy of St Mary at Denham in Buckinghamshire, although executed in stuccoed brick rather than stone.

Captain Brooks died on 16 October 1833, aged 68 years, after being gored by a bullock, and was buried in a vault on the property. Two years later his wife Christiana died, aged 59 years. The Brooks Memorial Chapel was erected following Christiana's death, in accordance with her will. Four hectares were alienated from the property, with 4000 square metres set aside for the chapel and burial ground, and the remainder for a rectory and glebe. The chapel, later renamed St Mary the Virgin Chapel, is one of the oldest private memorial chapels in New South Wales still used for public worship.

The burial ground surrounding the chapel was consecrated by Bishop Broughton on 26 March 1845 and includes a range of 19th- and 20th-century monuments. The Blomfield, Gavin, Gordon, McDonald, Holman, Kemp, Riley and Thirling families all have monuments here. The most substantial is the sandstone sarcophagus to the Blomfield family, descendants of Richard and Christiana Brooks. The Gordon / McDonald monument was removed from the Balmain Cemetery and relocated here in the 1930s.

NOTABLE BURIALS

- Captain Richard Brooks (1765–1833), of 'Denham Court', mariner and merchant
- James John Riley (1821–1882), first mayor of Penrith, 1871–74
- Frank Astor Penfold Hyland (1873–1948), governing director of Penfolds Wines

MORE INFORMATION
- J & JD Maxwell, *St. Thomas Mulgoa, Holy Innocents Church of England Rossmore, St. Mary the Virgin Church of England Denham Court: cemetery inscriptions*, Nepean Family History Society, St Marys, 1984.

Architect John Verge designed the memorial chapel, built 1833–39

HOLY INNOCENTS ANGLICAN CEMETERY, ROSSMORE

CHURCH STREET, OFF BRINGELLY ROAD, ROSSMORE

Burials: 1846–2011

Holy Innocents Church, Rossmore dates from 1848, when there were just 29 houses and 166 inhabitants in the entire district. The church and cemetery mark the centre of the original township of Cabramatta.

Remnants of an old timber picket fence, and substantial hardwood posts with decorative turned tops, mark the entrance to this quaint churchyard. The graves are located to the south and west of the small dark-brick Gothic Revival Church.

With its yews and cypress, and lush green grass, this churchyard has an English feel about it.

The earliest headstone marks the grave of Charlotte Hunt (d.1846). Another early sandstone headstone with deeply incised inscription commemorates John McKaughan (d.1848). Two headstones with refined Georgian fan motifs mark the graves of Thomas Simpson (d.1859) and Thomas Croxton (d.1851). The stonemason clearly had trouble with Croxton's unusual name, as the lettering shows signs of a mistake which was fixed up.

Tucked away in the corner are the Bell family graves, of 'Bellfield', which are marked with headstones and footstones and enclosed by an unusual tapering slate kerbing, forming a coffin-like shape.

One of the most substantial memorials stands by the porch entrance to the church. It is a trachyte obelisk to the Tyson family. The family were struck by tragedy, experiencing three deaths in two years: two accidental deaths followed by a son killed in action during the First World War.

The churchyard is well maintained but the church is no longer in use.

NOTABLE BURIALS

- Robert Bell (c.1799–1877), of 'Bellfield'
- James Douglas Tyson (1903–1917), accidentally killed at Croydon Railway Station
- Joseph Wilson Tyson (1895–1918), soldier, 'died somewhere in France'

MORE INFORMATION

- Jean McDowell Jones, *Nepean District Cemetery Records, 1806–1976*, Sydney, 1977.
- J & JD Maxwell, *St. Thomas Mulgoa, Holy Innocents Church of England Rossmore, St. Mary the Virgin Church of England Denham Court: cemetery inscriptions*, Nepean Family History Society, St Marys, 1984.

Left Georgian motif headstones from the 1850s

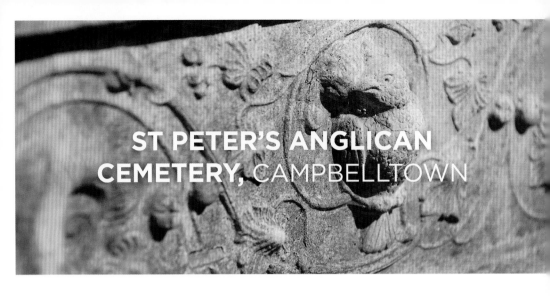

ST PETER'S ANGLICAN CEMETERY, CAMPBELLTOWN

**HOWE STREET, CAMPBELLTOWN
(ENTER CEMETERY VIA THE CHURCH CAR PARK)**

Burials: 1823–present

Governor Macquarie set aside land for a burial ground as part of his plan for Campbelltown in 1820, but it took several years to be surveyed and fenced, causing 'great inconvenience' to families in Airds and Appin. The first burial took place in 1823, but the cemetery was not fully marked out and enclosed until 1824.

This is the earliest cemetery in Campbelltown and you will see many gravestones dating from the 1830s to the 1850s. One strange feature of the cemetery is that the majority of graves face roughly north-west, suggesting a decision to orientate the graves to suit the lay of the land rather than the traditional east. The cemetery is still in use and a columbarium wall encloses the cemetery on two sides, which includes a section for the Returned Services League.

A cluster of prominent graves on the rise, including some of the parish ministers, look down over

Reddall family tomb

the rest of the cemetery. High cast-iron fences surround these family plots. Another cluster of early graves can be found at the bottom of the slope, including Henrietta and Edward Fletcher. Henrietta was born on the way to Botany Bay, a baby of the First Fleet. Her husband was a police constable at Minto.

Early gravestones in this cemetery demonstrate a common idea of the time that graves were a reminder of mortality, and the words memento mori appear at the top of a number of anthropomorphic headstones executed by local stonemason Shea.

The most unusual monument in the cemetery is to the child John Nimrod Monk (d.1864). Look closely at the classical pedestal and you will see lizards and birds carved below a lifelike bust of the boy (rather than the more usual cherub). Among the graves is a small stone to Mary Jane Lance (d.1885), an Aboriginal girl who died at the age of 16. It is said that Fred Fisher, of Fisher's Ghost legend, was interred here.

NOTABLE BURIALS

- Thomas Reddall (1780–1838) clergyman and educationalist, first incumbent of the parish, 1820–1838, and his second son Reverend Thomas Reddall, MA, (d.1860) also minister of the parish for 18 months
- Thomas Rose (d.1837) convict, baker, publican and water conservator

- John Warby (1774–1851) convict, first stockman at the Cowpastures protecting the wild cattle herd, explorer and guide, owner of 'Leumeah' estate
- Reverend Canon William Stack (1810–1871), clergyman, parish incumbent 1846–1855
- James Tyson (1819–1898) pastoralist, Australia's first great cattle king and an early millionaire, politician

MORE INFORMATION
- Verlie Fowler, *A Stroll Through St Peter's Churchyard*, Campbelltown and Airds Historical Society, Campbelltown, 1994.

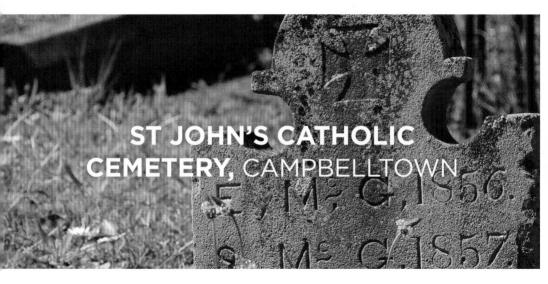

ST JOHN'S CATHOLIC CEMETERY, CAMPBELLTOWN

BROUGHTON STREET, CAMPBELLTOWN

Burials: 1827–present

This is the most picturesque cemetery in Campbelltown, located on a rise overlooking today's city. Early graves abound with a variety of memorial styles and quirky inscriptions. James Bourke donated the 2.2 hectares of land in 1825 and the consecration took place on 27 December 1826. One of the earliest headstones here is to John Masterson (d.1827). The Catholic Parish of Campbelltown, the second oldest parish in Australia, is historically associated with Father John Joseph Therry, who designed the simple Georgian-style church.

Pay attention to the inscriptions as you wander around. There is quaint phrasing and misspellings on several memorials. The Bourke family grave which encloses three memorials includes three variant spellings of the family name: Burk, Bourk and Bourke. James Ruse's headstone (d.1837) has been repeatedly quoted over the years, not just because of his fame, but also because of its quirky spelling. Ruse reputedly carved the lengthy inscription himself, leaving space for his death date and age. You'll find his headstone in the north-west corner.

St John's Catholic Cemetery is remarkable for the number of finely carved anthropomorphic headstones (many by the stonemason Shea), some fine cast-iron work, the survival of several timber surrounds, and two cast-iron crosses. Many people don't know that a number of exiles from the 1798 Irish Rebellion are buried here: Nicholas Bryan (d.1835), John Fowler (d.1833), Thomas Connor (d.1835) – all transportees of the *Atlas II* – Hugh Byrne (d.1842), cousin of Michael Dwyer, and Thomas Bourke (d.1833). Despite suffering vandalism over the years, the well-kept cemetery is a colonial survivor that exudes history.

NOTABLE BURIALS

- James Ruse (1759–1837), smallholder, father of wheat industry
- Matthew Healey (1760–1840), pioneer of Goulburn, built Riversdale Inn
- Irish exiles of 1798

MORE INFORMATION
- Jim Munro, *Where Pioneers Lie: St John's Cemetery Campbelltown*, Campbelltown and Airds Historical Society, Campbelltown, 1991.

PRESBYTERIAN CEMETERY, CAMPBELLTOWN

CAMPBELLTOWN ROAD, CORNER BROUGHTON STREET, CAMPBELLTOWN

Burials: 1838–1963

This small sunken cemetery below Campbelltown Road is a truncated shadow of its former self due to road widening. The original 2000 square metres of land was donated in about 1837 by Alexander McDonald (d.1847), a parishioner of St David's Presbyterian Church, following the death of one of his children.

The first burial recorded in the registers is just a surname – Harper, 8 March 1838, in an unmarked grave. Alexander McDonald's memorial records that he lost two children in 1837 and 1838 and these are the earliest deaths recorded on a headstone. The cemetery was closed to burials in 1963 and the church struggled to maintain the graves and landscape. The Department of Main Roads resumed over 50 graves in the 1980s when it widened Campbelltown Road, but some bodies remain beneath the roadway. The headstones relocated to the northern corner of the cemetery are easily spotted as they are close-set in concrete. Campbelltown Council took over cemetery maintenance in 1990.

Despite its modest size there are some substantial memorials here. Along the fence of Broughton Street, you can see the grave of the Reverend Hugh Robert Gilchrist (d.1852), the first minister of St David's Church; the headstone of the cemetery founder Alexander McDonald; and the Thomson family plot, which features a table top tomb enclosed with iron rails. Four altar tombs stand sentinel in the northern part of the cemetery, commemorating the Howe Family. These were moved at the time of the resumption. At least three Campbelltown

mayors are buried here, along with four Presbyterian ministers.

The most unusual memorial is the squat marble cannon with the relocated memorials that commemorates Captain Lachlan Macalister, of the British Army's 48th Regiment Foot. His descendants have erected a plaque outlining Macalister's life history including the fact that he was among the party of men that captured and killed Jack Donahue, the 'Wild Colonial Boy', in 1830.

TIP

Combine a visit here with St Peters Anglican Cemetery, just down the road.

NOTABLE BURIALS

- William Howe (1777–1855), settler, magistrate and owner of 'Glenlee'
- Lachlan Macalister (1797–1855), 48th Regiment Foot, soldier, magistrate, mounted policeman and pastoralist
- John Kidd (1838–1919), store-keeper, dairy farmer and politician

MORE INFORMATION

- Marie Holmes, *The Presbyterian Cemetery, Campbelltown*, Campbelltown and Airds Historical Society, 1996.

Captain Lachlan Macalister's (d.1855) memorial

CAMPBELLTOWN PIONEER PARK, CAMPBELLTOWN

ST JOHN'S ROAD, CAMPBELLTOWN

Burials: 1869–1959

This is a grim, little cemetery, now a tiny pioneer park tucked on a corner outside a school. There is little here for the ordinary cemetery visitor. But in order for me to be comprehensive, let me tell you about it.

Benjamin Warby donated the land for a Congregational burial ground in the 1860s. It later was also utilised by the Methodists. There are 127 known burials. Maude Charlotte Bocking (d.1869) is the earliest burial still marked by a gravestone. The last burial in the cemetery was William Robert Piggott (d.1959). Local aldermen, merchants, farmers, builders and undertakers are buried here.

This cemetery proudly bears a heritage plaque from Campbelltown City Council. Many of the 20 or so memorials that survive in the cemetery have been reset in concrete. Some have been laid on their backs (on a slight slope so the water can drain) to discourage vandalism and reconstruct broken bits.

Cars whizz along beside the main road and the cemetery has no atmosphere. It is hard to commune with Campbelltown's 'pioneers' in this soulless place. A withered wreath bearing the epitaph 'Lest We Forget' perches beside a headstone set in concrete, indicating some descendants still care.

TIP

While you are in Campbelltown visit the other cemeteries, and make sure you call in at the Campbelltown Arts Centre. It has an excellent courtyard café.

NOTABLE BURIALS

- Thomas Jenner Winton (1846–1887), Campbelltown's first town clerk
- William Webb (1848–1910), JP, newspaper proprietor, founder of *Campbelltown Herald*
- James Bocking (c.1830–1926), merchant, founding member of the Congregational church and Campbelltown mayor

MORE INFORMATION

- Marie Holmes, 'Congregationalism in Campbelltown: the cemetery', *Grist Mills: Journal of Campbelltown & Airds Historical Society*, vol. 17, no. 2, July 2004, pp. 20–40.
- *Pictorial Cemetery Register*, CD ROM, Campbelltown District Family History Society, Campbelltown, 2002.

NARELLAN CEMETERY, NARELLAN

6 RICHARDSON ROAD, NARELLAN

Burials: 1839–present

The Narellan Cemetery is undergoing a transformation. The protestant burial ground, was established in 1827 when Narellan township was surveyed. In 2008 the Lebanese Muslim Association purchased it to cater for the growing needs of Sydney's diverse Muslim community. The once St Thomas Anglican Cemetery will become the An-Nur Islamic Cemetery and Burial Ground, opening a new chapter in the history of Sydney's cemeteries.

The cemetery is located on a sloping site, with the protestant burials located on the high part of the site. The first St Thomas Anglican Church officially opened in 1839, and burials are recorded from this time. Many graves from the 1840s are now unmarked. The earliest gravestone that survives is to Sarah Linton, wife of William, who died on 14 September 1858.

A range of 19th- and 20th-century grave markers in sandstone, marble and granite all face east. Some of the earliest grave markers have fallen and lie on the ground. The most interesting memorial is a little child's grave enclosed by a bespoke wrought-iron fence which features stylised tulips and the inscription RIP Dianne May McFarland.

This is a unique grave marker.

The new Muslim burials are located on the lower part of the site. Significant landscaping works are currently underway. This will be an important cemetery for the Muslim community for years to come.

MORE INFORMATION

- *St Thomas Cemetery, Richardson Road, Narellan, NSW*, Camden Area Family History Society, Camden, 2009.

A unique grave marker for Dianne May McFarland

ST PAUL'S ANGLICAN CEMETERY, COBBITTY

COBBITTY ROAD, COBBITTY

Burials: 1830–2008

St Paul's is in the running for the most picture-perfect English-style churchyard in Sydney. The graveyard encircles this simple sandstone church with spire, designed by architect John Verge and constructed 1840–42. The cemetery features a range of headstones and grave plantings and an exuberant array of wrought-iron surrounds. Over the years the picturesque church has attracted artists, including William Hardy Wilson and Sydney Ure Smith.

The construction of the church was marred by tragedy. Edward Wise, a 24-year-old labourer, was struck by lightning in November 1841 while building the steeple. The gravestone recording his fate can be found in the churchyard and bears the epitaph: 'In the midst of life we are in death.'

There has been a chapel on this site since 1827. The Reverend Thomas Hassall, the minister of Cowpastures parish who was fondly known as the 'galloping parson',

Left Neoclassical pedestal tomb featuring the fine-grained local sandstone

built the Herber Chapel, naming it after Bishop Herber of Calcutta whose diocese encompassed the whole of Australia. The first burial in the cemetery was Samuel Otto Hassall, the brother of Reverend Thomas Hassall, who died in 1830.

The vaults in the cemetery provide a bit of a who's who in the district, with all the main estates represented. Many of these monumental pieces use a fine-grained local sandstone with distinctive dark swirls. This stone is also visible in cemeteries around Camden. The highly accomplished ironwork grave surrounds feature unique designs that were probably executed by the local blacksmith Sweyn Campbell and his son Hugh who carried on the local smithy business for many years. More

modern, but deserving of admiration, is a metalwork fence 'headboard' to Charles Gourlay (d.1963) which welds all the letters of the inscription to a fence. There are some standout symbolic carvings on headstones in the cemetery, including a delicate crown, broken flower and draped urn with downturned torch.

> ## TIP
>
> Plan your visit to coincide with the Cobbitty Markets held on the first Saturday of the month (except January and February) in the Cobbitty Public School grounds.

NOTABLE BURIALS

- Oxley family vault, descendants of John Joseph William Molesworth Oxley (c.1784–1828), surveyor-general and explorer, of 'Kirkham'
- Thomas Hassall (1794–1868), Anglican clergyman, inaugural minister of St Paul's, of 'Denbeigh'
- Jeremiah Frederick Downes (1818–1887), of 'Brownlow Hill'
- Charles Cowper (1834–1911), politician and police magistrate, of 'Wivenhoe'

MORE INFORMATION

- St Paul's Anglican Church Cobbitty, 'History', St Paul's Anglican Church Cobbitty website, 2016, <www.cobbitty.anglican.asn.au/history>.
- *St Paul's Anglican Cemetery: Cobbitty Road, Cobbitty NSW*, Camden Area Family History Society, Camden, 2009.

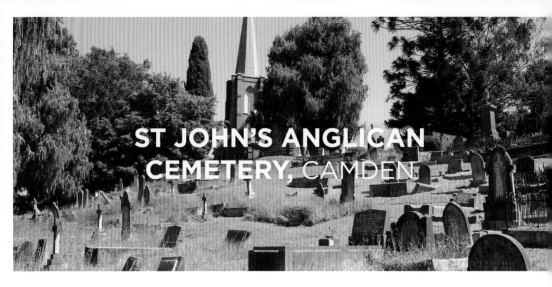

ST JOHN'S ANGLICAN CEMETERY, CAMDEN

MENANGLE ROAD, CORNER BROUGHTON STREET, CAMDEN

Burials: 1844–2000s

The iconic St John's Anglican Church, consecrated in 1849, sits commandingly atop a hill with picturesque views of the town and floodplains of Camden. When the Macarthurs of 'Camden Park' laid out the little village of Camden, they gave moral predominance to the Anglican Church. Its clocktower and spire dominate the landscape visibly and audibly; the clock still chimes on the quarter hour. The entrance way to the church from Menangle Road features a rare timber lychgate with bench. You can also approach the church and cemetery via stairs from Broughton Street.

The cemetery cascades down the steep slope to the east of the church. It is deceptively large, as it wraps around the hill and church. There are over 1800 burials here. Subsidence is an ongoing issue and monuments lean in all directions, giving the cemetery the unwarranted feeling of neglect. Notice how some of the iron grave fences

have been built to address the changing levels on the slope. I have not seen this innovation in any other cemetery.

The first burial occurred on 29 June 1844. Several early headstones with matching footstones date from the mid-19th century. Some of the most interesting monumental work and carving mark the graves of Camden's wives. An anthropomorphic headstone with finely carved inscription commemorates Mary Ann Greenfield of Narellan, who died on 24 August 1845. This appears to be the earliest surviving headstone in the cemetery. An extraordinary carving of a crown and broken anchor, along with classical decoration, adorns the headstone of Mary Rootes (d.1858), wife of well-known Primitive Methodist Sivyer Rootes of Camden. Elizabeth Waters was just 32 years old when she died in 1858. Her grave is marked by a tall sandstone Corinthian broken column with wreath, surmounting a pedestal and three-step base, a memorial that signifies a life cut short.

Seek out the large sandstone headstone (made from the distinctive swirled sandstone of the Nepean) erected by Margaret Hall to her husband William, who was accidentally killed in 1868 by a falling tree. The blunt epitaph still exudes the shock felt by Margaret at his death:

The hue of his cheeks and lips decayed
Around his mouth a sweet smile played
They looked and he was dead.

NOTABLE BURIALS

- Dr Henry Grattan Douglass (1790–1865), doctor of medicine and public servant
- Commander Alexander Martin (1784–1868), veteran of the Napoleonic Wars
- Eliza Pearson (1803–1879), first postmistress in Camden 1841–79
- Maximillian von Zglinicki (1828–1898), policeman and gaol governor

MORE INFORMATION

- Ron Clerke & Beverley Booth, *The churchyard cemetery of St John's Camden,* Illawarra Family History Group, Wollongong, 1989.
- Janice Johnson, *If gravestones could talk: stories from the churchyard of St. John's Camden,* Camden Historical Society, Camden, 2010.

Grave offerings

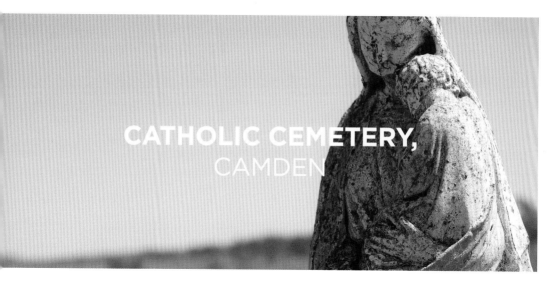

CATHOLIC CEMETERY, CAMDEN

CAWDOR ROAD, CAMDEN

Burials: 1843–present

You will find the Catholic Cemetery on the Cawdor Road just to the south of the Camden township. The cemetery is situated on a rise with bucolic vistas. We are on the outskirts of Sydney here. The cemetery is variously described as being in Cawdor or Camden.

The cemetery dates from the 1840s. The earliest marked grave is James Flynn, who died on 13 February 1843, and there are a few headstones dating from the 1850s among there smattering of sandstone and marble headstones. The majority, however, are 20th-century slab and desk monuments. The cemetery also features an array of vernacular, homemade memorials, an indication of the socio-economic status of Camden and Cawdor throughout the 20th-century.

The most fascinating memorial is a concrete tree trunk with some carvings that marks the grave of William Russell, an Aboriginal elder

Left Grave of William Russell (d.1914), an Aboriginal elder

from the Burragorang Valley. The Gundungurra people knew Russell, sometimes referred to by whites as 'King Billy', as Werriberrie. He died 4 April 1914 aged 84 years. Werriberrie was well known in the Camden district and had witnessed the expansion of white settlement through the floodplains and valley. Just before he died, local councillor and grazier Alfred Leonard Bennet helped him to publish his recollections under the name William Russell. They can be found in the Mitchell Library.

Three other graves are of particular interest. The parish priest Father Hogan died in 1926 and, after a public subscription, the parishioners of Camden and the Oaks erected a marble cross over his grave. The memorial, a tribute of their esteem and affection, was unveiled two years later at a special service attended by over 500 local residents and clergy. Look out also for two semicircular sandstone headstones. One records the accidental death of eight-year-old Frederick Rice, who fell from a horse in 1878; the other features an unusual carving error in the inscription – the stonemason has managed to carve the N backwards in Thomas Byrne's name.

You will notice some older headstones that are clustered neatly together down in the far left corner. These memorials were removed from Burragorang Valley prior to its flooding by the Warragamba Dam in the 1950s.

NOTABLE BURIALS

- William Russell (1830–1914), Aboriginal elder of Burragorang
- Reverend Arthur John Hogan (1876–1926), parish priest of Camden
- Graves relocated from Burragorang Valley

MORE INFORMATION

- Ron Clerke & Beverley Booth, *Camden Catholic Cemetery*, Illawarra Family
  History Group, Wollongong, 1995.

CAMDEN GENERAL CEMETERY, CAMDEN

CAWDOR ROAD, CAMDEN

Burials: 1903–present

Modern cemeteries are not dreary. On the contrary, they are full of colour and movement. Camden General Cemetery is a case in point. This thoroughly 21st century cemetery was dedicated nearly 120 years ago on 8 October 1898. The grave plots feature many personalised decorative elements: rugby league flags, coloured pebbles, strings of beads and lights, bunches of artificial flowers, whirling coloured windmills, photographs and statues. The close observer will appreciate the personalised tributes that display esteem and love for these deceased Camden residents.

The cemetery is divided into different denominational areas and a small baby's section pulls at the heart. The multicultural origins of the local community are evident in the grave decoration as well as the names. The number of young men that have sadly passed away through accidents also struck me.

Camden War Cemetery can be

found at the top of the hill, enclosed by a hedge and with formal brick pier entrance gate. Camden airport was used for RAAF training during the Second World War. Both the Central Flying School and the No. 71 squadron of the Royal Australian Air Force were based at Camden. The war cemetery contains 23 burials, mostly deaths from three separate fatal air training exercises in 1943, 1944 and 1945.

MORE INFORMATION

- Ron Clerke & Beverley Booth, *Camden General Cemetery*, Illawarra Family History Group, Wollongong, 1995.
- *Camden General Cemetery: Cawdor Road, Camden, NSW*, Camden Area Family History Society, Camden, 2005.

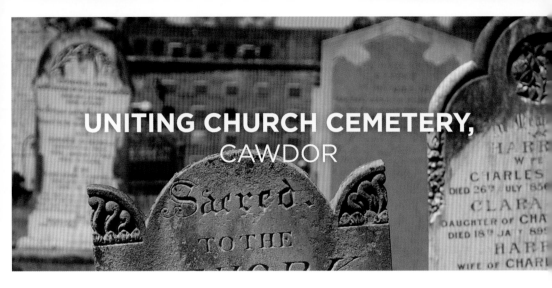

UNITING CHURCH CEMETERY,
CAWDOR

CAWDOR ROAD, CAWDOR

Burials: 1845–present

This peaceful and orderly little church cemetery is located beside the former Wesleyan, now Uniting Church, at Cawdor. A church has been on this site since 1850 and the first recorded burials were in 1853. Prior to that Wesleyans were buried in the Anglican cemetery at Camden. The current church, which dates from 1880, is still in regular use. The twittering birds and rural setting encourage quiet contemplation. The inscriptions with warnings from the grave and scriptural passages also encourage this state of mind.

The earliest headstone dates from 1845, although it was moved to the cemetery in 1888. The stone has been carefully reset after it was broken and is still perfectly legible. The plainly designed stone commemorates Martha Ward of 'Elderslie', who died 30 April 1845. Her inscription implies that death was a release from illness:

The winter of life is past
The storms of affliction are ov'r
Her struggle is ended at last
And sorrow and death are no more.

There are some excellent examples of finely carved symbolism on sandstone headstones dating from the 1850s and 1860s, some of which are signed by the monumental mason C Ransdale of Picton. See if you can spot the hand pointing to heaven, clutching a rose and ribbon bearing the words 'Thy Will Be Done', that decorates the gravestone of four of David and Ann Doust's children. Faith would be needed in such tragic circumstances. The headstone of local preacher Peter Gilks, beneath the cypress tree, has a marvellous rendition of acorns and a thatch of branches.

Flowers are carved on many graves too. Even the graves throughout the 20th-century have substantial marble and granite memorials. The Wesleyan congregation of Cawdor clearly invested in commemorating their dead.

The tragedy of young lives lost is reflected in a number of the early memorials. An obelisk on a substantial sandstone pedestal marks the grave of Frederick Cox who died in October 1856 at the age of 14. A broken anchor speaks of tragedy. Cox speaks from the grave with the popular verse:

All you that come my grave to see
Prepare yourselves to follow me
Prepare yourselves, make no delay
For I in haste was call'd away.

Further across in the cemetery you will find a more modest sandstone headstone to nine-year-old Stephen Doust who drowned in February 1857. His long epitaph fully quotes the Cox one before referring to it in a desperate personalised warning from the grave:

One Week Before This Grave Was Dug
From Yonder Tomb I Learn'd the above
Nor Did I Think I Should So Soon
By Sudden Drowning Be Call'd Home
Remember Death Ye Young and Gay
Prepare For it And Judgement Day.

Although located on the absolute outskirts of metropolitan Sydney, this fascinating church cemetery is well worth a visit.

NOTABLE BURIALS

- Martha Ward (1781–1845), of 'Elderslie'
- Peter Gilks (1813–1860), local Wesleyan preacher

MORE INFORMATION

- Daphne Koob, *Pioneers at rest: the Uniting Church Cemetery Cawdor*, the author, Emu Plains, 1998.
- Suzanne Voytas, *Snap shots of early Cawdor pioneers*, the author, Springwood, 2002.

Left Frederick Cox (d.1856): 'Prepare yourselves, make no delay, For I in haste was call'd away'.

NOTE ON CEMETERY LISTINGS

A number of other gravesites were visited during the research for this book but were not included in the field guide as they were lone graves, simple churchyards with only one or two headstones, or relocated headstones. Here's the list. For more information and photos, visit my blog Sydney Cemetery Adventures website at <sydneycemeteryadventures.wordpress.com>.

- St John's Anglican Cemetery, Pitt Street, Badgerys Creek (resumed for airport)
- Uniting Church Cemetery, Pitt Street, Badgerys Creek (resumed for airport)
- Lighthouse keeper grave, Barrenjoey Lighthouse
- St Patrick's Catholic churchyard memorials, Allawah Street, Blacktown
- Vault of William Carss, Carss Park, Blakehurst
- Gladesville Hospital Cemetery, Victoria Road, Gladesville
- Shadforth Memorial, former St Mark's Anglican Cemetery, Greendale
- Nathaniel Lucas gravestone, St Luke's Church grounds, Liverpool
- St John's Anglican Church, Pittwater Road, Mona Vale
- St Nicholas of Myra Catholic Church, High Street, Penrith
- Presbyterian Churchyard, 99 Bathurst Street, corner Buckingham Street, Pitt Town
- Anglican Churchyard, 110 Bathurst Street, Pitt Town
- Rodd Family Vault, Rodd Park, Henley Marine Drive, Rodd Point
- Baptist Churchyard, Rooty Hill Road South, Rooty Hill
- Lone Grave, William Harvey Reserve, Rouse Hill
- Baptist Chapel Cemetery, 742 The Horsley Drive, corner O'Connell Street, Smithfield
- John Howorth gravestone, St John's Church grounds, Wilberforce

GLOSSARY

ACROTERIA
Architectural detail placed on
corners, shaped a bit like
an orange segment.

ALTAR TOMB
Stone structure similar to a
church altar that usually sits over
a subterranean brick vault.

BROKEN FLOWER
A flower carved with a
snapped or broken stem to
symbolise a life cut short.

CHURCH CEMETERY
A burial ground set aside for one
particular church or religious
denomination. Sometimes located
beside the church but separated
from it, and thus distinct in design
from the churchyard. In Sydney
during the 19th century, the
church cemetery was increasingly
separated from the physical
church building with no visual
or spatial link. It was a precursor
to the general cemetery.

CHURCHYARD
A burial ground that encircles a
church. The term is sometimes used
interchangeably with church cemetery.

COLUMBARIUM
Wall (usually brick or concrete)
with slots for placing cremated
remains or ashes inside and covered
with a plaque. Also referred to as a
cremation niche wall. Introduced
into many closed church cemeteries
as well as general cemeteries to
continue commemorative practices
and to cater for the growing
rates of disposal by cremation.

CREMATORIUM
A building which contains ovens for
burning human remains. Crematoria
usually present public ecumenical

chapels for memorial services and are surrounded by memorial gardens and columbaria for the placement of ashes. The ovens are not on public display. The first Sydney crematorium was built at Rookwood in 1925.

CRYPT
Originally a subterranean burial chamber beneath a church. Since the late 20th-century the term also describes individual above-ground burial chambers, often placed within a wall.

DENTILS
Neoclassical architectural ornaments resembling teeth (from the Latin *denticulus*, a little tooth) that embellish the cornices of headstones and pediments.

DESK HEADSTONE
Lower style stele, often on a slope, resembling a writing desk. The term is often used more generically to describe all lower style stelae from the 1920s onwards.

DOWNTURNED TORCH
Neoclassical decorative motif inspired by the Greek torches – think Olympic torch. A secular symbol of immortality, the downturned torch could also represent a life (and light) extinguished.

DRAPED URN
Neoclassical style decorative motif inspired by Roman cinerary urn. Occasionally unadorned, more commonly depicted partially covered with mourning drapery or a pall.

FALLEN ROSE
A rose carved at the bottom or base of a headstone, seemingly fallen from a garland, wreath or bouquet.

FINIAL
An architectural detail (from the Latin finis, the end) used to describe a pinnacle. More specifically refers to the ornamental cluster of foliage that completes Gothic Revival–style pinnacles and pediments.

FOOTSTONE
A small upright stone placed at the foot of a grave. The outline of the stone usually mimics the headstone. A footstone usually faces inwards to the grave and bears the deceased's initials and year of death.

GARDEN CEMETERY MOVEMENT
Landscape design and burial reform movement established in Britain in the late 18th century to create large extramural burial grounds or 'cemeteries', severed from churches and carefully laid out with parterres, plantings and pathways. This cemetery

ideal was embraced in Sydney when the colony designed its burial grounds.

GENERAL CEMETERY

A large burial ground set aside by the government and divided into denominational sections. First established in Sydney in the 1860s; earlier in regional areas in New South Wales.

GOTHIC REVIVAL

Architectural design and decorative ornamentation inspired by art and architecture of the Middle Ages. Was the preferred style for sepulchral memorials among Catholics in 19th-century Sydney.

HEADSTONE

An upright memorial stone placed at the head of a grave. In earlier times the head of the grave faced east. Also known as a stele or stelae (plural).

IRON 'ETNA'

A cast-iron grave marker, often imported from Scotland, particularly from the Watson, Gow & Co's Etna Foundry in Glasgow. Some were manufactured locally. The inscription panel was usually left blank, so an inscription could be painted upon it. In New South Wales, mass-produced cast-iron grave markers could be ordered through mail order catalogues and easily transported across large distances. They were also much cheaper than stone grave markers. For these reasons, iron grave markers are more commonly found in isolated rural areas whose citizens lacked both money and access to monumental masons.

LAWN CEMETERY

A burial ground with commemorative plaques set into the lawn. There is no kerbing or pathways and usually no grave plantings. Introduced into Sydney in the 1960s.

LEDGER STONE

A large flat rectangular stone set in the ground that covers a grave. A ledger stone generally has a long inscription and epitaph but little or no ornamental decoration.

LYCHGATE

A covered entrance to a churchyard or church cemetery usually with a gabled roof and timber gate; sometimes with a bench located behind the gate providing refuge from the weather. An English churchyard tradition, the term derives from Anglo-Saxon lich, meaning corpse. The coffin bearers often paused beneath the lychgate before proceeding to the graveside for the interment.

MAUSOLEUM

A large above-ground burial chamber with an entrance door and shelves for coffins. From the mid-20th-century it was sometimes referred to as a vault. In the 21st century, mausoleum is also used to describe large multi-storey buildings with crypt burials.

MEMORIAL GARDEN

A rose or planted garden for placing cremated ashes.

MONUMENTAL AREA

An area within a modern cemetery that allows headstones (in contrast to the lawn cemetery area).

NEOCLASSICISM

Architectural design and decorative ornamentation inspired by ancient Greece and Rome, and to a lesser extent Egypt. It was the preferred style for sepulchral memorials among Protestants in 19th-century Sydney. Also known as Classical Revival, Greek Revivalism or Italianate.

OBELISK

A tapering rectangular column with a point. A popular neoclassical monument, inspired by Cleopatra's Needle.

PARTERRE

Formally designed garden beds.

PEDESTAL

A rectangular prism standing on its end that usually forms the base of monumental and figurative stonework.

SARCOPHAGUS

A neoclassical decorative motif that was inspired by the Roman sarcophagus (stone coffin), but it did not contain the body. Sometimes depicted partially draped in a pall.

STELAE

Upright memorial stones. Commonly referred to as headstones or gravestones.

TABLE TOMB

Flat ledger stone supported on legs. Looks like a table.

VAULT

In the 19th century a vault described large subterranean brick-lined graves in which bodies were placed in layered coffins (double or triple case coffins) on shelves. There was no earth within the vault and a slab on the ground, or a monument, covered access. The vault section was the most expensive burial area. In the mid-20th-century vault has become an alternative term for mausoleum.

BIBLIOGRAPHY

Each of the cemetery entries has a specific list of useful resources for more information. These are also compiled together in a Trove list: 'Sydney cemeteries' <trove.nla.gov.au/list?id=64285>.

Below is a select list of broader readings about the history of cemeteries, death and dying in Australia.

- Ashton, Paul, Hamilton, Paula & Searby, Rose, *Places of the Heart: Memorials in Australia*, Australian Scholarly Publishing, North Melbourne, 2012.
- Curl, James Stevens, *A Celebration of Death: An Introduction to Some of the Buildings, Monuments, and Settings of Funerary Architecture in the Western European Tradition*, rev. edn, BT Batsford Ltd, London, 1993.
- Gilbert, Lionel, *A Grave Look at History: Glimpses of a Vanishing Form of Folk Art*, John Ferguson, Sydney, 1980.
- Gilbert, Lionel, *The Last Word: Two Centuries of Australian Epitaphs*, Kardoorair Press, Armidale, 2005.
- Jalland, Pat, *Australian Ways of Death: A Social and Cultural History 1840–1918*, Oxford University Press, South Melbourne, 2002.
- Jalland, Pat, *Changing Ways of Death in Twentieth-century Australia: War, Medicine and the Funeral Business*, UNSW Press, Sydney, 2006.
- Kellehear, Allan (ed.), *Death & Dying in Australia*, Oxford University Press, South Melbourne, 2000.
- Killion, Martyn CH & Garnsey, Heather E, *Cemeteries in Australia: A Register of Transcripts*, 3rd edn, Australasian Federation of Family History Organisations, Sydney, 1994.

- Liveris, Leonie B, *Monuments and Masons: Cemeteries at Karrakatta, Fremantle, Guildford, Midland*, Metropolitan Cemeteries Board, Claremont, 2009.
- Loudon, John Claudius, *On the Laying Out, Planting, and Managing of Cemeteries and on the Improvement of Churchyards*, facsimile edn, Ivelet Books Ltd, Redhill, Surrey, 1981 (1843).
- Murray, Lisa, 'Cemeteries in Nineteenth-Century New South Wales: Landscapes of Memory and Identity', PhD Thesis, Department of History, University of Sydney, 2001.
- Murray, Lisa, '"Modern Innovations?" Ideal vs. reality in colonial cemeteries of nineteenth-century New South Wales', *Mortality*, vol. 8, no. 2, 2003, 129–143.
- Murray, Lisa, 'Remembered / Forgotten? Cemetery landscapes in the nineteenth and twentieth centuries', *Historic Environment*, vol. 17, no. 1, 2003, 49–53.
- Nicol, Robert, *At the End of the Road: Government, Society and the Disposal of Human Remains in the Nineteenth and Twentieth Centuries*, Allen & Unwin, with Centennial Park Cemetery Trust Inc. SA, St Leonards, 1994.
- Nicol, Robert, *This Grave and Burning Question: A Centenary History of Cremation in Australia*, Adelaide Cemeteries Authority, Adelaide, 2003.
- National Trust (NSW), *Cemeteries: A National Trust Policy Paper*, 1st edn, National Trust of Australia (NSW), Sydney, 1987.
- National Trust (NSW), *Guidelines for Cemetery Conservation*, 2nd edn, National Trust of Australia (NSW), Sydney, 2009 <nationaltrust.org.au/wp-content/uploads/2015/09/cemetery_conservation_guide.pdf>.
- Sagazio, Celestina, *Cemeteries: Our Heritage*, National Trust of Australia (Victoria), Melbourne, 1992.
- Sagazio, Celestina (ed.), *Conserving Our Cemeteries: An Illustrated and Annotated Guide Based on the ACNT National Guidelines for the Conservation of Cemeteries*, Melbourne, 2003.
- Whittick, Arnold, *Symbols for Designers: A handbook on the Application of Symbolism and Symbolism in Design for the use of architects, sculptors, ecclesiastical and memorial designers, commercial artists and students of symbolism*, Crosby Lockwood & Son Ltd, London, 1935.
- Worpole, Ken, *Last Landscapes: The Architecture of the Cemetery in the West*, Reaktion Books, London, 2003.

ACKNOWLEDGMENTS

This cemeteries field guide draws upon two main strands of research that I have undertaken over the last twenty years: historical research for my doctoral thesis completed in 2001 and the many field trips and discussions developed through the National Trust (NSW) Cemeteries Conservation Committee. The National Trust (NSW) has been a leading light in the appreciation and conservation of our cemeteries. The Cemeteries Conservation Committee brings together a diverse group of volunteers who together research, assess, advise and lobby for the preservation and care of cemeteries. I have enjoyed the support and encouragement of many committee members over the years.I would particularly like to acknowledge the expertise and intellectual stimulation of Stephen Davies, Katherine Brooks, Matthew Devine, Chris Betteridge, Siobhan Lavelle, George Gibbons, Michael Lehany, Sue Clarke, the late Gordon Brown, and all my current colleagues on the cemeteries committee.

I wish to acknowledge the extraordinary research undertaken by dozens of volunteers in historical societies and family history groups to document and transcribe our cemeteries. Martyn Killion and Heather Garnsey recognised their contribution many years ago by compiling a register of cemetery transcripts for the Australasian Federation of Family History Organisations. The Society of Australian Genealogists has an unsurpassed collection of cemetery transcripts, surveys and research papers. I spent many hours fact-checking in their library and thank their staff and volunteers for their unstinting help and interest. Of course, these days many cemetery transcriptions are appearing online. I particularly drew upon the Australian Cemeteries Index website and the Hawkesbury Net cemetery transcript website, both of which are compiled by volunteers. These are great resources and I tip my hat to the compilers of these works.

I wish to recognise the extraordinary resource of the *Australian Dictionary of Biography* online. Thousands of biographies have been meticulously researched by historians, many noting places of burial. This proved an absolute goldmine for identifying persons of interest. The *Australian Dictionary of Biography* is one of the nation's greatest assets. So too is the National Library of Australia's *Trove*, especially the digitised newspapers. It is shameful the federal government has cut funding to *Trove*. It is a world-leading digital resource that enables thousands of Australians to discover our history and heritage. This book would not have been possible without *Trove*.

A number of fellow historians and librarians pointed out details to me that enhanced my work. I wish to express my particular thanks to Ian Hoskins, Deborah Beck, Mari Metzke, Tom Richmond, Michelle Nichols and Melissa Jackson for your collegiality. My gratitude also to my City of Sydney colleagues, Laila Ellmoos and Sasha Baroni, whose quiet support made this book possible.

There are a number of historic photographs, plans and drawings reproduced in the book. Thank you to the staff at the City of Sydney Archives, National Library of Australia, Royal Australian Historical Society, Society of Australian Genealogists, State Library of NSW, State Library of Victoria and Sydney Living Museums for their assistance with reproductions and permissions.

My sincere thanks to Phillipa McGuinness at NewSouth Publishing for commissioning the guide and giving me the opportunity to share my love of Sydney, history and cemeteries. Your enthusiasm for the project is greatly appreciated, Phillipa. Emma Driver has been a relaxed and reassuring project editor, keeping me to deadlines and facilitating my involvement throughout the entire publishing process, which has been marvellous. Copy editor Victoria Chance has applied her historical knowledge and keen eye to make the text sparkle. It has been great to work with Victoria; our history networks go way back. The designer Emma Bennetts has done a stunning job, creating a practical book that is beautiful to browse, and Neil Radford produced the index with aplomb and good cheer under pressing deadlines.

But the final thank you deservedly goes to my partner and fellow historian Mark Dunn. Mark visited all 101 cemeteries with me and captured their unique qualities in the gorgeously evocative photographs that illustrate this guide. Thanks for your support, love and devotion, Mark, and thanks for avidly embracing the Sydney cemetery challenge.

IMAGE CREDITS

All photographs by Mark Dunn unless otherwise credited below:

p. 13: A.G. Foster collection, Royal Australian Historical Society. p. 15: *Illustrated Sydney News*, 29 May 1875, p. 4, courtesy National Library of Australia. p. 20: State Library of NSW. p. 21: Dixson Galleries, State Library of NSW. p. 24: Vaucluse House Collection, Sydney Living Museums. p. 36: SPF, State Library of NSW. p. 41: State Library Victoria. p. 52: State Library of NSW. p. 54 (left and right): A.G. Foster collection, Royal Australian Historical Society. p. 60: Mitchell Library, State Library of NSW. p. 81 (left): Photographer: Charles Bayliss, National Library of Australia. p. 84: Photographer: Milton Kent, City of Sydney Archives. p. 110: Photographer: Charles Pickering, State Library of NSW. pp. 111, 120: Burton Family Album, Society of Australian Genealogists. p. 126: Photographer: American & Australasian Photographic Company, Caroline Simpson Library and Research Collection, Sydney Living Museums. p. 143: City of Sydney Archives. p. 146 (right): Houison collection, Society of Australian Genealogists. p. 149: *Sands' Sydney and Suburban Directory*, 1889. p. 285: *Illustrated Sydney News*, 7 January 1887, p. 20, courtesy National Library of Australia. pp. 288, 290: Burton Family Album, Society of Australian Genealogists.

INDEX

Page references in *italics* indicate illustrations.

Opposite St Thomas' Anglican Cemetery, Enfield